A FRACTURED LIBERATION

A
FRACTURED
LIBERATION

KOREA UNDER
US OCCUPATION

Kornel Chang

THE BELKNAP PRESS OF
HARVARD UNIVERSITY PRESS
2025

First printing

First Belknap Press of Harvard University Press hardcover edition, 2025

Epigraph quoted from Bruce Cumings, *The Origins of the Korean War*,
vol. 1, *Liberation and the Emergence of Separate Regimes, 1945–1947*
(Princeton, NJ: Princeton University Press, 1981), 68.

Library of Congress Cataloging-in-Publication Data

Names: Chang, Kornel S., 1976– author.
Title: A fractured liberation : Korea under US occupation / Kornel Chang.
Description: Cambridge, Massachusetts : The Belknap Press of Harvard
University Press, 2025. | Includes bibliographical references and index.
Identifiers: LCCN 2024008850 | ISBN 9780674258433 (cloth)
Subjects: LCSH: Korean reunification question (1945–) | Korea—History—Allied occupation,
1945–1948. | Korea—Politics and Government—1945–1948.
Classification: LCC DS917.52 .C428 2025 | DDC 951.904/3—dc23/eng/20240523
LC record available at https://lccn.loc.gov/2024008850

Sinparam expresses the pathos, the inner joy,
of a person moved to action not by coercion
but by his own volition. *Param* is the sound of
the wind; if a person is wafted along on this wind,
songs burst from his lips and his legs dance with joy.
A *sinparam* is a strange wind that billows in the
hearts of people who have freed themselves from
oppression, regained their freedom, and live in a
society of mutual trust.

—**Chŏng Kyŏngmo**

Contents

Note on Transliteration and Language

Korean words and names are transliterated in the McCune-Reischauer system, Japanese in the Hepburn system, and Chinese in the Pinyin system, except for those widely known in English by other spellings, such as Seoul, Busan, Jeju, Syngman Rhee, Kim Il Sung, Tokyo, and Chiang Kai-shek. As is customary with East Asian names, the surname appears first, unless the author writes in English, in which case the surname appears last.

In some direct quotations in the book, racial epithets for people appear. I chose to leave in those terms in order to convey the language and attitudes of the time.

A FRACTURED LIBERATION

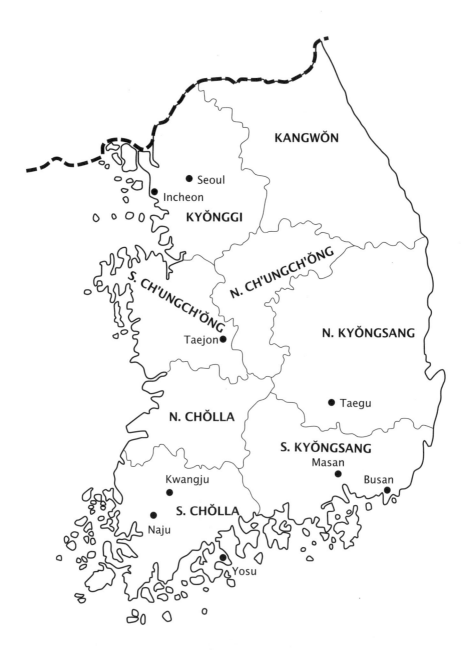

KANGWŎN

● Seoul
● Incheon
KYŎNGGI

S. CH'UNGCH'ŎNG

N. CH'UNGCH'ŎNG

N. KYŎNGSANG

Taejon ●

● Taegu

N. CHŎLLA

S. KYŎNGSANG
Masan
●
● Busan

Kwangju
●
S. CHŎLLA
● Naju

Yosu

Provinces and major cities of South Korea.

● Jeju

Prologue   A Family Debate

Growing up in Queens, New York, my South Korean immigrant parents never spoke directly to me about the division of the Korean peninsula or the Korean War. They saw no good reason why my sisters and I should know. But there were random nights when I was awoken by conversations at a whisper. On one night, half asleep, I overheard my parents and my grandmother, who was living with us at the time, recollect the American soldiers who had stayed with them during the Korean War. They told stories of good and bad soldiers but I couldn't make out most of the details—Korean school once a week only gets you so far.

When I woke up the next morning and asked my father about what I'd heard, he told me it was "nothing important." The nothing important, as I later learned, included how my grandparents had fled south in 1946 with their only child at the time, my aunt, leaving behind their extended family in Pyongyang—family they would never see again.

It would be many more years before I learned how war and division shaped my family's life. But I started to get an inkling in the summer of 1994 when the war came home to our family gathering at my oldest uncle's house. In the preceding months, the Korean peninsula had become the most dangerous flashpoint in the world. For decades, it had been divided into two starkly different countries: a communist North and a capitalist South. The two had been at war my entire life—a war that started in 1950 when Northern forces invaded the South in an attempt to reunify the peninsula, cost some five million lives over the following three years, came perilously close to involving nuclear weapons, and technically never ended. There had been an armistice in 1953, but never a peace treaty. Now, in 1994, a standoff over

North Korea's nuclear program threatened to tip Koreans back into combat. On the evening news they spoke of a Second Korean War. There was every reason to think that it would be a bloodbath. Indeed, a US war game simulation estimated 50,000 American military casualties and over a million Korean deaths in the first three months of the conflict.

News anchors focused on the demilitarized zone (DMZ)—the narrow strip of land that divides Korea at the 38th parallel. It was, they explained, the most militarized border in the world. Viewers were told that 70 percent of the North Korean Army was amassed at the DMZ.[1] The South, meanwhile, was peppered with US military bases. The Cold War seemed to be over everywhere in the world but in Korea. Thinking about my parents' homeland then, I couldn't fathom how it had ever been one country. The Korean peninsula seemed hopelessly, permanently divided.

"All wars are fought twice, the first time on the battlefield, the second time in memory," Viet Thanh Nguyen writes.[2] But what happens when the war never ends? In my family, we rekindled it over dinner. As a recent high school graduate that summer of 1994, I had been promoted to the adult's table, albeit at the outside edge. The pearly floral design on the traditional black folding table was barely visible, now covered by an array of Korean dishes and *banchan* (side dishes), arranged in neat, inviting rows. As I ate my fill of *galbi* (grilled short ribs) and *japchae* (stir-fried glass noodles), I heard a family argument I would hear at every gathering from then on. My oldest uncle, the patriarch of the family, would champion the United States' hardline policy—no negotiating with a "crazed" regime, is how he would put it. Other relatives would chime in, arguing that the US military presence had propped up authoritarians in the South and aggravated tensions all over the peninsula.

The debate continues today, and it usually goes back and forth until my oldest uncle blurts out: "Well, if it wasn't for the Americans, we'd all be living under the communists now!" This is where the argument ends, with the blunt choice that all Koreans face: North or South, totalitarianism or American military bases, communism or capitalism.

I leave the table full, but with a question. Were there no other options?

Introduction   Korea's Asian Spring

Around noon on August 15, 1945, a voice—stilted and high-pitched—that Koreans had never heard before came through the airwaves. In villages and towns across Korea, crowds gathered around a neighborhood radio to hear an urgent message from the Japanese emperor and their imperial overlord. There were excited murmurs rippling through the crowd saying the emperor was planning to announce Japan's surrender from World War II. But no one was certain. They'd been hearing rumors of Japan's imminent defeat for months now. Adding to the confusion, just the night before, Japanese soldiers had gone door to door, exhorting Korean residents: "We are winning the war right now. If you contribute your possessions in making weapons, we will win the war."[1]

For nearly four decades, Koreans had lived under Japanese rule. As colonized subjects, they were forced to take on Japanese names, learn Japanese, and participate in Shinto rituals—the Japanese state religion—honoring the emperor.[2] Each family was also required to have a picture of the emperor in a place of honor in their homes. The Japanese enforced these rules and regulations through a massive police state, a 60,000-strong force, who terrorized Koreans with arbitrary arrests, draconian surveillance, and torture.

The colonial government also censored Korean art and writing, suppressed Korean resistance and dissent, and conscripted millions of Koreans for war and work throughout the Japanese empire, which stretched from Manchuria to French Indochina to the Dutch East Indies at its zenith. This mobilization included young Korean girls to serve as "comfort women"—a Japanese euphemism for sex slaves—for the imperial army. "Ever since we have been old enough to remember, all we've had is forty years of shame. To us there were no pleasure of love, no glory of youth, and no honor in art," is how one Korean writer summed up the colonial experience.[3] For a great majority of Koreans, the forty years of shame was all they had ever known. In 1945, more than 80 percent of the population was less than forty years old. The thought of an independent Korea must have seemed inconceivable.[4]

The Koreans who gathered to hear the broadcast that day could be forgiven if they resisted getting their hopes up. The emperor's speech, played back from a phonograph recording taken the night before, was staticky and the reception was poor. Moreover, the Japanese they heard wasn't quite what Koreans—and for that matter, most Japanese—were familiar with. The colonial policy that forced Koreans to adopt their rulers' tongue did not include the formal Japanese that was being spoken by the emperor. Confounded, the crowd turned to each other and exchanged confused looks. Then, all of a sudden, another voice came through the radio. This time it was in Korean. They soon recognized it was a Korean translation of the emperor's speech. But after hearing the four-and-a-half minute message in Korean, they still weren't sure what it meant. They heard something about Japan accepting the joint declaration of the Allied powers, but there was no mention of a surrender or Korea being freed. It must have felt like a cruel tease. The confusion was mercifully cleared up moments later when a Korean explanation of the emperor's message followed: Japan had indeed surrendered. Tense crowds all across Korea erupted into cheers and chants.

Thinking back to that glorious day, Kang Ch'angdŏk remembers: "The fact that Korea was liberated excited everyone." He had been sitting in a prison cell for dodging conscription into the imperial army only days before the emperor's historic announcement. He was released just in time to hear the surrender and partake in the celebrations. He recalled the euphoric scene of throngs of Koreans pouring into the streets shouting, "Hurrah Korean independence," "Land to the farmers," and "Long live the proletariat." At the time, Kang believed he was witnessing "our world" being ushered in.

Other Koreans, like Chŏn Sukhŭi, took a quiet moment to let the news sink in, even savor it. Chŏn, who had recently given birth to a son, thought at first it must be a dream after hearing the surrender on a small transistor radio tucked away in her husband's office. "Could there be a miracle like this one?" she marveled. With that thought, she sank into the couch and felt the happiness wash over her, perhaps while imagining her newborn son growing up free in an independent Korea.[5]

The collapse of the Japanese empire ushered in an extraordinary—indeed, a once in a lifetime—opportunity for Koreans. After nearly forty years of foreign rule, this was their chance to start over. It kindled hopes of what a future Korea could be: freer, better, and more equal and just. The electrifying sense of possibility jolted Koreans into action. Peasants occupied Japanese-owned farmlands, workers seized control of the factory floor, villagers chased the former colonial police out of town, and women demanded political and economic equality. The explosion of activities made it seem as if Koreans had readied for this moment their whole lives.

The countless initiatives that surfaced after August 15 were seeded during the dark years of the colonial period. Japanese rule spawned Korean struggles for independence, both at home and abroad, beginning with the 1919 March First Movement, which saw two million Koreans participate in nationwide protests against colonial rule. (My great-grand uncle was arrested and imprisoned for reading aloud the Declaration of Korean Independence during the March First Movement.) Nationalists of various political stripes organized the Korean Provisional Government—Korea's government in exile—in Shanghai, after Japanese authorities had violently put down the protests.

The colonial years also witnessed the explosive growth of communism and socialism in Korea's cities and countryside. Preaching the gospel of revolution, activists mobilized peasants and workers (and to a lesser degree, women) to rebel against inequality and exploitation. "Our national emancipation movement is merely a step toward the ultimate purpose of social revolution," their manifesto declared. "This is our belief and the common objective of all the toiling masses of the world."[6] Their calls for land redistribution, workers' rights, and women's equality were among the core demands for independence after the fall of the Japanese empire.

At the same time, Japanese rule sowed new divisions and exacerbated old ones among Koreans. Colonial repression and factionalism divided nationalists and left them fighting bitterly over who were the true heirs to the March First Movement. Communists and socialists bickered over doctrine and orthodoxy. And rank-and-file workers and peasants pursued their own goals that put them at odds with activists and their agendas. The divide between the Korean landed elite and the peasant masses that predated Japanese rule grew deeper and more complex as a result of colonial policies.

Japanese rule also established new fault lines within Korean society by furnishing political and economic opportunities for some of their colonial subjects. This included prominent businessmen, landowners, poets, novelists, and local officials who were detested for abetting Japanese rule. Coming to terms with colonial-era collaboration would pose one of the most vexing challenges in a liberated Korea.[7] As much as Koreans wanted to imagine independence as a brand-new start—a tabula rasa, if you will—the colonial past threatened to haunt the liberatory present. These divides ensured that when Koreans emerged out of colonialism, they would not share a single, pristine vision of independence. The meaning of liberation would have to be worked out, perhaps even fought over. The great uncertainty around what would come next worried Koreans like Kang, who wondered, "What would this country become in the coming future?"[8] He remembered the question consuming him, as the exhilaration of liberation gave way to anxiety over an unknown future.

Could Koreans rise above their differences to rebuild their nation? Could they make the transition to independence without spiraling into chaos and violence? Using both carrot and stick, Japanese colonial rule had kept a lid on both Korean aspirations and conflicts—that is, until August 15, 1945. With the sudden collapse of the Japanese empire, hopes, visions, and fractures that had been bottled up for nearly forty years erupted into Korea's Asian Spring. If Koreans deserved anything after nearly four decades of colonial rule, it was the chance to determine their own futures.

The blooming of Korea's Asian Spring was cut short by the arrival of foreign occupying armies. Shortly after Japan's surrender, US and Soviet officials agreed to establish two military occupation zones, one in the South run by the Americans and the other in the North directed by the Russians. The US occupation government, led by Lieutenant General John R. Hodge, carried out a hard-line, anti-communist agenda that largely preserved the pre-liberation status quo below the 38th parallel. This involved, among other things, reconstituting the hated colonial police and rolling back the changes that had been initiated by Koreans during the three-and half-week interlude between Japan's surrender and the arrival of American forces. In contrast to postwar Japan, where Americans, according to historian John Dower, "proceeded to dismantle the oppressive control of the imperial state," the US occupation in Korea maintained much of the colonial system and dealt with Koreans with a heavy hand.[9] In one of the great ironies of the immediate postwar, Japan, the hated wartime enemy, received democratization and reform, while Korea, a liberated country, got the hard line and discipline.

Following this storyline, most accounts of Korea just after World War II look at these years for the origins of the Korean War. Highlighting the forces of repression and polarization, scholars show the United States adopting a "reverse course" policy—to create an anti-communist bulwark in the South—from the very outset in Korea. The Cold War looms large: the partition of Korea in August 1945 becomes the "first postwar act of containment," and General Hodge, the leader of the US occupation, a "premature Cold War warrior." The decisions of Hodge and his military high command, these accounts suggest, entrenched divisions among Koreans and made reunification virtually impossible. The result: an inexorable march to war.[10]

There are good reasons for seeing postwar Korea in this way. The Cold War continues to rage on the Korean peninsula after all—seventy-five years and counting—as an anachronism that refuses to die. But was the occupation period only a prelude to the Korean War? Did all roads have to lead to schism and war?[11] The haste to get to the Cold War has sidelined Korea's Asian Spring to the margins of history. As a drama moving relentlessly toward division and war, the actions of the great powers—especially of the United States—occupy center stage. They have left little room for the voices and struggles of Koreans and the possibility that things could have turned out differently. Even in the few cases in which Korean experiences are considered, they are typically captured in binary terms: communism versus capitalism, left versus right, and revolutionary versus reactionary. Viewing their actions and ideas strictly through a Cold War lens has oversimplified Korean hopes and ambitions and flattened the complexity of their postliberation experience.[12]

This book is meant to capture a moment alive with promise and possibility, when Koreans were seized by dreams of freedom and starting anew. It looks at what Koreans at all levels of society in the South—from political leaders and activists to ordinary peasants, workers, and women—aspired to, at the independence they envisioned, and at how they sought to make it a reality. My book also reveals the tensions and clashes that arose as Koreans pursued their diverse goals for liberation. Watchwords like "revolution," "freedom," and "independence" meant different things to different people—they were moving targets that inspired a wide range of initiatives and ideas. This singular opportunity to work out the meaning of independence both inspired and divided Koreans, giving rise to a kaleidoscopic postliberation experience.

The ongoing, seemingly endless, conflict on the peninsula makes it hard to imagine Korea beyond North and South. But this is not the way it had to be. Koreans pursued alternative visions for their country. In fact, the choice Koreans faced at the end of 1948, between a one-party communist state and an autocratic liberalism, was between two options that had very little support at the beginning of the occupation. Between the two extremes was a social democratic majority that demanded a more egalitarian society without necessarily calling for a revolution.

Virtually all Koreans wanted land redistribution, labor rights, and a reckoning with their collaborationist past. But most Koreans, not being strict idealogues (many of them were not aware of what political labels meant), were not rigidly dogmatic about how to achieve these goals, nor were they against compromise or cooperation. After liberation, many of them pursued incremental changes to improve their daily lives. Tenant farmers secured long-term leases or bought land at a steep discount from their landlords. Workers demanded and received higher wages and better working conditions. Women negotiated nursing at work and maternity leave. And the most popular refrain among workers at the time was "Capitalists will sacrifice their money, technicians their skills, and workers their efforts for reindustrialization."[13] This also applied to a good number of activists, who adopted a pragmatic, even cautious approach to liberation, especially once they learned that the United States would be occupying the South. That is to say, it was not revolution or nothing for most Koreans. As sprawling and contentious as Korea's Asian Spring was, it had a social democratic spine running through it.

What is more, the core aspirations of the Korean majority had the backing of American and Korean reformers in the military government, who had been sent to Korea by the State Department. They included New Deal liberals, Christian socialists, and trade unionists who challenged Hodge's hard-line, anti-communist approach. They proposed land redistribution, New Deal-style trade unionism, and voting rights, and advocated removing collaborators from public life. Despite the high command's efforts to reduce Korean aspirations to Cold War binaries, these reformers knew that their ambitions were broader and more diverse. Their stories reveal the paths not taken. In telling them, I seek to restore contingency to a narrative that looks ahead to division and war as an inevitable endpoint: North and South is not the way it had to be.

This then begs the question, If there was a majority of Koreans who wanted social democratic style reforms, and their aspirations had the support of

American and Korean reformers in the military government, why did South Korea end up with an authoritarian regime led by Syngman Rhee? Historians have pointed to Hodge's early support of reactionary rightists, including industrialists, landlords, and businessmen—people who were associated with Japanese rule. As Bruce Cumings has argued, "The Occupation made critical choices in the last months of 1945 that shaped the conditions in which a rightist autocracy could emerge triumphant more than two years later."[14] There is no doubt that these early decisions contributed to the tragic outcome in the South and Korea more broadly. However, they did not seal Korea's fate: there was still time and opportunity for Americans to shift course.

It wasn't very long before Hodge himself recognized the error of backing Rhee. In the summer of 1946, he authorized talks with moderate leftists and rightists to create a "true coalition of democratic parties," leaving the Far Right and Left outside looking in. With Hodge's support, liberal advisers thought a third way was a genuine possibility. Carving a path between North and South would not be easy—there were challenges, for sure. US policymakers had to contend with Korean expectations, Soviet competition, and Rhee's constant brinkmanship. But just because it was hard doesn't mean things had to turn out the way they did.[15]

My book highlights the key moments, where a different choice, firmer resolve, and a twist or turn in favor of unity, could have led to alternative outcomes. I also explain how and why these key moments became missed opportunities. Each failure had a compounding effect, leaving policymakers with fewer and fewer good options, until there was none. By the fall of 1947, a palpable sense of resignation and gloom had settled over the American Occupation, with one State Department official remarking, "Whatever we do now in Korea is bound to be bad. Our only hope is not to do worse."[16] These bad and worse policy options were made stark in a top-secret State-War-Navy Department memo: "The United States is obliged to decide whether it will continue to occupy South Korea for an indefinite period, or whether it will withdraw and permit the Soviet Union to dominate the entire peninsula. . . . If the US determines that its interests will be better served by remaining in Korea, it will have to face up to the responsibility it is assuming in regard to the Korean people."[17]

Boxed in by Korean aspirations, on one side, and Soviet intransigence—real and imagined—on the other, Hodge was prepared to cut bait and withdraw from Korea. That was his recommendation to the War Department.

But the State Department, which had consistently criticized the military government's hard-line approach, now believed holding on to half the peninsula was necessary to contain the spread of communism and secure American national security interests in Northeast Asia. US policymakers, therefore, developed an exit strategy that would allow the United States to maintain a foothold in Korea without the liabilities of a military occupation. The US would call for elections with the intent of establishing a separate, anti-communist client state in the South. Elections would be held in May 1948, a constitution would be ratified shortly thereafter, and a formally independent South Korea would be established by the end of the year. This exit strategy, as everyone involved in the planning knew, would leave Korea indefinitely divided.

The decision to create a separate South Korea empowered the reformers who had been sidelined by the military high command for most of the occupation. Their proposals, which were previously rejected, were either enacted or given a place of prestige within the occupation's agenda. They passed land redistribution, labor rights, and democratic reforms in the lead-up to the elections. It is perhaps the height of irony that these progressive changes were implemented only after the United States decided to pursue a separatist policy that would permanently divide Korea into two. And, for better or worse, reformers worked toward both progressive and separatist objectives.

The last-minute reforms ensured that it would not be a liberation completely denied. This was not immediately apparent. The newly established South Korea comes under authoritarian rule, after all. And the Korean War would follow two years later, burying Korean hopes in rubble and ashes. With hindsight, however, we can see that more Korean aspirations in the South were realized, with warts and all, than has been generally thought.[18] But whatever democratic gains these reforms have inspired over the years, South Korea remains one half of a whole. Koreans are still haunted by an unfinished liberation.

1 Pursuing Liberation

What do you do after you've been freed from nearly forty years of foreign rule? In Kaesŏng, villagers searched furiously for metalware to bring to the celebration at Manwŏltae, the former site of the Koryŏ Dynasty Royal Palace. Foreign invaders had burned the palace to the ground multiple times during the Koryŏ period (918–1392). It was rebuilt after the first four invasions, but after the fifth sacking, the king of Koryŏ fled, abandoning the royal residence for good. Memory of the fallen palace became a source of national pride and grievance in Korean lore. The people of Kaesŏng chose to celebrate their first evening of freedom on hallowed grounds.

But there was one problem: the people lacked the brass gongs that were traditionally played to mark special occasions like this one. Poorer substitutes—spoons, chopsticks, and even handrails—were also in short supply. In the last days of the war, desperate Japanese authorities had confiscated almost all metalware for war material.[1] Yet, this did not stop Koreans in Kaesŏng from fully celebrating what was one of the most monumental days of their lives. Pak Munchae remembered they improvised, using tin shop signs to reproduce the traditional festive sounds to sing and dance to, deep into the night.[2]

But celebrating is not all they would do that evening. At one point during the festivities, someone in the crowd shouted, "Let's go! Let's go to X's house." Upon this prompt, the revelers quickly turned into an angry mob. "Everyone stormed that house, destroying things, confiscating them." Who was X and what did he or she do to elicit such a violent reaction? We don't know for sure, but we do know that the villagers thought the house belonged to a pro-Japanese collaborator. For the crowd, retributive justice was a long time coming.

It took other Koreans longer to accept—and, thus, respond to—the reality of Japan's defeat. On the morning of August 16, the day after the emperor's historical announcement, Yi Ilchae was still pondering whether he should report for his draft assignment. He received his draft notice to enlist in the Japanese imperial army, Unit 774, several days before Japan's surrender. As one of the last of the two and half million Koreans who were conscripted, Yi would not be sent to the front lines. Instead, he was assigned to security detail in downtown Taegu, located 150 miles southeast of Seoul, not too far from where he lived and worked.[3]

What was his hesitation? The empire was no more, so why would he show up for duty? It wasn't that straightforward, however. For a twenty-two-year-old Korean, Japanese rule, which began formally in 1910, would have been all he had ever known. Under colonial policy, Yi was forced to adopt a Japanese name, learn Japanese in school, and participate in Shinto rituals to honor the emperor. An independent Korea was unfathomable to members of his generation. Rumors had also been swirling for months about Japan's imminent defeat and nothing ever came of it. If Japan had surrendered, why were there still armed Japanese soldiers roaming the streets?

Then came August 16, 1945, the day *after* Japan surrendered. Yi reported for security detail at the Taegu railroad station and stood guard for two days. It was only after his Japanese commanding officers had disappeared that he felt safe to believe the unbelievable: Korea was free. But what now? Perhaps in his excitement, Yi ran into the crowded streets to join other jubilant Koreans. Downtown Taegu was flooded with people holding banners declaring Korean independence and waving the Korean flag, which had been previously banned by colonial authorities. It is unclear whether Yi would have recognized the flag if he saw it. It might have been the first time he had seen the *T'aegŭk* (blue and red circle) surrounded by the four-tri-gram design of the Korean flag.

What we do know is that after Yi left his post, he returned to the Mitsuwa Chemical Company, where he had been working prior to being drafted. There, he discovered his Korean colleagues had negotiated severance payments from their Japanese employers and were in the midst of organizing a self-management committee in which workers would take control of the operation of the company. As part of a transition to a peacetime industry, they

Koreans celebrate liberation in 1945.
National Archives (111-SC-212019)

planned to convert the wartime plant that produced chemicals used to enhance the efficiency of military radars into a toothpaste factory. In a matter of days, Yi went from a colonial conscript to a worker-manager who would now help with the running of a factory floor once owned by the Japanese.[4]

Yi's story of a world turned upside down captures the radically different and better futures that he and many other Koreans imagined and pursued after August 15. But his response to the news was just one of many. The writer Hyŏn, Yi T'aejun's autobiographical protagonist in "Before and After Liberation," was on a bus traveling from the countryside to Seoul on August 16, 1945, when he learned of Japan's surrender.[5] His driver had hailed an oncoming bus and pulled up next to it to talk to the other driver.

"What's up?" Hyŏn's driver asked the other driver.
"What do you mean, what's up?" The other driver responded.

"You got the paper in Chŏlwŏn didn't you?"

"It's just like they broadcasted yesterday."

"We couldn't really make it out because of the static. But it was an unconditional ceasefire."

Upon hearing this, Hyŏn jumps up from his seat and interjects into the conversation.

"What are you talking about?"

"They say the war is over."

"The war?"

"Yes. It's over."

"What do you mean, over?"

"Japan lost finally."

"It's true. It's finally over!"

As the words sank in, Hyŏn was overcome with joy, on the verge of tears. But when he turned around, searching for Korean commuters to share the moment with, all he saw through his welled-up eyes were stony faces and blank looks. Thinking perhaps the other riders hadn't heard the conversation, he asked, "Didn't you hear what the driver said?" His question was met with silence. Nobody even turned around. Dejected by the indifference of his fellow Koreans, Hyŏn sank back into his seat, returning to his "tired, subdued, sunken-eye look."[6] It was as if nothing had changed.

For some Koreans, liberation had, in fact, brought little change to their daily lives. Mun Chean, who worked for the Seoul Central Broadcasting Station, recalled that "the administrative system of the colonial era in which the station operated was actually maintained until the arrival of the U.S. military on September 9."[7] Employees were still required to follow the reporting guidelines of the *Directory for Forbidden Items* and get approval for news content and broadcast programs in advance from the Ministry of Communications. Thus, Mun, along with everyone else at the station, continued to be censored after August 15. Airing the proceedings from the Yalta (1944) and Potsdam conferences (1945), for instance, where the Allied powers had discussed the terms of Japan's surrender, was still strictly prohibited. The broadcasting of Korea's national anthem also continued to be forbidden. For weeks, Mun experienced liberation in name only.

Other people found the changes brought by liberation to be unsettling, at least initially. Ch'oe Yisan wrote about his first day back in school after Japan's surrender:

> At the beginning of the first session of classes, the teacher called attendance. Going down the list of names, he changed the names that had been revised to Japanese under colonial policy back to Korean. Most name reversions were simple, as there was only one more character added to the second letter to the surname. For the original Korean names that were harder to guess, the teacher asked the student.

His classmates, Ch'oe recalled, paused, to consciously remember to answer in Korean instead of Japanese. "Everyone had answered 'hai' during the colonial era, but now were to answer 'ye.'" It felt awkward to respond in Korean, and so students would cut the tension by bursting into laughter after answering.[8] Liberation would take some getting used to.

Yet, while responses ran the gamut, most Koreans embraced liberation. They were determined to make the most of the opportunity, even if they didn't completely agree on what it meant. And so, a remarkable number of people worked with a concerted sense of mission and purpose from the moment they heard the emperor's staticky broadcast. Kang Ch'angdŏk, who was stuck in a prison cell for evading conscription only days before Japan's surrender, remembered that "all kinds of organizations began to form" after August 15; he himself joined a youth organization that went around to rural areas to demand land for peasant farmers.[9] For Kang, along with many other Koreans, liberation had breathed life into the ideal of being part of something greater than oneself.

An Hoenam's 1946 semiautobiographical story, "Fire," captured the remarkable sense of purpose that fueled Koreans after Japan's surrender. It is about a Korean man, Mr. Yi, who returned to Korea after having been forced to work overseas on Truk Island in the Pacific for the Japanese empire.[10] He would have been among the 4.3 million Koreans stranded in North China, Japan, and Sakhalin at the end of the war. They all naturally hoped, with liberation, to return home to be reunited with family and kin. Yi described the outpouring of emotion after setting foot in his homeland for the first

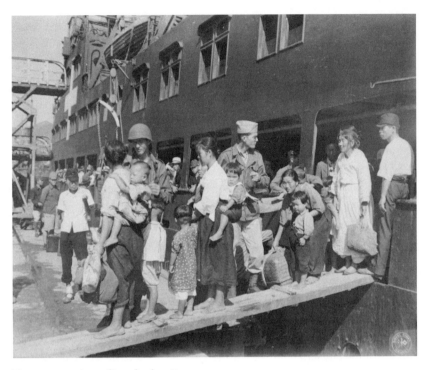

Korean repatriates disembark at Busan.
National Archives (111-SC-290547)

time in four years. "When I first landed in Busan, I cried rubbing my hands across the soil."

However, upon returning to his village, Yi learns his father had passed away, his six-year-old son had died from smallpox, his wife had left him for another man, and his home had fallen into disrepair. Embodying the national suffering of Korea under wartime Japan, he had lost everything while he was away. "On the day he returned, his weeping was heard from far off as I sat in my own room," his neighbor, Mr. An, recounts in the story. "Whenever I reluctantly started off to his house to see him, sounds that pierced one's lungs and tore one's intestines would come to mind, making me retreat back home."

The two men eventually meet at the village Lunar New Year celebration. Mr. An relates that Yi told harrowing stories of comrades perishing from illness, hunger, and suicide and of the nonstop US aerial and naval bombardments that consumed Truk Island in a sea of flames: "There was a blackened rash on his face, while his protruding cheekbones and furrowed brow made his tale of hardships particularly impressive and convincing to anyone who heard it." The hell Yi experienced as a conscript—and then returned to—hardened him, made him cynical. "On the face of a simple peasant was always a spiteful look of malice, and even after we became acquainted, he didn't lose the contemptuous eyes with which he watched me." An's impression of Yi is that of a "selfish backroom dealer," certainly not the "pure" peasant he expected.

While talking, they observe villagers—young and old, men and women—playing *pul nori* (fire game) to mark and prepare for the beginning of a new planting season: "The vast field swarmed with people, wherever you looked—those setting things on fire, the flame, the smoke that shot through the sky. Some children produced fire while others chased after them to put it out." Yi eagerly joined in, swinging "a massive fire stick and inflamed almost as many spots as his footsteps." This annual ritual of hope and renewal took on added meaning after August 15, 1945. As An observed, "I wondered if the euphoria after Korea's liberation had been compressed all into this one game because *pul nori* this year was a greater success than any other previous year." Enchanted by the flames, Yi decides to commemorate his own rebirth by burning down the only thing he has left: "The terrifying flames were shooting up toward the sky, and the roof of the house was already starting to burn." An, who did not witness Yi's pyromania but had premonitions of it, envisioned "him setting the fire to his house and then climbing the nearby hill to watch it burn while the moonlight soaked his body to the skin."

The two meet one last time, right before Yi leaves his hometown forever. An encounters a person transformed. "He seemed sharper and more composed than before. It seemed as if he was changing into a different person every second." Despite his profound losses, Yi speaks of finding a bright future. "The fact that I'm back in my hometown like this really means that I've come back from the dead. But now that I'm back it's not possible to live as I used to anymore. My parents, my wife, my son, my house, my possessions, they're all gone now." He resolves to "live not only for himself but also for others, dedicate his life to working for Korea's future, in whatever shape or form." In his parting words, he tells An, "a wonderful new world must be just around the corner, since Korea is now liberated."

If liberation meant anything, it was the chance to start over.

Son Kijŏng, gold medalist at the 1936 Summer
Olympics, Berlin, Germany.
Der Spiegel / Wikimedia Commons

In Seoul, longtime nationalist Yŏ Unhyŏng led efforts to rebuild a new nation. He had spent considerable time in prison in the 1920s and 1930s advocating for Korean independence. After being released in 1932, Yŏ became
editor for a Korean newspaper and again came to the attention of Japanese
authorities when he published a photo of Son Kijŏng, head down, clutching
a young oak tree to cover up the Japanese flag on his jersey during the medal ceremony at the 1936 Berlin Olympics. Son had won Korea's first Olympic gold but had done so as member of the Japanese delegation. Olympic
officials raised the Japanese flag and played the Japanese anthem during his
turn at the podium. Colonial officials shut down Yŏ's newspaper and had
him arrested and imprisoned for printing the "subversive" photo.

When Yŏ emerged from prison yet again, he worked toward building an underground independence movement, first with the Korean People's Liberation Party and then with the National Foundation League (NFL), which Yŏ established, along with other independence activists, in 1944. The league built a clandestine network of organizers who fanned out across Korea to gain adherents among peasant farmers, conscripted soldiers, workers, women, and the youth.[11]

Yŏ's record of principled resistance gave the organization considerable stature. As one Korean historian explained, "Yŏ Unhyŏng was almost the only person in Korea who had public recognition and prestige at a time when young people hoped for the emergence of national heroes who would lead the independence and founding of Korea at the end of the Japanese colonial era."[12] The league had close to seventy thousand members by the time of the emperor's announcement.

On the evening of August 14, Endō Ryūsaku, the second highest-ranking official in the Japanese colonial government, requested urgently to meet with Yŏ the next morning. At their 7:00 a.m. meeting, Endō told Yŏ the emperor would be announcing Japan's surrender at noon. He asked him to take charge of preserving the peace during the transition, which meant, above all else, ensuring the safety of the hundreds of thousands of Japanese residents in Korea. Why did Endō want a dedicated anti-Japanese fighter to lead this effort? From years of colonial surveillance and persecution, Japanese officials knew Yŏ had broad popular support. It was why colonial authorities spent so much time and effort to quiet him. And it was why, Endō felt, Koreans would follow Yŏ's lead.

Yŏ agreed to the request on the condition that the colonial government immediately release the thousands of political prisoners held in its jails. He also wanted assurances from Endō that his organization, and other allied groups, would be left alone to carry out its mandate without interference from the Japanese. In no position to negotiate, being only a few short hours away from Japan announcing its surrender, Endō quickly acquiesced to all of Yŏ's demands.[13]

Almost immediately, Yŏ went to work mobilizing a peacekeeping force to maintain law and order, as he had promised. But he would not stop there. Building on the networks and infrastructure of the NFL, Yŏ organized the de facto government of Korea, first the Committee for the Preparation of Korean Independence (CPKI) and then the Korean People's Republic (KPR) several weeks later. Yŏ envisioned a broad coalition—a united front—to

Yŏ Unhyŏng, longtime advocate of Korean independence.
Mongyang Memorial Museum

lead a free and independent Korea, saying, "Unification must happen as quickly as possible. The paradise where all of us can live well together will occur by gathering each person and each party including workers, capitalists, democrats, and communists."[14] Within weeks, over a hundred CPKI branches and people's committees appeared across Korea.

Rivals and critics denounced Yŏ as a political opportunist who offered something to everyone in order to acquire power. There were even whispers he had collaborated with the Japanese. This charge had almost no basis in fact, and accusations that Yŏ was an opportunist ignored his long record of pragmatism and willingness to work with different groups to achieve Korean independence. He had been a member of the Communist Party *and* Sun

Yat-sen's Chinese nationalist party. Yŏ also counted American missionaries among his friends, who considered him a Woodrow Wilson–style liberal, if anything. If there was a center in Korean politics during this time, Yŏ might have been it. He remains one of the very few Korean figures who is revered in both North and South Korea.

In September, the KPR released a twenty-seven-point program that outlined the group's aspirations for liberation. The highlights included:

- Confiscating lands from the Japanese and national traitors and redistributing them to poor Korean farmers.
- Nationalizing major industries like mining, shipping, banking, and manufacturing.
- Enacting labor reforms to end child labor and establish maximum work hours and a minimum wage.
- Providing the vote to Korean men and women over the age of eighteen (excluding Koreans who collaborated with the Japanese).
- Offering women equal rights.
- Guaranteeing the rights of free speech, assembly, and religion.

In a warning shot to foreign powers, the KPR insisted on "complete autonomy and independence" for Korea as it worked toward building an "authentically democratic state."[15] In sum, Korean leaders demanded political autonomy and freedom, economic redistribution and equality, and redress for colonial injustices.

This was the stuff of liberation.

Right around the time Yŏ was launching the CPKI, a group of thirty Korean women established the Founding Women's Association (FWA) to much less fanfare. It was led by Yu Yŏngjun and Pak Sunchŏn and a sixteen-member executive committee. Many had cut their teeth on the women's rights movement as part of the Kŭnuhoe (Rose of Sharon Society). Formed in 1927, the Kŭnuhoe represented a remarkable alliance of Korean socialist, communist, and Christian nationalist women. And for several years, it had been a force in independence struggles as well as women's rights. The women-only organization opened over sixty chapters in Korea and abroad with membership numbering in the thousands.[16] In 1931, however, it collapsed under

Japanese colonial repression. A number of its socialist and communist leaders were imprisoned or exiled. Those remaining went underground, where they struggled to maintain the nucleus of the movement.

It was this remnant that emerged in the hours after the emperor's historic announcement to start the FWA. Like its predecessor, the FWA sought to unite women of all stripes—radical communists, social democrats, and conservative nationalists—in a fight for liberation and women's rights. "We women will actively participate in the total struggle for the liberation of all citizens," they declared. Reflecting the diversity of the organization's membership, the platform ranged widely, from political to economic to social rights. It called for women's suffrage and the right to hold office, equal pay for equal work, the abolition of licensed prostitution and sex trafficking, investment in women's education, and public assistance for pregnant women and mothers. This was a program of comprehensive change that they believed would liberate women and the nation simultaneously.[17]

Korean women had played an important role in the independence movement going back to the March First Movement. It was a sixteen-year-old female student, Yu Kwansun, who organized some of the earliest protests against Japanese rule and inspired a nation. In March 1919, starting with her hometown, Yu went from village to village to organize public demonstrations against the Japanese. She recited passages from the Korean Declaration of Independence, handed out homemade Korean flags, and led crowds in chants of "Long live Korean independence!" Her activism helped fuel protests across the country.[18]

Colonial authorities quickly arrested Yu for sedition and tortured her in prison—she would eventually die from the injuries. "Even if my fingernails are torn out, my nose and ears are ripped apart, and arms are crushed, this physical pain does not compare to the pain of losing my nation," she wrote from prison before her death.[19] (Yu's story continues to resonate with Koreans around the world. In January 2019, the New York state legislature introduced a bill to designate March 1 as Yu Kwansun Day.)

The focus on *national* liberation made a lot of sense. It was the one issue that all Korean women, whatever their background, could agree on. But the FWA insisted that true national liberation could not be achieved without women's emancipation—the two, they argued, were inseparable: "Only when the national problem facing Korea is completely liberated, our woman problem will at last be resolved. Conversely, if our woman problem is not solved, then the national revolutionary problem will also not be solved."[20]

Yu Kwansun in Sŏdaemun Prison in Seoul, where she died from torture wounds at seventeen.

Korean History Database / Wikimedia Commons

But Koreans, men and women, did not wait for liberation to be handed to them. They didn't need a formal party platform or a multipoint program to spur them to action. Nearly forty years of hopes, dreams, and grievances came rushing out in spontaneous celebrations, uprisings, and retributions in which ordinary Koreans would give meaning to liberation in their own diverse ways—big and small, organized and chaotic, high-minded and self-interested. These countless individual acts ushered in Korea's Asian Spring—a sprawling moment ripe with promise and possibility when almost anything seemed possible.[21]

Among the most pressing goals was land reform. In fact, even before the KPR's platform became public in the first week of September, Korean peasants had begun seizing and occupying some of the 875,000 acres of Japanese-owned lands. Held mostly by the Oriental Development Company, chartered by Japan in 1908, these lands constituted close to 50 percent of all farmland in the southern half of Korea, including some of the richest rice paddies. As a colonization company, the Oriental Development Company encouraged Japanese migration and settlement, as well as extracted and transferred resources from the colony to the metropole. It rapidly acquired land to facilitate both aims, becoming far and away the largest landowner in Korea. A big portion of the rice the Japanese ate came from its prized colony. The Korean peninsula, as critics put it, was Japan's rice bowl.

Not surprisingly, the development company became one of the most hated symbols of colonial rule. In 1927, Korean nationalist Na Sŏkju attempted to blow up the company headquarters in Seoul. He failed. But he did gun down several office employees before killing himself, which earned him martyrdom—today several statues of him stand in Seoul. The Japanese authorities, on the other hand, denounced him as a terrorist for attacking unarmed civilians.

Forty years of colonial rule had produced crushing poverty and widening inequality in the Korean countryside. "As we look over rural conditions here, we find that seventy-five percent of the farmers are tenants or part tenants," reported Arthur C. Bunce, a YMCA missionary based in Korea. The system, he wrote in 1933, "keeps the tenant farmer very poor and unable to save enough to ever buy his own land and, in many cases, the tenant is little better than a serf."[22] In an overwhelmingly agrarian society, nearly 80 percent of the native population worked on a farm. Tenant farmers paid at least half and as much as 90 percent of their harvest in rent to their landlords, which left them with very little at the end of the season. With no long-term leases, they also struggled with chronic housing and work insecurity.

Ch'oe Chŏnghŭi described the plight of the tenant farmer under Japanese rule: "They had worked this land which belonged to the landlord and each year had returned his quota of rice. What remained was far from enough for one year, six months, or two months. In fact, it wasn't sufficient for even one month." During the spring, peasant women—mothers, grandmothers, and daughters—with a basket in hand and a *pojagi* (a colorful, stitched cloth covering) wrapped around their waists foraged for edible greens like *minari*, dug up roots, and stripped the barks from trees to try to make up some of the deficit. But, whatever the landless peasants did, the threat of hunger lingered. Death seemed to be the only escape: "When someone died the only comment made by those who watched the funeral procession was, 'Now you won't have to starve, that's good.'"[23] These conditions, resulting from colonial policy, drove hundreds of thousands of Korean rural families off the land. Uprooted, they wandered to Japan, Manchuria, and Siberia in search of work or food.[24]

Landless peasants raided government rice storages almost immediately after Japan's surrender.[25] They must've taken great pleasure from gorging on quota rice that for a generation they had to turn over to the Japanese (rice was a luxury item for most Koreans, to be had on special occasions, if they were lucky). But after they satiated their hunger pangs, they turned to bigger aspirations. Thousands of peasant families acted swiftly to take over lands owned by the Japanese and those of Korean "traitors," who were more often not, absentee landlords, the thinking being that if you were a Korean who accumulated land and wealth during this time, you must have collaborated with the Japanese. Peasant leaders and activists established unions, federations, and committees to try to redistribute the land more systematically—to instill order to the process. But this occurred after the fact: land seizures themselves were largely spontaneous.[26] From the outset, peasants were clear about what they wanted. After forty years of exploitation and suffering, they set about taking back what was once theirs. As the peasants saw it, they had earned the land with their toil, and they would take it.

Seizing land was a messy business, sparking conflict. But it was also exhilarating, stirring feelings that had been long buried or forgotten. Han Saengwŏn, from Ch'ae Mansik's 1946 classic story "Once Upon a Rice Paddy," captured the sublime happiness peasants felt upon reclaiming their lands: "To think that . . . the land he had turned over to the Japanese, like a dream, would be returned and be his again. . . . There could be nothing in this world so wonderful and rare."[27]

Peasants marked the occasion with continuous dancing and singing—and not a small amount of drinking—for several days straight. Indeed, the *makkŏli*—unrefined Korean wine made from rice and barley—was flowing. There were more than a few reports of drunken naked men screaming and hollering on tabletops. Some peasants took an additional step to try to guarantee their landholdings. Like all imperial powers, Japanese colonizers sought to rationalize, classify, and standardize Korean society, making a census and land surveys and insisting on new weights and measures. These things made the colony more legible to the Japanese, and thus, easier to rule.[28] In agricultural areas, the Japanese made property maps, created land registers, maintained tax records, and imposed rice quotas. These instruments of imperial statecraft helped determine how much land there was in Korea, who owned it, and how much it was worth. And this, in turn, helped Japan extract Korea's rice.[29]

For peasants, Japanese records were an albatross, and so, they stormed the government buildings and played *pul nori* with them. Pillars of black smoke from the burning paperwork could be seen from all directions across the countryside. By destroying them, peasants sought to eliminate the paper trail that might challenge their ownership of recently usurped lands. They also wiped out the debts they owed, whether they be taxes or rice, in a single swoop. There was rhyme and reason in the chaos.

Taking their land back was important to Koreans, but it wasn't all that mattered. Retribution was in the air. In fact, some people pivoted swiftly from celebrating to seeking revenge. They went looking for collaborators who sided with the colonizers. But exactly who or what was a collaborator? What about the Japanese, the people who actually colonized Korea? There were some 700,000 Japanese in Korea immediately after surrender.[30] Between Yŏ Unhyŏng's effective peacekeeping and the presence of armed Japanese soldiers, Japanese settlers escaped almost completely unscathed (the same could not be said of the Shinto shrines and their property). Koreans showed more anger at their fellow countrymen for collaborating than at the Japanese colonizers. As Pak Munchae explained, "The most hated group of people at the time were less Japanese than pro-Japanese collaborators."[31]

Collaborating could take many different forms, depending on how one chose to define it. Yi Kwangsu, colonial Korea's most famous writer, argued (self-servingly, as he was accused of collaboration himself) that anyone and everyone was a collaborator, if taken literally, by "paying taxes to the Japanese government, registering one's household, following the law, flying the rising-sun flag, taking an oath to the Empire, worshipping at a shrine." "If one didn't collaborate," he insisted, "one would be dead or imprisoned."[32]

But after liberation, Koreans targeted three groups of people in particular for their traitorous actions. First were the Korean landlords who threw in their lot with the colonizers. The Japanese needed native cooperation to effectively rule their colony—despite their military superiority, they were massively outnumbered by the Koreans. And so, early on, they entered into a bargain with the Korean landed elite. Colonial authorities would preserve the traditional landlord system and the class privileges that came with it. In return, Korean landlords helped maintain colonial rule by staunching resistance from revolutionary nationalists and peasant rebels.[33]

This arrangement polarized class relations in the countryside, as the gulf between the rich and the poor grew, with the landholding elite gaining at

Korean comfort women held by the US military.
National Archives (111-SC-262580)

the expense of the peasants. And the peasants took notice: the Korean land-lords, as they recalled bitterly, "ate sumptuous meals in peace, wore hand-some clothes, and lived happily," even while "an entire village was trans-formed into a living hell with everyone weeping because of drafting and requisition and National Protection Corps and conscription and student soldiering."[34] The anger ran deep, and not even the young were immune from it. After liberation, children of tenants could be seen chasing down and assaulting children of landlords.[35]

Second were the village leaders who had enthusiastically championed Ja-pan's war aims and worked closely with colonial authorities to accomplish them. This included recruiting Korean men and women for the draft, in-cluding girls to serve as "comfort women" for the imperial army during the war. In Chang Tŏkjo's "Hamsŏng" [Shouts], a mother desperately tries to rescue her daughter from conscription into the Women's Volunteer Corps: "The mother of Chŏmsun let down her hair and furiously demanded an explanation while the police and township clerks assured her it would bring glory and honor to her family."[36] This is a scene that could have taken place in just about any village at the time.

Memories of being unable to protect their sons and daughters and the feelings of shame and humiliation it brought back—as well as the fear of not knowing if they were still alive or safe—fueled smoldering hatred for the village elders that erupted into violence when Japanese rule collapsed. Villagers ransacked and burned their homes, running them out of villages with nothing but the clothes on their back—that is, if they were lucky. "Those who fled survived," explained Pak, "but those who stayed were caught and killed."[37]

The third group Koreans turned on was the police. During the colonial era, the Japanese drew policemen from the native population to maintain order. The police worked hand in glove with the landlords to collect rice and put down revolts. Anytime a dispute arose between a landlord and tenant, the police sided with the landlord, acting, essentially, as a private security force.

As daily enforcers of Japanese authority, the police were the face of colonial rule. And they were nearly everywhere. For every four hundred Koreans, the Japanese had employed one policeman, so nearly half the police were Koreans. One of the most notorious police stations was led by Yi Kwi-bun, who reportedly killed thousands.[38] But more than anything, it was the daily torments that ordinary Koreans despised. The failure to meet the rice quota, for example, resulted in a slap in the face, or worse, a beating. Some corrupt police inflated the quota to skim off the top. In unannounced home visits, police checked whether the picture of Emperor Hirohito was in the required place of honor in the house.[39] Those deemed in violation were publicly flogged and, in some cases, imprisoned without a trial. "This they frequently did," one US official later reported. "There were none of the restraints from arbitrary action such as the writ of habeas corpus." He added, "Wiretapping, the use of informers, searches without arrests, and torture were commonplace."[40]

So, when the chance presented itself, liberated Koreans went on a beating spree of the Korean police, chasing many of them out of town. Detective Yi's home in Kaesong was wrecked after liberation. (His home might have been the aforementioned "X's house.")

Not all Koreans took justice into their own hands. Some villages established "people's courts" to try suspected collaborators right after liberation. These courts were locally inspired and set up with protocols and standards for reaching judgment, which suggests some Koreans had been grappling with the issue long before the end of colonial rule.[41]

Identifying and punishing "collaborators" was necessary if Koreans were going to reverse the legacy of colonialism, but it was never going to be easy. An informant who hunted down Korean resistance fighters, like the one portrayed by Lee Jung-jae (of *Squid Games*) in the 2015 blockbuster Korean film *Assassination*, was unequivocally a collaborator. But was the young Korean man who volunteered for the imperial army because he had no real alternatives a collaborator? "I didn't want to go because I might die in the military," said one former solider. "But because we were so poor."[42] What about the *kukch'irang*—the Korean women accused of betraying the nation for consorting with the Japanese? Outside of village elders and the police, they received the harshest treatment, including public floggings and shaming. Coming from impoverished families, these women often exchanged sexual favors with Japanese men for food, clothing, and other sustenance.[43] Were they collaborators?

People's courts took the first stab at answering some of these thorny questions by establishing rules, norms, and standards. Some were rudimentary, but they provided a basic structure, and, because people's courts were administered locally, they could take into account nuances and complexities often overlooked by abstract legal definitions. Yet at times these proceedings devolved into "show trials" in which guilt and punishment were predetermined. Still, the fact that some local communities took the time and effort to establish a system to render judgment in an orderly and not totally arbitrary fashion was remarkable. This was, after all, following forty years of colonialism and when they could've just opted for extrajudicial means. They seemed to understand that exorcising the colonial past would not be achieved through a fit of violence or rage. Retribution, in other words, was not the same thing as justice.

Meanwhile, in the cities, Korean workers, being of the same mind about ownership as the peasants, seized "enemy" property in mass. At the rubber and paper factories down the road from Yi Ilchae's in Taegu, workers banded together to take control of their respective plants. They used their new managerial prerogative to implement an eight-hour workday, provide daily rations for employees, improve meals, and update facilities used by workers.[44] In Seoul, Korean workers in several industries held company presidents and managers captive until they paid out severance bonuses and transferred the factories to the employees. Workers saw the severance payments as merely recouping "what had been plundered by imperialist Japan over the last thirty-six years."[45]

The "workers' self-management" movement, as scholars would later call it, began spontaneously in August as workers seized control of a handful of factories. But as the news of the seizures traveled, takeovers spread rapidly throughout the peninsula, so much so, that by November, some 80,000 workers had assumed control of more than 700 factories, offices, and mines in the South alone.[46] What did they hope to achieve by seizing the factory floor? Some of the takeovers were led by communist, anarchist, and socialist activists who had recently emerged from prison or the underground after Japan's surrender. They envisioned the seizures as the start of a workers' revolution that would throw off capitalist as well as Japanese rule. "The ethnic chains have been cut off," wrote the revolutionary poet Yun Gon Kang, "but the class chains remain."

Under colonialism, the communists were some of the most dedicated fighters for workers' rights and Korean independence.[47] They were activists like Yu Pyŏnghwa, who learned about communism through his father, who read to him the *Communist Manifesto* the way a devoted Christian father would the Bible. By the time he was thirteen, Yu could recite communist doctrine by memory. In 1944, he fled with his family to Manchuria after being questioned by the colonial police on suspicion of promoting Korean independence and communist ideas. Yu returned to Korea in 1945 and became a labor organizer for the railroad union.[48]

But in most cases, rank-and-file Korean workers took over factories and businesses without formal guidance or organizing. For these workers, seizing the factory floor was less about revolution and more about reform, driven by bread-and-butter concerns—higher wages, safer working conditions, and more control over their labor. In addition, women workers in the textile and rubber shoe industries, many of them teenagers and younger, sought paid leave for childbirth, dedicated time for breastfeeding on the job, and exemption from night work. Largely ignored by male union activists, Korean women workers frequently had to organize on their own to make their demands heard, going back to colonial times. And if you go by the numbers, women workers protested and struck as often as their male counterparts.[49]

One of the landmark protests of the colonial era was inspired by a rubber shoe worker, Kang Churyong, better known as the "woman-in-the-sky." Kang was among forty-nine women workers at the P'yŏngwŏn Rubber Factory in Pyongyang, who went on strike to protest the factory's plan to cut their wages. The cuts would come on top of wage reductions that were enacted just a year earlier. The owner fired the striking workers and replaced them with new ones. The fired workers responded by going on a hunger strike while occupying the factory floor. Shortly thereafter, the police were called in to forcibly remove the protesters, ostensibly ending the standoff.[50]

Kang, however, refused to see their struggle end this way. She first considered suicide to draw attention to the worker's cause, but ultimately decided on a different tack. At the crack of dawn on May 29, 1931, two weeks into the strike, Kang made a rope of cotton cloth, tied a stone around one end, threw it to the roof to anchor it, and climbed up the Ŭlmildae Pavilion, thirty-six feet high. Morning commuters heard her yell out that she would not come down until the owner of the factory showed up and promised, face to face, to abandon his plan to cut wages. "If he fails to do so," she said, "it will be my great honor to die as a representative of the working populace."[51]

Kang's daring protest received enormous public attention; her image covered the front page of all the major dailies. The Korean media marveled at Kang's moxie, ingenuity, and eloquence. Facing public pressure, factory executives agreed to do away with the wage cuts and hired back most of the previously fired workers. (Nearly eighty years later, Kim Chinsuk, a welder for Hanjin Heavy Industries, in a reprise of Kang's "sky-high sit in," spent almost a year perched atop a 115-foot crane in protest of the company's decision to lay off hundreds of its workers. On the 309th day of her protest, the company agreed to reinstate the fired workers.)[52]

Yet, as exceptional as Kang and her actions were, she was not alone in her devotion to the cause of the women workers. In fact, six of Kang's female colleagues, who struck alongside her, went to prison for their activism.[53]

To achieve their goals, workers—whether men or women—didn't necessarily see the need to overturn the capitalist system. But they wanted to fundamentally alter the relationship between management and labor if they were going to preserve the distinction. At the Chosŏn Leather Factory and the Mishin Company in Seoul, workers found "conscientious" Korean shareholders and financiers to buy a stake in their companies after assuming control. The investors would run the company and make business decisions, but workers would be represented at the management table in an arrangement resembling codetermination. They would thus have a say on wages and salaries, work hours and conditions, and the overall direction of the company. In some instances, workers, intent on obtaining a fair share of the fruits of their labor, negotiated profit-sharing with investors.[54]

Liberation, in short, took many forms.

As was the case with peasant land seizures, most of the properties workers targeted were Japanese owned. In some ways this couldn't be helped, since over 90 percent of the largest businesses in Korea were owned by the Japanese minority—this fact alone spoke to the highly unequal colonial relationship. Fresh memories of being conscripted to work in factories, mines, and construction in Korea and across the Japanese empire during the recent war also inspired the mass takeovers. Korean workers justified the seizures as an act of compensatory justice (what we might call reparations today)— back pay for decades of colonial exploitation.

Yi Kyuwŏn wrote a fictionalized account of his experience as a worker at the Mitsubishi Steel Company.[55] His story, "Haebang kongjang" (Liberation factory), provides a glimpse into what workers might have experienced in the hours and days after liberation. The novel begins with the protagonist, Kim Yonggap, a smelter at the factory, responding defiantly to his manager. "No. I can't run your machine. Starting today, your orders won't work at this factory. We have the right to order." From here, Kim emerges as the unlikely leader of a ragtag group that includes Yi Talgwan, an electrician who had lost two fingers while operating a lathe; Cho Ŏkman, a boiler who went deaf from the roar of a malfunctioning machine; and Song Ch'an, a technician who was fired after losing his left arm in a work-related accident.

None of them, including Kim, had prior experience leading or organizing. In fact, when Kim steps forward to call for worker unity, he is unnerved by the sight of the hundreds of factory workers and forgets the speech he had spent days rehearsing. Indeed, much of the early organizing is impromptu and not very well coordinated. They are not professional activists. There is no grand strategy.

And yet, the workers manage to form a committee to stop the Japanese executives from carrying away and selling factory machinery and assets, destroying factory records and blueprints, and hoarding cash and supplies. And they come up with a petition demanding back pay and severance for the five hundred workers at the soon-to-be shuttered factory. The committee goes to the home of the company president to present their demand. He summarily rejects it, enraging the workers. The sight of oversized clay pots filled to the brim with rice doesn't help matters. Workers drag him and other Japanese executives back to the factory and lock them up in the air defense shelter. After two days, the president reluctantly agrees to a 1.5 million *won* settlement. He also signs papers transferring ownership of the factory to the workers' committee.

"This was the moment," Yi explains, "when they felt a sense of liberation." Workers commemorate the takeover by renaming the factory P'alwŏl Kong-jang (August Factory) to represent "the sun of August, the passion of August," but most of all, "the liberation of August." They create a sign with the new name and proudly hang it up at the front gate of the factory.

Instead of distributing the funds as severance payments, Kim proposes to use the money to keep the factory open. He is confident the workers could run and operate the factory without the Japanese capitalists. "Let's show the power of workers!" he declares. The plan is to convert the munitions factory into a peacetime industry in which "machines are no longer blocks of steel, but creatures that move through the heat and sweat of the workers."[56]

Being a Korean owner did not make one safe from labor uprisings. At the largest textile factory in Seoul, workers faced off with its powerful president, Kim Yŏnsu. Along with his brother, Kim Sŏngsu, he headed the Kyŏngsŏng Spinning and Weaving Joint Stock Company, the largest Korean industrial enterprise during the colonial era. Their company was, in many respects, the first *chaebol*, the family-run conglomerate (like Samsung or Hyundai) that later would come to dominate South Korean economic life. The Kim brothers were among a select group of Korean businessmen who benefited under—some would say collaborated with—Japanese rule. Their company was only able to get as big as it did because of easy access to loans through the colonial government.[57] Kim Yŏnsu was put on a trial for "anti-national-ist" activities in 1949. (His brother, Kim Sŏngsu, was classified as a pro-Japanese collaborator by the Presidential Committee for the Inspection of Collaboration for Japanese Imperialism in 2009.)

Kim's factory in Seoul had a long history of conflict between management and labor, including worker demonstrations in 1926 and 1931. Both of these instances ended with managers calling on the colonial police, who doubled as strikebreakers, to put down protesting workers. Sounding almost envious of the Korean company's heavy-handed tactics, one Japanese newspaper called the end of the strike in 1931 an "overwhelming defeat" for the workers in an article with the blaring headline "A Victory to the Company."[58]

Sensing a shift in the balance of power after Japan's surrender, workers quickly organized to make new demands on the company's president. On

August 31, 1945, the fourteen hundred textile workers held a convention where they called for an eight-hour workday, improved facilities, education classes, and a year-end bonus equivalent to a year's salary. Young women and girls, who comprised a significant portion of the workforce, added equal rations for equal work to the list of demands—previously, men received higher rations then women regardless of the time put in.

Workers formed a self-management committee as a negotiating ploy to increase their bargaining power with the company—they didn't have any intention of actually taking over the factory. Ever the imperial executive, Kim Yŏnsu agreed to only the eight-hour workday in a take it or leave it offer. Unsatisfied, workers occupied the factory floor where they threatened to remain until their other demands were met. Kim responded by shutting down the factory, which caught workers by surprise, but they were not completely unprepared. The managerial committee formed to gain leverage at the bargaining table was now directing the operation of the plant on the fly after the lockout.[59]

With the end of forty years of Japanese rule, Korea's future brightened, like the sky after a long storm. Electrified by the possibilities, Koreans acted swiftly to realize their hopes and aspirations, seizing the moment to claim their independence, right past wrongs, and pursue equality. One could say they were moved by the *sinparam* that writer Chŏng Kyŏngmo described as "the strange wind that billows in the hearts of people who have freed themselves from oppression, regained their freedom, and lived in a society of mutual trust."

Yet in the midst of the effervescence and idealism lurked fractures and divisions. Korea's Asian Spring was not a monolith. As Koreans pursued their diverse visions for liberation, their differences would become more and more apparent. The schisms ignited contests over the meaning of liberation and how its promise should be fulfilled. The struggles took place at every level of Korean society, touching almost every facet of Korean life. And, as they bubbled up, they threatened to throw liberation into turmoil and violence.

Liberation, it turns out, also divided Koreans.

2 Fractures Appear

Mr. Yi's transformation in "Fire" captured the hope and idealism of liberation. Yi was the former conscript who lost everything while he was away. But while playing *pul nori* back in his hometown, he imagines a fresh start, a new life. The fire fills him with optimism that a radically different future for him and Korea was "just around the corner." So much so he's willing to set ablaze all his remaining possessions in a baptism of sorts and begin again with nothing. And why not? Free from colonial rule, Koreans now controlled their own destiny; happier times surely lay ahead.

But a closer reading of the story also reveals the perils and challenges of liberation. After the end of the Lunar New Year festivities, Mr. Yi and Mr. An walk back to their homes. When they reach Yi's house, he tells An to wait for a moment. Yi goes inside and emerges initially with a dresser but then goes back inside several more times and comes out with another household item each time. It becomes clear that Yi is bringing out all of his personal belongings in order to burn them. An restrains Yi, telling him, "You must hang on. . . . Korea's been liberated, things will get better from now on." Yi breaks down and starts sobbing uncontrollably. An comforts him for a while before leaving for his own house.

An has trouble sleeping that night. The way Yi talked about and played with fire, as if he was possessed by it, gives him nightmares: "It summoned up images of a dozen houses in Seoul razed to the ground by fire; it recalled the mountain tops and dikes scorched by *pul nori* earlier." "I was gripped," he confessed, "with a grotesque anxiety that a fire might suddenly break out in my own house." Unlike Yi, An has a wife, a job as a writer, and a peaceful home. In other words, he has things to lose.

After Yi burns down his house, An admits as much: "He was less fortunate, and thus, he has destroyed the old and begun anew." He praises Yi for having the courage to make a fresh start while chastising himself for being a coward for fearing the fire. But the truth was, An felt enormous relief when he learned the fire was confined to Yi's house.[1]

Not everyone wanted to start over.

Koreans may have envisioned liberation as a new beginning but that didn't mean they shared the same vision for what came next, whether it was for themselves or their country. This was because they didn't all have the same interests and goals, their collective yearning for independence notwithstanding. And even when they did, they didn't always pursue them in the same way—approaches differed. Korean responses to the end of colonial rule ranged widely, revealing important differences in how they imagined liberation and sought to fulfill its promise.

Take the struggles and aspirations of peasant farmers. Many of them had confiscated Japanese-owned lands and those of Korean collaborators right after liberation and claimed them as their own. But what might come as a surprise, just as many peasants—probably more—didn't take anyone's land. Why not? Seizing Japanese-owned lands, in some respects, was the low-hanging fruit, simply because, in most cases, there was no one around to stop it. Japanese landlords were largely absentee, more likely to be suits in an office, working for the likes of the Oriental Development Company, which had office buildings in all the major cities in Korea. They hired managers and foremen to oversee the day-to-day affairs. And these employees on-site, some of them Korean, were hardly going to put up a fight now that Japan had surrendered. Indeed, many of them, fearing retribution, fled their positions soon after the emperor's announcement.[2]

But Japanese-owned lands made up "only" half of the total land in Korea. The other half belonged to Koreans, who were, for the most part, present and living nearby. And appropriating their lands was much harder. How much pause did this give peasants? Quite a bit in some areas. Consider the region known as the "rice bowl" in south central Korea, which mainly included areas in the North Chŏlla, South Ch'ungch'ŏng, and North Kyŏngsang provinces. It boasted some of the highest tenancy rates, some of the richest rice paddies, and the largest landlord estates on the peninsula. Yet peasants seized fewer estates here than almost anywhere else in Korea.

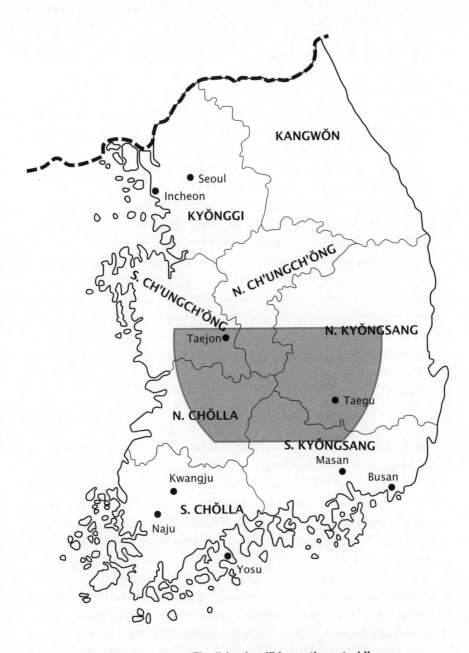

The "rice bowl" in south central Korea.

Rural chronicler Ch'oe Chŏnghŭi observed the power dynamics in the "rice bowl" and explained how they came to be: "It was taken for granted that life in the big house was one way and for the peasants another way." "This way of thinking," she contended, "had become second nature," the result of "hundreds of years of living like slaves" in which "generation after generation watched and learned."[3] Her depictions of peasant passivity obscured the long history of peasant revolt and resistance in Korea, most notably the Tonghak Rebellion of 1894, when peasants came close to overthrowing the Korean landed elite.[4] But the cumulative power she describes landlords amassing, over decades and even centuries, was quite real and would not dissolve so easily, even with the rupture of liberation.

In the areas outside the "rice bowl," peasants felt freer to usurp land after liberation. There, Korean landlord power had been weaker and peasants had more of a history organizing, forming peasant unions to collectively fight high rents and taxes and exploitative practices of the landlords. Just as power begets power, resistance begets resistance. What this tells us is prior conditions, under Japanese colonial rule and going further back, shaped what peasants imagined to be possible, which, in turn, affected how they would respond to liberation.[5]

That did not mean that peasants in landlord strongholds settled for the status quo. For one thing, some did seize lands there, just not as often. And even when they didn't, they still demanded and won significant reforms. Some tenant farmers negotiated lower rents, cutting them by half or more in many instances. Others who had previously worked—and lived—with the uncertainty of land tenure obtained long-term security from their landlords. Peasants also extracted other concessions, including pushing the cost of fertilizer, water, equipment, and taxes to the landlord.[6] These reforms irked landowners, who saw their grasp slipping. Yi Sŏndal, the wealthy landlord in "Sorrow of Peasants," complained, "How can a landowner survive when the only farm rent that he receives is 30% of the harvest? Tenant farmers don't let go of their land as meekly as before when landowners ask them to leave either!" He lamented, "Today the world is one in which landowners cannot live . . . only tenant farmers can."[7]

Peasants also obtained land by another method: they purchased it. Fearing their lands would be eventually expropriated, Korean landlords offered to sell their tenanted lands at heavily discounted prices (rumors of a Soviet

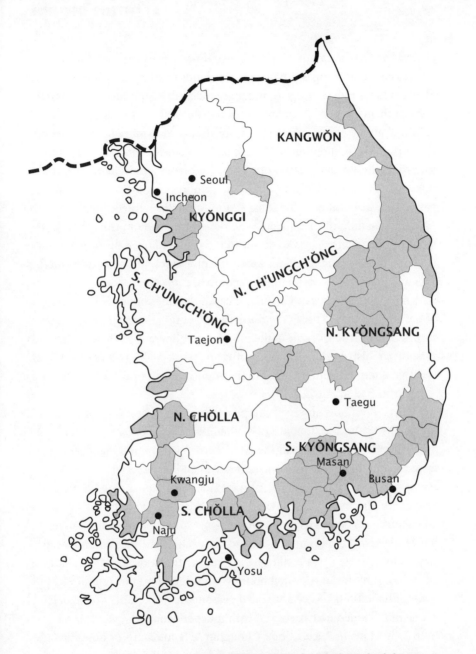

Red peasant unions during the colonial era.

occupation, circulating in August, drove down prices for land dramatically). Peasants unwilling or unable to seize lands outright now had a choice.
They could wait for a new government to redistribute the lands and possibly
acquire them without payment—this was not out of the question, as the
KPR had already promised to do so—or they could secure land right away
for a price. The first option carried risks. Fortunes had undoubtedly shifted
toward tenant farmers but no one knew for certain what the future would
hold. Like everyone else, they heard the rumors of a possible foreign occupation that cast doubt on the prospects of immediate independence.

Many tenant families mitigated the risk by buying land from their landlords, pooling their money to do so. Some borrowed from the local money-
lender. Other peasant families sold off their livestock and household goods.
This was their once-in-a-lifetime chance to become landowners—they were
determined to find a way. Ordinary peasant families bought up a majority
of the lands sold by Korean landlords, who put up more than 60 percent of
their tenanted lands for sale in the months after liberation. The sales ignited
a massive redistribution of land constituting perhaps the greatest transfer of
wealth from the rich to the poor in the country's history. Without knowing
it, peasants had initiated land reform.[8]

Internal divisions, however, complicated this story of empowerment and
uplift. The economic situation of Korean peasants had varied under Japanese rule. Some farmed land that was theirs, others rented land as tenant
farmers; and then there were the farmhands and servants who made up the
landless proletariat.[9] These groups were not equally positioned to take advantage of the mass selloff. Hired farmhands and servants, for example,
who were too poor to lease, let alone own, were without the resources to
buy land even at the lower prices. And their ranks had swelled under Japanese colonial rule. As a result, the poorest of the rural poor were largely
excluded from the land buying boom. "Would money fall from the sky because of liberation?" asked frustrated peasants, for whom the dream of land
ownership seemed no closer even with independence.

In "Ritual at the Well," Ch'oe Chŏnghŭi tells the story of how the land
purchases fractured one Korean village. It begins with villagers gathered for
the annual ritual at the communal well. This was a day for performing cer-
emonial rites to ask the spirits for a bountiful water supply for the upcoming season. In between rites, the villagers eat, drink, and talk. The troubles
begin when a Korean *ajumŏni* (middle-aged woman) brings out a plate of

bread. In a mad scramble to get a piece, the villagers knock the plate over and bread pieces fly everywhere.

One of the villagers later accuses Haksu, a young man, of taking more than one piece. She suspects he had taken the extra piece for his girlfriend, Mongbun. Haksu tells her and the other villagers, who had now gathered around him, that he took the bread piece to his mother but they don't believe him. Hearing the quarrel, Haksu's mother comes racing out with a rag in hand, yelling, "That son-of-a-bitch! It would've been better if he hadn't ever been born." Once she gets in striking distance, she winds up and swings the rag at her son with all the force she can muster. Choe describes the rag being blacker than ink, soaked with urine, a stench so noxious it made peoples' eyes twitch. After catching her breath, she tears into Haksu's alibi. "You said you hid the bread to give to your mother? What a liar. So then why yesterday did you hide a sweet potato in your load of wood and take it to her house if you are so concerned about me? You're no son of mine. And, of all people, why that slut? The daughter of our worst enemy, why to that wench?"

Living nearby, Mongbun's mother hears the insults and emerges from her home to confront Haksu's mother. But before she can say or do anything, Haksu's mother pulls the pin out of her neatly bunned hair and begins pulling on it with both hands. When she finally lets go, we learn the reason for Haksu's mother's rage. Predictably, it had nothing to do with the bread or how her son lied about it or even Mongbun. "All of that land out there to be sold, so why in the world did you have to take the land that we had worked?" Haksu's mother screams. Mongbun's mother, who had held back until now, finally speaks up, "For goodness' sake! Who told you not to buy it? When you said you weren't going to buy it, the landlord was selling it elsewhere. So then didn't we sell our iron pot, our soy sauce and kimchi pots and even the pig which we had fattened. We sold everything and bought the land. If you felt that way, why didn't you sell everything and hold on to it no matter what? Why go after me?"

This does not sway Haksu's mother one bit: "So what? You sold your iron pots, kimchi pots, soy sauce pots, and your pig, too, all of that and bought the land that someone else couldn't. So what? Is that what you have to do in order to feel good? You just wait. I'll raise a pig, sell the piggies and I'll buy the very land that your family has slaved over. You wait and see!" Ch'oe recalled being unable to feel hatred for Haksu's mother. But she thought her anger was misplaced. "Although Haksu's mother insists that they are starving because of Mongbun's family, it is not so. The one responsible for your starving is another. It is the landlord. For decades you worked like slaves on the land from which you got your food. Although the coming of liberation made your situation better, the landlords found things difficult. They felt threatened by their former servants and sold the very land upon which you had slaved so long and hard."[10]

Divisions caused by the land purchases complicated the future of land reform. It was not clear that the peasant families who purchased and now owned land would support wider land redistribution. Mongbun's family, for instance, now owned land. Would they support land reform for Haksu's family now they had theirs, and if so, under what terms? The KPR proposed confiscating land from the big landlords without compensation and redistributing them to poor farmers for free. But some peasant families, like Mongbun's, paid for their land by selling off most of their possessions. Would they now support other families receiving land for free? Things could get messy.

In late August 1945, a fight between Kungsam-myŏn peasants broke out in Naju, a farm region on the southwest tip of Korea. Raised voices turned into yelling and then escalated to armed conflict, leaving several participants injured. The conflict had been brewing for weeks. The Kungsam-myŏn peasants had laid claims to Japanese lands in Naju owned by the Oriental Development Company, contending that they were ancestral lands stolen by the Japanese. They had records—reams and reams of documentation going back decades—to prove it. No one seemed to dispute their claim. What was the issue?

The local branch of the KPR, the Naju's People's Committee, sympathized but it believed the peasants' demands should be pursued under its direction as part of a comprehensive program for independence. The longtime leader of the Kungsam-myŏn peasants, Na Chaegi, respectfully disagreed. After several attempts to reach a compromise failed, tensions flared resulting in the violent clash between supporters of the two groups.

Unlike most justifications for the takeover of Japanese lands, the Kungsam-myŏn peasants made their claim as a restitution for *pre*-colonial injustice that went back almost sixty years. In the late 1880s, a local Korean official, Chŏn Sŏnch'ang, cheated Naju farmers—the parents and grandparents of the Kungsam-myŏn peasants—out of their lands. The farmers accepted what they thought was a loan from Chŏn to help pay for taxes; a drought had put them behind. What they didn't know was that Chŏn had conspired with other local Korean officials to accept the tax payments as proof of transfer in ownership—to him.

Outraged, the farmers petitioned the local government office, but their appeals went ignored. After several years of being denied, they submitted a formal request to the central high court in Seoul in September 1896. Less than a year later, the high court ruled in the farmers' favor, agreeing that the lands in question were illegally usurped and ordered the lands returned to them. Just as it seemed justice would prevail, the Korean royal family suddenly announced that they had acquired the lands from local officials. As the acquisition was deemed a legal transaction, the Naju farmers were left with no recourse for redress.[11]

It seems Korea's problems with inequality and injustice were not entirely of Japan's making. The Korean royal family collected rent on the land from 1898 to 1910, before it was seized by the Japanese colonial authorities and put up for sale. The Oriental Development Company eventually purchased the lands.[12]

In October 1925, at a 1,400-person mass meeting, the region's peasants decided to organize a league to lead a land reclamation campaign against the Japanese company. The executive committee selected Na Chaegi to head the investigation division because of his reputation for integrity and honesty with the peasantry. A longtime resident of Naju, Na exemplified the commoner-landowner (what might be called the yeoman farmer in America) who emerged in Korea during the late nineteenth and early twentieth century.[13] As a landowner himself, he was keenly aware that the loss of land represented more than a financial blow, it deprived people of their sense of independence and dignity. As head investigator, Na went around Naju assisting peasants with documenting and filing their claims, which formed the basis for two court petitions in the 1920s. Both cases resulted in unfavorable rulings.

When the Japanese empire collapsed, the peasants in Naju immediately organized the Kungsam-myŏn peasant union and unanimously chose Na as chairperson. More than two decades of tireless devotion to their cause made Na a beloved, hero-like figure among the farmers in the region. Peasants were prepared to take back the land by force, but Na convinced them that taking a legal approach based on careful documentation would be better. He understood that most peasant claims to Japanese lands after liberation appealed to abstract ideals of social justice and anti-colonial nationalism. But he thought the claims of the Kungsam-myŏn peasants were different—they were more concrete. The lands in Naju were definitively theirs, stolen first by corrupt Korean officials and then by Japanese colonizers. They had an absolute legal right to recover them.[14]

Meanwhile, in the cities, workers had their own conflicts and struggles to contend with. At first glance, it didn't seem so. Korean workers had seized the factory floor in plant after plant, over seven hundred in total, giving the appearance of a unified working-class response to liberation.[15] But not all factory takeovers were the same. Some workers believed they were making revolution, just as the communist and socialist activists had spoken about. They had gained control of the means of production, after all. But as much as idealism was everywhere, it was practical concerns that drove most workers, who were now facing an uncertain future. Their Japanese owners were already, or soon to be, gone, and without them, it was unclear who would run the factories. If they shut down, what would the workers do? How would they make a livelihood? "The activities of the workers' control committees," as one US occupation official later explained, "were a natural improvisation to keep plants in operation which in many cases would otherwise have been shut down."[16]

The first stage of the takeovers looked very similar in most plants, resembling events out of Yi Kyuwŏn's "Liberation Factory." Workers formed self-management committees to protect company property, including machinery, raw materials, and finished products, from being plundered by looters or carried off to Japan by the owners. These committees were empowered to negotiate (and coax, if need be) severance payments and bonuses from their employers, which workers frequently reinvested back into their factories, in the hopes of keeping them open. These negotiations often ended with the owner signing over the factory to the workers.

But this is where the similarities ended. Some worker control committees made the transition to management seamlessly, even raising the level of productivity in some cases, which raised the question of why there was ever a distinction between labor and management. Others, however, quickly realized they didn't have the capital or the managerial and technical expertise to run a company (executives and engineers were almost always Japanese). Consequently, they went in search of "progressive" or "conscientious" Korean investors and managers to help run their factories.[17]

The decision didn't sit well with all workers. Some remained convinced they could operate the company on their own and thought the other workers were giving up too easily. They also didn't trust they could identify "conscientious" or "progressive" investors. In their experience, capitalists were capitalists, whether Korean or Japanese. And by handing the controls over to them, they were restoring the former system of exploitation.

Yi Tonggyu's popular 1945 short story, "Older Brother and Lover," highlighted these tensions. The story depicts a Korean woman whose loyalties are torn between her brother, a worker-activist in the self-management movement, and her love interest, an office worker at her brother's factory. Chaesun meets her boyfriend, Pyŏngch'an, several days after liberation. She soon learns that he works at the same factory as her older brother, Chaedŏk. When Chaedŏk and the other factory workers decide to form a self-management committee and oust their employer, Pyŏngch'an organizes the office staff to support them.

Yet, very quickly, Pyŏngch'an comes to believe the interest of the factory and its workers would be better served with a Korean investor at the helm. "I am, of course, on Chaedŏk's side and I identify with his views," he tells Chaesun. "But when we think about our factory's financial circumstances it will require a massive infusion of capital to continue operating it." Pyŏngch'an argues that, as a worker, Chaedŏk simply doesn't know everything involved in running a factory—financing, managerial functions, the technical expertise required.

He also mentions to Chaesun that the prospective owner is a well-respected Korean nationalist who was imprisoned during the 1919 March First Movement. "His love for his countrymen is second to none, and when he manages the factory, he will not exploit the workers like the Japanese capitalists used to, but rather he will share the profits along with the workers." For these reasons, Pyŏngch'an and the other office workers support him to be the company's new director. But Chaedŏk and the other factory workers oppose his recommendation, supposedly "without knowing these facts."

Chaesun speaks to her brother later that evening: "You know, listening to Pyŏngch'an's explanation, it seemed to make sense. . . ." Chaedŏk cuts her off, saying, "Even if he has a point we simply cannot compromise. Since August fifteenth, there have been numerous other factories where workers took over from the Japanese besides us, and we're at a moment where this kind of problem will be confronted by many other places in the future. But if we accept the new director and set a precedent, can you understand the ramifications that it will have upon others? For this reason, we must fight on behalf of other factory workers, even if accepting the new director is actually in our interest."[18]

Hearing her brother's arguments, Chaesun is troubled. Pyŏngch'an had been on her brother's side from the very beginning and the workers' lack of capital and experience seemed like legitimate concerns. Had the idealism of her brother and the other factory workers blinded them to the practical reality of managing a company? On the other hand, she learns that Pyŏngch'an recently accepted a 2,000-wŏn payment from the prospective director. Was that a bribe?

To resolve her inner conflict, Chaesun feels she must choose a side. She regrets that she has to choose between her brother and her lover. But then she hears the news that Pyŏngch'an has been hospitalized. Having got wind of the payment, factory workers had beaten him at a meeting held by the self-management committee the night before. When Chaesun visits him at the hospital, Pyŏngch'an is remorseful and admits he had been wrong. He also resolves to help the workers operate the factory on their own as an act of atonement. Chaesun feels vindicated: Pyŏngch'an is a good man, after all. On her way out of the hospital, she bumps into Chaedŏk, who is there to visit Pyŏngch'an. They smile at each other, and she feels an enormous sense of relief. Everyone was now on the right side, and the right thing seems obvious.

In reality, the choice was not so straightforward. In fact, many self-management committees, for the very reasons Pyŏngch'an cited, opted to bring in outside capitalists. They expected the new owners to make a profit but under a power-sharing arrangement in which labor would have input into wages, benefits, and work conditions. Some agreements included profit-sharing and a workers' stake in the company. For example, the 140 workers of Chosŏn Misin, formerly a Japanese-owned company, partnered with Korean investor Na Sanggwŏn to jointly manage the company. The workers at the Chosŏn Land & Sea Transport Company and the Chosŏn Leather Company in Seoul did the same. The workers seemed satisfied with the arrangement.[19]

The communist intelligentsia viewed the dizzying array of bottom-up initiatives with suspicion. They saw revolutionary stirrings in them, to be sure. As Pak Hŏnyŏng, Korea's leading communist, wrote in his 1945 *August Theses*: "The revolutionary passions of the Korean people are exploding nationwide, with farmers and workers at the forefront of these struggles." But a genuine revolution required focus, organization, and, above all else, enlightened leadership. What Pak observed instead was a series of ad hoc responses—headless and incoherent. "This spontaneous struggle of the people," he wrote, "is not following the correct political line and is proceeding without nationwide revolutionary guidance."[20]

Part of this perception stemmed, ironically enough, from a class bias. Coming from elite backgrounds, many of them educated in Japan, leftist activists doubted that "ignorant" workers could lead a factory, let alone a revolution. They had even less regard for farmers, with one activist opining the "normal cultural level of Korean peasants is the lowest out of all classes."[21] As a result, communists had a hard time fully supporting either the land or factory seizures. They smacked of capitalist desires for ownership, which, they warned, would fracture class solidarity.

Hwang Sunwŏn, one of Korea's great storytellers, famously critiqued workers' petit bourgeois aspirations in his colorful satire, "The Story of Liquor." Chunho works in a Japanese-owned distillery factory in Pyongyang. As a young man he started at the bottom, then eventually worked his way up to become the chief secretary. In the days after liberation, he vigilantly keeps watch over company equipment and stock from the factory's night-duty room. One evening, he single-handedly prevents the Japanese owner and his goons from making off with it. The other distillery workers recognize his bravery and devotion by choosing Chunho to be the interim manager, while they decide on the factory's future.[22]

As part of his new position, Chunho is allowed to stay in the company house, once the residence of the Japanese manager, Nakamura. The first thing Chunho does is remove all vestiges of the Japanese: hanging scrolls, picture frames, the wardrobe made of Paulownia wood, and the potted plum tree cherished by the former manager. He also proudly cuts off the head of the stone statue in the garden. Satisfied, he takes a warm bath and treats himself to the company soju. This becomes his nightly ritual.[23]

But after a while, his new home begins to feel empty. He thinks it's because he put everything away. "Why should the furniture be blamed?" he tells himself. "It's not right to leave the rooms as empty as these for such a big house." He brings out the hanging scrolls, the picture frames, the wardrobe, and the potted plum tree and puts them back in their previous locations. He also places the statue head back in its original position. The home now looks *exactly* as it did when Nakamura was the resident.

Sitting in front of the potted plum tree, Chunho feels content. But he has a nagging feeling something is missing. "Right! I should print a self-portrait of mine as big as the manager's and hang it on the wall of the drawing room." He puts on a suit and heads to the photo studio. When he returns, he looks over all of his new possessions with pride. They make him think that "the sufferings he endured were not in vain and from now on he'd be able to live more comfortably."

The next morning, Chunho gets disturbing news from comrade Kŏnsŏp, who leads the self-management committee. They want the distillery to be run by a union. Immediately, Chunho's mind races for a solution: "I should hurry and find wells of money and furnish it [the distillery] with capital. Whom could I contact?" An answer comes to him: "Ah! Yes! There's P'ilbae, who's become an upstart through clothing manufacturing. Why didn't I think of this good idea before?" The following day Chunho tells Kŏnsŏp that he has found a Korean investor for the distillery. Kŏnsŏp sees right through Chunho's plan: "That's what I thought. Already there are many who think that if a Korean becomes the manager of a factory or a company then he'll soon become like Nakamura from before. If the factory is financed by an individual manager, then there'll be a disaster. Our distillery should be managed by a union."

That night Chunho drinks heavily alone at the factory. While stumbling around the empty distillery, he cries out, "Who's going to feed you bastards? Fine, you left me out like that . . . I'll kill all you bastards." He sees the light on in the night-duty room and rushes over and swings the door wide open. There's no one there but that doesn't matter to Chunho, who is out of touch with reality at this point. "Put your hands up!" he shouts, while holding a kitchen knife. "I'll catch you bastards and throw you all in here!" Petit bourgeois aspirations had turned a model worker—a comrade—into a depraved capitalist.

There was something to this critique. Just as the peasant land purchases created tensions, activists were not wrong to be concerned about potential divisions. But the idea that ordinary Koreans would pass up an opportunity for land or self-management to follow the direction of an enlightened revolutionary vanguard, was, to put it mildly, unrealistic. It made light of their yearnings for freedom, dignity, and security after nearly four decades of colonial rule. The fact was, workers had their own expectations and ideas for liberation, which they were happy to pursue with or without the Communist Party.[24]

The alliances and tensions between the activist intelligentsia and the rank and file could be traced back to the colonial period. Ever since the 1920s, the communists, along with their socialist and anarchist allies, played a key role in creating the labor movement in Korea. Their activism, which included organizing drives, educational campaigns, and direct action, mobilized Korean workers after the First World War. Owing in no small part to their efforts, Korean workers went on hundreds of strikes per year between 1925 and 1935, demanding everything from wage increases to maternity leave.[25]

Some of the most famous communists were women, including the dynamic duo of Hŏ Chŏngsuk and Chu Sejuk. Given their backgrounds, they made an unlikely pairing. Hŏ came from a prominent Korean family in the North. Her father was Hŏ Hŏn, a wealthy communist, who would later become chairman of North Korea's Supreme People's Assembly. As a rich landowning leftist, Hŏ Hŏn was in the minority in Korea, but not a trivial one.[26] In contrast, Chu came from more modest means. When Hŏ met and recruited Chu to the communist cause in Shanghai in 1921, she was basically broke. Yet the two would join forces to make their indelible mark on feminism and the class struggle in Korea.

Eloquent, provocative, and beautiful, the duo became a public sensation that made them some of the first celebrities in Korea. Their latest relationships and outspoken political views were fodder for the Korean tabloids. (Chu Sejuk went on to marry Pak Hŏnyŏng, and they became *the* revolutionary power couple.) What received less attention, except from colonial authorities, was their grassroots work among women workers and students. Chu, for instance, worked diligently to organize women workers in the factories in Inch'ŏn, a port city located slightly west of Seoul. Seeking to raise a new generation of women cadres, she and Hŏ also mentored student leaders at girls' high schools.[27] The two also worked together to launch the Korean Women's League in 1924, the first socialist women's organization in Korea.[28]

Japanese colonial officials wasted little time in suppressing this wave of activism and dissent. Communist and socialist activists bore the brunt of the repression—many were rounded up, imprisoned, tortured, or forced underground or into exile.[29] At the height of the crackdown, Chu and Pak were in Moscow, when the communist leadership suddenly asked Pak to go to Shanghai. The cosmopolitan city had become home base for anti-colonial Korean nationalists after the March First Movement. The couple decided to leave behind their only child, Vivian, in the care of a trusted comrade

Chu Sejuk and Pak Hŏnyŏng with their daughter, Vivian, in
Moscow in 1929.
Seoul Shimbun

and go to Shanghai together. But the mission went awry when Japanese
authorities caught up to Pak in 1933 and sent him to a colonial prison in
Korea, where he spent the next six years.

Thinking her husband was dead, Chu returned to Moscow, where she
eventually married Kim Tanya, another rising communist star, who had
worked closely with Pak to build the party. In fact, the three of them were
together at a safehouse in Shanghai when Pak was arrested. The Japanese police were there to apprehend Kim, but Pak distracted them so that Kim and
Chu could escape.[30] In 1937, the couple became victims of Stalin's purges—
Kim was executed and Chu was sent to a gulag for being Japanese spies. She
was carrying her second child when they were arrested. Her first child, Vivian, would grow up as an orphan in Moscow; her second, Kim's child, would
die in the labor camp where Chu was held.[31]

Communists often became martyrs for the liberationist cause. They had put in the work and made the sacrifices—in some cases, like Chu, the loss of a husband and a child. If they felt entitled to lead Korea after liberation, it was not entirely without cause. Yet, at the same time, the rank and file often initiated strikes, boycotts, organizing drives, and work slowdowns without help from the intelligentsia. For some, this wasn't necessarily by choice. Many women workers, largely ignored by labor organizers who were mostly male, had to mobilize on their own if they wanted to gain redress, as did the female workers at the P'yŏngwŏn Rubber factory. In other cases, however, differences over strategies, tactics, and vision led workers to part ways with communist organizers and act on their own.

Some of these disagreements foreshadowed the conflicts that would come after independence. Indeed, the clashes over labor self-management and industrial cooperatives can be traced to the early 1930s, when rubber workers in Pyongyang struck deals with "conscientious" Korean capitalists to co-own and co-run several factories. With an equal stake in the company, workers received an eight-hour workday, better working conditions, and a share of the profits.[32] The communists opposed the arrangement, criticizing industrial cooperatives as a reformist compromise that dulled revolutionary zeal while keeping an exploitative system in place. The workers, as they would do later, went ahead anyway, joining forces with nationalist investors. The Korean labor movement may have bore the mark of communist leadership, but it was also defined by a powerful streak of workers' independence.[33]

Activists were not the only ones at odds with the rank and file. Organizers also confronted divisions within their own ranks over vision and strategy. Unlike the communists, anarchists and moderate socialists supported industrial cooperatives and, more broadly, incremental reforms. They viewed cooperatives as laboratories where workers, as equal stakeholders, could learn skills to operate a factory. These activists imagined industrial cooperatives as way stations to full socialist control of production. They didn't see cooperation with Korean capitalists as capitulation, especially if it was initiated by the workers.

These disagreements came from something more fundamental: anarchists opposed the communists' top-down methods of organizing and their tendency to centralize authority within the party apparatus. As their name implied, anarchists were naturally suspicious of concentrated power and wanted to see more rank-and-file control. They loathed the idea that local workers' aspirations had to be vetted by "professional" organizers (i.e., communists) from the outside. This hierarchy, they argued, made them tone deaf to the desires of the rank and file. So it is unsurprising that the anarchists created organizations to rival the Communist Party during the colonial period.[34]

The intra-left disputes raised questions about the relationship between the party/state and workers. Workers wondered if they should pursue their goals under a communist party or state as part of broader socialist agenda or preserve their independence by creating their own institutions. These questions were largely theoretical and low stakes under Japanese colonial rule, when the left was suppressed and there was no Korean state to speak of. But after liberation, when there was an actual chance of the left coming to power, they took on real importance.

One Korean socialist staked out an early position following independence: "The union does not operate under the direction of the party," he stated emphatically. "The opinion that the party is heavy and the union is light must be thoroughly liquidated. Each organization can be expanded and reinforced only when the party exerts its function and identity as a party and the union fully demonstrates its function and identity as a union." He, along with a number of other leftist activists, didn't trust the state—even a socialist one—to protect the rights and interests of workers.[35]

Such divisions went to the very top. The rapid formation of the KPR and the rollout of its detailed platform gave the illusion of party unity. Behind the scenes, however, Pak Hŏnyŏng and Yŏ Unhyŏng were locked in a power struggle over control of the party. This was a contest between two competing visions for Korean independence.

When Yŏ left the meeting with Endō on August 15, he reached out to both prominent rightists and leftists to join the Committee for the Preparation of Korean Independence (CPKI). In describing his approach, Yŏ compared the nation to a park: "You have to plant sakura, plant pine trees, plant mugunghwa (rose of Sharon), make mountains, make ponds to have a good park, not just sakura." Applying this analogy to an independent Korea, he called for national unity: "We must above all make the unified front and do the utmost to become united in full independence."[36]

He invited the distinguished communist Hŏ Hŏn to be part of the committee and also considered Pak Hŏnyŏng but didn't know his whereabouts (Pak had gone into hiding after being released from prison in 1939). Making good on his promise of inclusion, Yŏ also recruited staunch conservative An Chaehong, the owner of the *Chosŏn ilbo*, a major Korean daily, to be the vice-chairman, which made him second only to Yŏ within the CPKI. An was a wealthy Korean rightist, but in Yŏ's mind, a patriot, because he had a record of opposing Japanese occupation. Being a nationalist is what mattered most to Yŏ. As long as you didn't collaborate with the Japanese, you had a place in an independent Korea.

Born to a *yangban* (elite gentry) family, Yŏ made his first political statement when he dramatically freed his family's slaves in 1910 and burned all existing records to guarantee their emancipation. After the March First Movement (1919), Yŏ cofounded the Korean Provisional Government (KPG) in Shanghai. During this time, he also served as the Korean representative to the Paris Peace Conference, where he, along with other nationalists from the around world, tried in vain to hold American president Woodrow Wilson to his promise of self-determination.[37]

He quickly found himself on the outs at the KPG. Yŏ despised the elitism and divisiveness of the rightist members and wasn't afraid to show it. He threw a chair at Kim Ku, head of the provisional government, in a meeting at which he accused Kim of secretly working to turn the KPG into a right-wing cabal. He left the provisional government for good after that incident. Yŏ felt more affinity for the communists and their values, joining the party in 1921. He would become friendly with Pak and other leading cadres, considering them allies. But he found their fidelity to doctrine too rigid, and eventually left the party.[38]

After liberation, Yŏ tried to bring the different factions together into a coalition government. Bridging these divides would be challenging, to say the least. The conservatives, led by An, wanted a supermajority of 70 percent in the CPKI, which was a non-starter for Yŏ. Given that the left emerged from the colonial period with overwhelming popular support, it was an unreasonable ask. But conservatives worried that without a majority, they would not be able to stop the radical changes that the left envisioned. And as much as they wanted to believe Yŏ's talk of a "united front," they saw him as man of the left and a class traitor. He had renounced his *yangban* status by liberating his family's slaves after all.[39]

The real challenge to Yŏ's authority came from the Left. Many of the communists vehemently opposed the inclusion of landlords and capitalists in the CPKI. The idea that Yŏ would embrace reactionary forces, groups who "supported the murderous and invasive war of Japanese imperialism," made little sense to them.[40] They thought it a mistake to include people who could thwart the revolution. If anything, they thought the CPKI should be led by the revolutionary vanguard who could guide the popular masses. Pak was obsessed with following proper doctrine. He and his communist allies seized control of the committee, when unknown assailants, on the evening of August 18, 1945, attacked Yŏ on the streets. He sustained serious injuries to his head that required home rest. It would be the first of more than a dozen attempts on his life. During Yŏ's absence, Pak orchestrated a palace coup. Yŏ may have been the most popular political figure in Korea, but Pak, with his uncompromising stance, had the allegiance of the activists.[41]

On his return to the CPKI on August 25, Yŏ once again reiterated the need for a united front—capitalists, democrats, and communists—and not just "progressive" (i.e., leftist) forces. But Pak and his communist allies ignored him, drafting a vision statement that read like a declaration of war against the non-Left. Two weeks later, they dissolved the CPKI and announced the formation of the Korean People's Republic. They insisted it was merely an extension of the CPKI, but the leadership profile of the new organization showed this not to be true. Two-thirds of the KPR's Central Committee were now made up of members from Pak's communist faction.[42]

Grasping at straws, Yŏ tried to delay the opening of the KPR by refusing to sign off on the new cabinet. But the communists ignored his objection and pushed forward with the announcement. Yŏ was appointed chairman of the KPR but it was a title in name only—he was effectively marginalized within the organization. On September 7, a second attempt was made on his life when a would-be assassin planted a bomb near his home. Yŏ survived the blast. He suspected Pak and his allies of being behind the attack.[43]

Yet, Yŏ remained with the organization and continued to work with Pak. Despite his public stature, he had no political party to fall back on, and building one would take considerable time and effort. And the truth was, the communist's agenda contained many of Yŏ's policy preferences. Like Pak, he wanted to redistribute land to poor peasants, enact workers' rights and reforms, and remove collaborators from public life. There were, of course, differences in degree. When it came to collaborators, for instance, Pak wanted to cast a wider net by defining it exclusively in class terms. But

Yŏ didn't think they were insurmountable and he believed he could have a moderating influence on the communists. He also had a personal relationship with Pak—in fact, Yŏ had officiated at his first wedding, to Chu Sejuk. So, he stayed on, clinging to the hope that party (and country) unity remained possible.

Meanwhile, news began circulating that would upend nearly all these efforts, and the politics of liberation more broadly, in the South. Its impact could be detected in the slight—yet distinct—uptick in land prices in the South at the end of August.[44] It could also be seen in the exodus of conservative women members from the Founding Women's Association in Seoul in early September. Three weeks earlier, these same conservative women had joined leftist women activists to develop an agenda for women's liberation in Korea, including obtaining the right to vote, ending gender wage discrimination, abolishing licensed prostitution and red-light districts, and establishing social services for pregnant women.[45]

The women also recently worked together to clean the streets, provide aid to the poor and recently released prisoners, and begin preparations to hold classes at the Chungang Women's Vocational School. Their collaboration provided hope that Koreans—left, right, and center—could unite in working toward the liberation of women and the nation. But on September 6, several prominent rightist members suddenly quit to form the Korean Patriot Women's Association. What had changed their calculations about working with leftist women activists? And what was the connection between this development and the rebounding land prices in the South?

3 The Race to Korea

The sudden collapse of the Japanese empire gave the Soviet Union the inside track to Korea. US officials discovered this on August 10, 1945, the day after the United States had dropped a second atomic bomb on Japan, leveling the city of Nagasaki. US military intelligence estimated that the closest American forces were at least a month away from reaching Korea. The Soviet invasion of Manchuria on August 9 placed their forces in striking distance of the Korean peninsula.

Based on those projections, the Soviet Union would beat the United States to Korea to accept Japan's surrender. And by the virtue of being the first there, they—not the Americans—would exert political control over the peninsula. This is what happened in Eastern Europe, where the Red Army established local control and what was about to occur in Japan, where conquering Americans would assume the role of sole occupying power. Officials in Washington viewed Soviet-control of Korea as a threat to security—and American interests—in Asia. The Pentagon quickly came up with a plan to administer Korea through two separate military occupations, one directed in the North by the Soviets and the other in the South by the Americans. The arrangement was supposed to be temporary.

The War Department assigned army colonels Dean Rusk and Chris "Tic" Bonesteel the task of dividing Korea into two zones. "Working in haste and under great pressure," Rusk recalled in his memoirs, "we had the formidable task to pick a zone for the American occupation."[1] Rusk would go on to become the secretary of state under Presidents John F. Kennedy and Lyndon B. Johnson and played an important role in crafting US foreign policy in Asia. In the late hours of August 10, however, he was a young, bleary-eyed junior officer who only had a vague idea where Korea was located on a map and knew virtually nothing of the country's history. "Neither Tic nor I," Rusk admitted, was "a Korea expert."[2]

Looking over a *National Geographic* map of the Korean peninsula, the two men frantically scanned it for a convenient dividing line but nothing made sense. Why would it? Korea had been a single, unified polity for centuries and maybe millennia depending on who you asked. Needing to report back something, they settled on the 38th parallel. Their recommendation would keep the Korean capital of Seoul, which was south of the proposed line, on the American side. Otherwise, the choice, as Rusk later admitted, "made no sense economically or geographically."

The War Department took their recommendation and, without giving it much thought, offered it to Soviet Premier Joseph Stalin. US officials, including Rusk, were skeptical that he would accept it. Their proposal would give the United States control over a larger portion of the peninsula, even though the Soviet military position was stronger because their troops were closer to Korea.[3] To understand the Americans' pessimism, we need to jump ahead a week. On August 18, 1945, President Harry S. Truman denied a Soviet request to land troops in Hokkaido, the northernmost island of Japan closest to Russia, which effectively locked the Soviet Union out of the occupation of Japan. Stalin was told Americans forces would accept the surrender of all the islands of Japan.[4]

To everyone's surprise, Stalin quickly agreed to the proposed dividing line without asking for changes or other concessions (he didn't know the Americans would rebuff his request for a shared occupation of Japan a week later). After the war, Stalin sought to maximize security for the Soviet Union without risking war with the United States, the world's lone atomic power. As a consummate realist, he focused on areas that directly impacted postwar Soviet security, which meant, above all else, controlling Eastern Europe. Korea was not Poland. It wasn't even Finland or Austria, which maintained independence after the war. Stalin had little interest in provoking the United States over half of a country he considered secondary to Soviet national interests. Simply put, Korea was not the hill he would die on. This did not mean Stalin didn't have *any* national security interests on the peninsula. He feared that Korea might be used as a staging ground for a future attack on the Soviet Union and so, at the very least, Stalin wanted an independent Korea that was not hostile to the USSR.[5] But he could achieve this goal by controlling half the peninsula. What is more, Stalin believed he needed American cooperation to achieve his postwar security goals—keep in mind that the Cold War was not inevitable at this point. This is why he agreed to joint occupation even though full control of Korea was in his grasp.

And just like that, an ancient nation with a deeply rooted history was split in two. Astonishingly, not a single Korean was consulted in the decision.

Dividing the country into two occupation zones was not the Americans' original plan for Korea. At the 1943 Cairo conference, the first meeting of Allied powers, the United States, Britain, and China put out a joint declaration stating, "The aforesaid three great powers, mindful of the enslavement of the people of Korea, are determined that in due course Korea shall become free and independent." This was the first time international powers had pledged support for Korean independence since it had been annexed by Japan in 1910. But it was unclear what the clause "in due course" meant.

More precise language had appeared in an earlier American version of the declaration. The first draft called for Korean independence "at the earliest possible moment after the downfall of Japan." President Roosevelt subsequently revised the passage to read "at the proper moment after the downfall of Japan." In Cairo, the Allies changed the wording on Korean independence for a third time, incorporating the British suggestion to add "in due course" in the final text.[6] Koreans took offense at the implications of the clause. One nationalist in exile wrote: "Some Americans and Europeans who are not acquainted with the Koreans' historical background, question—'Can they govern themselves?'" "When the ancestors of northern Europe were wandering in the forests, clad in skins and practicing rites, Koreans had a government of their own and attained a high degree of civilization," was his retort.[7]

British prime minister Winston Churchill cared little about Korean independence. However, he saw the talk over decolonizing Korea as a slippery slope that could lead to wider calls for the dismantling of empires everywhere, including India, the crown jewel of the British Empire. Churchill was overheard saying, "As long as [I am] prime minster . . . [I will] not yield a single scrap of British heritage."[8] British officials, therefore, sought to delay and create uncertainty around the process. The Allies would promise Korea independence but defer it to an indeterminate future. Korea would be stuck in what historian Dipesh Chakrabarty has evocatively called the "waiting room of history."[9]

Roosevelt agreed to the British language for several reasons. First off, he didn't want to cause friction between allies over a few words in the middle of a war. But more importantly, the British wording, "in due course," was close to Roosevelt's formulation "at the proper moment." The likeness reflected Roosevelt's reservations with granting independence to Koreans—and for that matter, *any* colonized people—too quickly. Roosevelt genuinely despised European-style colonialism, believing it to be brutal in most cases. He also thought it was one of the major causes of the Second World War. But his disdain for imperialism was matched by his doubt about the readiness of colonized people to govern themselves.

Channeling his favorite cousin, Theodore Roosevelt, FDR believed the colonized world in Asia, Africa, and the Middle East would require a period of tutelage—"civilizing" is the word his older cousin would have used—before they could run their own affairs. It was Theodore Roosevelt, as president in 1905, who signed off on Japan's control of Korea in a secret agreement with the Meiji government. (The deal came to light twenty years later when a historian discovered the secret memorandum while going through TR's presidential papers.)[10] Teddy Roosevelt admired Japan's rapid rise on the world stage and thought that as a modern power, it had a duty to tutor its "lesser" neighbor, Korea, in civilization. In addition, Japan agreed to recognize America's imperial claims to the Philippines in return. Bringing this family history full circle, FDR touted the US colonization of the Philippines as a model for the gradual emancipation of Korea. "I like to think that the history of the Philippines Islands . . . provides a pattern for the future of other small nations and peoples of the world," Roosevelt said in a 1942 radio address.

The United States had acquired the Philippines, along with Puerto Rico and Guam, as part of an agreement to end the Spanish-American War in 1898. The settlement ended the war with the declining Spanish Empire but not with its colonial subjects, who demanded immediate independence. This started yet another war, this time with Filipino nationalists, lasting three years. When Teddy Roosevelt triumphantly announced the end of the US-Philippine War in 1902, close to 800,000 Filipinos had perished. FDR's rosy assessment of US imperial rule in the Philippines left out much, to say the least.

Nevertheless, FDR, along with Congress, did agree to Filipino independence in 1934, marking a rare occasion when an imperial power voluntarily gave up its colony. They set a ten-year transition period that put the Philippines on track to gain full independence by 1945, which altogether amounted to forty-seven years of tutelage.

The Filipinos' forty-seven year path to independence was roughly the time-line Franklin Roosevelt proposed for the Koreans at the Yalta conference in February 1945, where the three wartime leaders of the Soviet Union, United States, and Great Britain met to plan for the postwar world. However, unlike in the Philippines, there would be more than one tutor for Korea. Roosevelt envisioned the Allied powers—the Soviet Union, United States, Great Britain, and China—administering Korea jointly as part of a multilateral trusteeship until it was deemed ready for self-government. Roosevelt imagined trusteeship as an instrument for tutelage without the evils of colonialism. He made clear that trusteeship would not involve the stationing of foreign troops in Korea. Here, then, was the process by which the Allies would fulfill the promise made to the Korean people in the Cairo Declaration.

At Yalta, Stalin expressed support for trusteeship, but he told Roosevelt, "The shorter the period the better," after hearing the president's timeframe for Korean independence. Stalin grasped that Koreans would not wait long for their independence.[11] Roosevelt's secretary of state, Cordell Hull, doubted the Koreans would wait at all. "Koreans wanted their independence immediately," he said, "not in due course."[12] The first US intelligence report on the political situation in Korea, written on September 15, 1945, showed Hull was way closer to the mark. "It was discovered from the beginning the Korean translation of the term 'in due course' in the Cairo Declaration has been the equivalent of 'in a few days' or 'very soon,'" US political adviser H. Merrill Benninghoff explained.[13]

Roosevelt was asking Koreans to wait forty years for independence after having gone through forty years of Japanese colonial rule. He had a hard time shaking the Philippine example—perhaps one too many conversations with his cousin Teddy. It is possible that Stalin's counsel opened Roosevelt to a shorter timeline, but we will never know, as FDR died shortly after the Yalta conference. The president's death and the sudden collapse of the Japanese empire scrambled postwar plans for Korea. Instead of a multilateral trusteeship with no foreign military presence, Korea was divided into two zones, each run by a different occupying army. Was Roosevelt's vision for trusteeship in Korea now dead? How would Korea obtain its promised independence under these conditions?

The Supreme Commander of the Allied Powers, General Douglas MacArthur, ordered the XXIV Corps of the Tenth Army in Okinawa to secure Japan's surrender in Korea and establish a military government south of the 38th parallel. Among American forces in the Pacific theater, the XXIV Corps was the closest to the Korean peninsula. Time was still of the essence. Despite the agreement with Stalin, officials in Washington worried that a prolonged power vacuum would tempt the Red Army to advance south and capture the entire peninsula.

The XXIV Corps was led by Lieutenant General John Hodge. As the highest-ranking US officer, he was poised to become the de facto leader of fifteen million Koreans. He could not have possibly imagined this growing up as a farm boy in Golconda, Illinois. Hodge had attended the Army Officers Training School at Fort Sheridan, Illinois, graduating in 1917. Without the elite pedigree of Douglas MacArthur, Dwight Eisenhower, or George Patton, who all went to West Point, he started out in infantry reserve and slowly worked his way up the military ranks. By the eve of World War II, he had attained the rank of lieutenant colonel and was chief of staff of the Seventh Army Corps.[14]

Hodge's stardom rose sharply during World War II. He took part in the famous island-hopping campaign that saw some of the bloodiest fighting in the Pacific theater. Hodge was wounded fighting in Papua New Guinea and narrowly avoided a shrapnel from a bomb in the Philippines—he was sleeping when the fragment tore through his tent. In July 1943, he commanded his own division for the first time, fighting the Japanese on the Solomon Islands. His unit suffered heavy casualties but it successfully captured New Georgia in the central Solomon Islands. He received the Distinguished Service Medal for his leadership and bravery. The citation noted he had "inspired his troops by his constant presence at the front and was primarily responsible for the forward division which brought the entire operation to a successful conclusion."[15]

Successful military campaigns in Leyte and Okinawa netted Hodge the Air Medal and a Purple Heart, further fueling his legend. War correspondents began referring to him as the "Patton of the Pacific." But he mostly shunned the spotlight. Perhaps because of his humble background, Hodge was more comfortable with his men or reading alone in his quarters. He was a man without "pose or affectation," known as a "soldier's soldier," according to the official history of the XXIV Corps. True to his reputation, Hodge would share his more lavish housing in Seoul befitting his status as head of the military government with his junior officers.

In this way, Hodge was the polar opposite of his commanding officer, General MacArthur—a legendary narcissist who craved adulation. As jour-

Lieutenant General John R. Hodge, commander of the US military
government in south Korea.
Alfred Eisenstaedt / The LIFE Collection / Shutterstock

nalist David Halberstam has written of MacArthur, "It was virtually impossible to take a photo of him that was not posed; he was aware every moment
of where the light was best, of how his jaw should jut, and the cap could be
displayed at the most rakish angle."[16] Consistent with this image, MacArthur
left behind a mountain of records documenting his every word and deed.
Over two million documents are held at his Archive and Library in Norfolk,
Virginia. And there's no shortage of public statements, including his fare-
well address to Congress in 1951, when he famously said, "Old soldiers never
die, they just fade away." By contrast, Hodge left behind neither a shred of

personal paper nor a single interview about his tenure in Korea, to the everlasting chagrin of historians. He seemed to have no trouble fading away.

Yet, for all his ego and vanity, MacArthur demonstrated surprising flexibility as the head of the occupation in Japan. Despite being a staunch, anti–New Deal Republican, MacArthur supported a robust agenda of demilitarization and democratization in Japan. His surprising burst of progressivism came in no small part from a messianic delusion that only he could cure the Japanese of their militarist ways and transform them into a peace-loving people. Nevertheless, under his auspices, US officials implemented wide-ranging reforms, including purging the National Police and securing workers' rights to unionize, land redistribution, universal suffrage, and permanent disarmament.[17]

Hodge had neither MacArthur's messianic zeal nor his flexibility. In fact, Hodge was rigidly principled and uncompromising, someone who naturally saw the world in black and white. This served him well as a military commander. But what about as the leader of an occupation who had to guide fifteen million Koreans to independence?

Japanese colonial officials had primed Hodge for his arrival in Korea. On September 1, 1945, Lieutenant General Kōzuki Yoshio in Seoul radioed the US military command in Okinawa to alert them of rapidly deteriorating conditions. He spoke about mob violence against the police, striking workers paralyzing the economy, and armed communists threatening revolution. He urged American forces to get to the peninsula as quickly as possible. The next day, Kōzuki warned ominously that "red" unionists might try to sabotage the landing of American troops.[18]

Hodge accepted the words of a hated enemy from only a few weeks ago at face value. He told Kōzuki to do everything in his power to maintain law and order. Later that day, he drafted a letter to the Koreans, which American bombers dropped on southern Korea over the next four days—300,000 leaflets in total. Addressed "To the People of Korea," the letter opened with, "The armed forces of the United States will soon arrive in Korea for the purpose of receiving the surrender of the Japanese forces, enforcing the terms of surrender, and insuring the orderly administration and rehabilitation of the country." The tone of his message quickly turned stern, as if he were a school teacher lecturing a naughty student: "How well and how rapidly these tasks are carried out will depend upon the Koreans themselves. Hasty and ill-advised acts on the part of its residents will only result in unnecessary loss of life, desolation of your beautiful country and delay in its rehabilitation."[19] The furthest thing from what a liberated people wanted to hear.

Before setting sail for Korea on September 5, Hodge cabled MacArthur about the possible revolutionary situation his forces might face upon their arrival. MacArthur gave Hodge full authority to act as he saw fit. As the Supreme Commander of the Allied Powers (SCAP), MacArthur was technically head of the occupation of Korea as well. But consumed by his vision to remake Japan, MacArthur showed little interest in the former colony— he visited Korea exactly once, even though it was not a long flight from Tokyo, and then only in the last days of the occupation.[20]

As a result, Hodge exercised command over almost all aspects of the occupation, with the authority to make policy by fiat. Though he did not hold the same power in Korea that MacArthur had in Japan—Hodge had to answer to Washington more than MacArthur did—it came close.

The imposing twenty-one ship convoy carrying the XXIV Corps arrived at the port of Inchŏn on September 8, 1945, three weeks ahead of the original schedule (the entry date was pushed up twice). The next day, Hodge formally accepted Japan's surrender at a ceremony in the Government-General building in Seoul. After the signing, Americans moved outside to watch the Japanese flag lowered and replaced with the stars and stripes of the United States.

Koreans had lined the streets hours ahead of time to welcome American troops following the ceremony. They cheered, waved American flags, and held signs hailing passing soldiers as liberators. The crowds lingered afterward to celebrate the formal end of colonial rule, chanting and dancing nonstop for hours. In the midst of the enthusiasm, however, there were troubling signs. Koreans were not invited to the surrender ceremony, and the American flag—not the Korean T'aegŭkki—flew above the Government-General building. They were bitter reminders that Koreans had not liberated themselves. Pak Hŏnyŏng, who learned that the United States would occupy the South in late August, lamented that "we experienced liberation on August 15 as if we received steamed rice cakes [a celebratory Korean treat] in the middle of the night." Kim Ku, the longtime leader of the Korean Provisional Government in Shanghai, worried that "our voice in the international community will be weak in the future because we had not done anything in this war."[21] In 1944, Kim had requested arms from the

In front of the Government-General building in Seoul, US soldiers lower the Japanese flag (*left*) and raise the US flag (*right*), 1945. National History and Heritage Command, 80-G-391464/80-G-391465

In September 1945, a Korean crowd in Seoul cheers the arrival of Allied soldiers.
National Archives (111-SC-212002)

United States and asked FDR to formally recognize Korea as an independent nation. The first request was denied and the second ignored.[22]

Koreans watched as the tactical troops of the XXIV corps began to disarm Japanese soldiers and secure the southern zone for the establishment of a military government. It would be filled by hundreds of civil affairs officers with expertise in commerce, law, and public health in the weeks and months to come. Most of these officers had trained for the occupation of Japan (including learning Japanese), but when General MacArthur decided to use the existing bureaucracy there, they were reassigned to Korea.[23] In an ironic twist, Korea—the former colony—received the occupation that had been meant for Japan.[24]

"This is essentially a story of improvisation," wrote Philip H. Tayler, a graduate of the Harvard University Civil Affairs Training School, who participated in the planning of the occupation of Japan. "Korea, the one country in the Pacific theater over which a real military government was established, was the only important area occupied by American troops in the Pacific for which some study or preparations had not been made."[25] Grant Meade, a civil affairs officer stationed in South Chŏlla Province, remembers receiving a total of one hour of instruction on Korea during his nine months at the military government school. He thought it reflected "the lack of seriousness with which the United States regarded the commitments made to establish a free and independent Korea."[26]

The American occupation would replicate what it did in Seoul—accept Japanese surrender, disarm Japanese soldiers, and establish a military government— in every province in the South. You could call it occupation federalism, with each province getting its own military government, which had, at least initially, a fair amount of autonomy to act as it saw fit. However, the process of installing US military rule in the South would take time. And the farther an area was away from Seoul, the longer it would take, extending the interlude in which local Korean groups were left in charge.

The most remote province in the South was Jeju Island, which was located fifty miles off the southern coast of the Korean peninsula. The United States didn't have military government teams on the ground there until mid-November 1945. In fact, some islanders were surprised to see the Americans when they finally arrived—news didn't travel fast from the mainland to the island. If there were to be foreign troops, they had expected them to be Soviets. A small group of American officers had flown into the island earlier, in late September, to formally accept Japan's surrender, but it seems most islanders were unaware of their visit, perhaps because the ceremony took under fifteen minutes and the officers were soon back on a plane to Seoul.[27]

In the meantime, the Jeju's People's Committee (PC) emerged as the acting government on the island. It assumed power after defeating rightist groups in a series of violent clashes that left more than a hundred people injured. The heads of the Jeju's People's Committee had led the resistance against the Japanese during the 1930s, which earned them widespread popular support after liberation. One of its leaders, Mun Tobae, spent three years in prison for organizing Haenyŏs, Jeju's famous women divers, against their Japanese employers. Over a thousand Haenyŏs participated in this struggle, which was suppressed by the Japanese colonial government in 1932. Because US military rule came late, the victorious PC had an opportunity to carry out its vision for independence. Jeju thus offers a glimpse into what could have been in Korea had there been no foreign occupation (or had it ruled with a lighter touch), and Koreans were left alone to work out their own futures.[28]

The Jeju's PC used its newfound authority to remove pro-Japanese collaborators from public life, take Japanese properties into custody, and re-open and build new schools, all the while maintaining public order. The organization took a surprisingly lenient approach with collaborators, only expelling those they considered the most notorious. In some of these cases, the PC assembled a people's court to prevent revenge-minded villagers from taking justice into their own hands. All in all, it pursued a moderate course that led to a largely peaceful transition to independence. It probably helped that there were few big landed estates—Japanese or Korean—to fight over in Jeju.[29]

When the military government team finally arrived on the island in the form of the US Fifty-Ninth Army, it was pleased with how the People's Committee had governed, so much so that they left them in power. As Grant Meade explained, "the Committee was highly cooperative, and the military government supported it wholeheartedly." With the government's backing, the people's committee ran the island effectively, collecting taxes, distributing rice, managing the outbreak of cholera, and maintaining public safety. The chairman of the committee, who had a distinguished record of anti-Japanese resistance, was thought to be "very pro-American."[30]

What was remarkable about this partnership was that the Jeju's People's Committee leaned solidly to the left (occasionally even straying into anti-American rhetoric) and American officials knew as much: "They are still the mild leftist socialistic minded people," wrote one American adviser, after his visit to the island in December 1946. And yet, he acknowledged, "Police, American personnel, and the general public all say that there has never been any trouble or riot on the island."[31] If Americans could support the Jeju's People's Committee to realize independence in a peaceful manner, one would think they could have worked with the other people's committees in the South, which tended to be more conservative on average. The Jeju's People's Committee was firmly on the left side of the political spectrum among PCs in the South. In other words, there was nothing inevitable about American policy in Korea. Just like the US Fifty-Ninth Army in Jeju, General Hodge and his military government had choices to make in Seoul about which Koreans they would work with and how.

4   Reversing the Tide

General John Hodge's tenure in Korea got off to rocky start. In his first press conference, on September 9, 1945, he went out of his way to praise Abe Nobuyuki, the Japanese general-governor of Korea, for keeping the peace after Japan's surrender. His words would have stung Koreans regardless, but given they came on the heels of Japanese soldiers firing on a Korean crowd who came to Inchŏn to welcome the Americans, killing two and injuring eight, made Hodge's comments especially tone deaf.[1] But that was not all. He was also quoted saying that Koreans were "the same breed of cats as the Japanese." Hodge claimed his comments were taken out of context and that he was referring only to Koreans who had collaborated with the Japanese, but the damage was done.[2]

It went from bad to worse the next day when Hodge announced that the occupation government would keep Abe and the rest of the Japanese colonial staff in place, albeit under American supervision. Already seething from Hodge's earlier comments, Koreans exploded in protest. One group called the decision "a slap in the face."[3] A Korean newspaper thundered they would rather be governed by "some chief from Borneo" than by the Japanese.[4] The fallout was swift. General MacArthur ordered Hodge to reverse the policy and remove all Japanese officials as rapidly as possible. It was a rare instance of MacArthur stepping in to countermand a decision made by Hodge. The White House also went into damage control mode, distancing itself from Hodge's decision. Truman declared "emphatically that the decision to retain Japanese overlords in positions of authority over the people of Korea was entirely a matter for the theatre commander." Acknowledging it was a mistake, Truman promised that the Japanese would be removed from Korea as soon as possible.[5]

What was Hodge thinking? As a lifelong military man who prized law and order above all else, he didn't like what he was seeing in Korea. The colonial government was shut down, factories were idle, prisons were empty, and the police were nowhere to be found. He also didn't much like the sweeping changes taking place all around him. He blamed the Korean People's Republic (KPR) for the social upheaval, accusing the organization of being a front for Soviet-backed radicals, which was untrue. If there were "communist agitators" within the KPR, they were homegrown.[6] Nonetheless, this judgment led Hodge to the ill-fated decision to keep the Japanese colonial machinery in place. As far as we know, he did not consult anyone—certainly not any Koreans—about his decision, though his political adviser, H. Merrill Benninghoff, agreed that southern Korea was a "powder keg ready to explode at the application at a spark."[7]

But not everyone in the military government saw things this way. Liberal advisers praised the Committee for the Preparation of Korean Independence (CPKI) and the KPR for preventing looting, bloodshed, and rioting in the weeks before the arrival of American forces. As they pointed out, not one Japanese was killed by a Korean after the surrender. On the other hand, more than thirty Koreans were killed by the Japanese police during the same period.[8] As one US official explained, "The Japanese had good reason to fear the Koreans. It was due to the leadership of Yŏ [Unhyŏng] and his associates that their worst fears were not realized."[9] They also commended Yŏ and his allies for efficiently distributing food and reopening schools during the interlude.

What is more, these advisers saw the KPR genuinely representing Korean aspirations for liberation. "If the People's Republic exhibited radical tendencies," Grant Meade wrote, "it only reflected with reasonable accuracy the views of the Korean majority."[10] The same opinion held for the local people's committees. "It is safe to say that for the most part the local People's Committees in these early days were of the genuine grassroots democratic variety and represented a spontaneous urge of the people to govern themselves," wrote Richard Robinson, a civil affairs officer in the Department of Public Information.

These different viewpoints failed to make a dent in Hodge's thinking. He was convinced that southern Korea was on the brink of anarchy no matter what anyone said. And he believed that the only way to avoid falling over the precipice was to preserve as much of the colonial system as possible. Unable to retain Japanese officials, Hodge would have to find Koreans to run it. But if not the KPR, who?

Hodge's advisers thought they had found a suitable alternative in the recently formed Korean Democratic Party (KDP). "The most encouraging single factor in the political situation," Benninghoff wrote, "is the presence in Seoul of several hundred conservatives among the older and better educated Koreans." Educated in the United States and American missionary institutions in Korea, many of its members spoke English and professed a desire for an American-style democracy. These were two big pluses on their side.

The problem was that they weren't nearly as popular as Yŏ and the KPR. William Langdon, another State Department adviser in Seoul, called the KDP "unrepresentative," conceding to his superiors in Washington that "we may have picked out a disproportionate number of rich and conservative people."[11] Some of its members also had close ties to the Japanese, which tainted the KDP as the party of collaborators. Benninghoff, however, shrugged it off as a minor issue. "Although many of them have served with the Japanese, that stigma ought eventually to disappear," he wrote to the secretary of state, without giving further details.[12]

The KDP, in turn, considered the Americans a godsend. For basically all of August, Koreans assumed that the Soviet Union would accept Japan's surrender. It was an unhappy prospect for the Korean elite, and it showed in their actions. Big landowners sold off their properties at a steep discount, industrialists made numerous concessions to their workers, and conservative political leaders compromised on policies they would have otherwise opposed. For example, conservative women members of the Founding Women's Association did not much like the economic reforms proposed by the organization but they went along with them because a majority of the mostly leftist-leaning membership supported them.

However, the southern elite believed fortunes had shifted in their favor after they learned that the United States would occupy their half of Korea in late August. They didn't know exactly how much US occupation might help them, but they liked their chances better with the Americans than with the Soviets. One could see the change already in land prices, which rose steadily after the news broke, and in the actions of the conservative members of the FWA, who left the group to form their own organization, the Korean Patriotic Women's Association, with a more conservative agenda stripped of the goals for equal pay for equal work and economic independence for women.[13]

These elites would be proven right. Within days of landing, the US military government received and consulted KDP leaders, who provided much of the early intelligence for the incoming Americans. Among them was Harvard-educated Yi Myo-muk, who would go on to become Hodge's personal translator. When asked about the KPR, they all said the same thing: its leaders were communist *and* pro-Japanese. If it sounded like they were reading from the same script, they were. The day before Americans arrived in Korea, the KDP had prepared and disseminated a document calling the KPR leaders "running dogs of Japanese imperialism."[14] They made this accusation even though the party's leading lights, Yi Myo-muk and Kim Sŏngsu, had a record of pro-Japanese activities during World War II. Both men were identified as pro-Japanese collaborators by the South Korean government in 2009.[15]

The KPR didn't get a chance to refute the charges until a month later. "We are waiting to be called forth," Yŏ told a *New York Times* correspondent in Seoul.[16] When he finally did get his meeting with Hodge in October, he was given the third degree. What were his ties to the Japanese? How much money did he receive from colonial officials?[17] Having to defend himself from the charge of collaboration must have been a bitter pill to swallow for the longtime independence activist. An internal military government investigation conducted in 1946 found that Yŏ "was always anti-Japanese."[18] The tense meeting ended with Hodge telling Yŏ that the United States was the only legitimate government in southern Korea. This was his way of denying recognition to Yŏ and the KPR.

Shortly after the meeting, the military governor, Major General Archibald Arnold, Hodge's second in command, announced the creation of an advisory council. It would be composed of prominent Koreans who would give Arnold advice on Korean matters on an "honest and non-partisan basis."[19] He invited Yŏ to be one of its ten members. However, when Yŏ walked into the first meeting and saw that the other nine people were KDP members or supporters, he stormed out. Yŏ wasn't opposed to working with conservatives but nine to one was not his idea of nonpartisanship, nor did he think it came close to being representative of the Korean people.

Arnold chastised KPR leaders in a statement that on his order was published on the front page of nearly every south Korean newspaper. (The military governor shut down the *Maeil sinbo* for refusing to publish the statement, despite Hodge's earlier pledge to maintain a free press in Korea.)[20] In the statement, Arnold likened KPR leaders to children throwing a tantrum after not getting what they wanted. He also belittled them for thinking they could govern Korea on their own, calling it "play-acting on a puppet stage with entertainment of questionable amusement value." He demanded they "pull down the curtain on the puppet show."[21]

The KPR published a pamphlet, "The Traitors and the Patriots," in response to Arnold's blistering public criticisms. It argued that the KPR—the patriots—was "the duly constituted organ of the Korean people," and by not recognizing it as such, Americans risked ignoring the will of the Korean people. It also said that the military government was being advised by traitorous Koreans. To prove the point, the pamphlet quoted extensively from anti-American speeches made by KDP leaders during World War II, including one of its founders, Kim Sŏngsu, who called Americans "vampires" and "enemies of humanity." (Kim Sŏngsu was the older brother of Kim Yŏnsu and a major shareholder in the Kyŏngsŏng Spinning and Weaving Joint Stock Company.) The KPR blasted Arnold's statement as an "insult to the Korean people."[22]

Hodge had the publication of all handbills and pamphlets in Korea banned immediately. His spokesperson said that this decision "was brought about by Communist faction handbills, which were both disturbing to the peace and critical of the occupation policies."[23] Ironically, the pamphlet uproar improved the standing of the KDP. To Hodge and his conservative advisers, the incident showed that the KPR was not serious about working with Americans. In contrast, the "Conservative Group," Benninghoff wrote, "[is] willing to cooperate with the military government."[24]

The US high command spent the early months of the occupation tilting the scales in favor of the KDP, its preferred party.[25] Among other things, occupation authorities supported KDP requests for the return of the Korean Provisional Government, including conservatives Kim Ku and Syngman Rhee. Their record of fighting for Korean independence—Kim in China, Rhee in the United States—would provide the KDP a much-needed shot of nationalist prestige. While Hodge and his senior advisers seemed not to care much about their collaborationist past, KDP leaders knew that the Korean people would.

Unable to keep Japanese officials, Hodge did the next best thing: he promoted the Koreans who had worked under them. His closest advisers insisted that the policy was born of necessity, since not enough skilled Koreans without the stain of Japanese collaboration remained to do the job. Occupation authorities filled out the rest of the government—tens of thousands of

From left to right: Syngman Rhee, Kim Ku, and General John Hodge after their
first meeting.
National Archives (111-SC-223972)

positions—with people recommended by American missionaries and
the KDP. Its own members occupied key positions within the military
government. Filled largely by educated, English-speaking Christians, it
became known disparagingly as the "interpreter's government." The vast
majority of Koreans was not Christian—Christians accounted for less
than 3 percent of the population in the South in 1945—and few spoke
English.[26]

Hodge's personal translator and KDP leader, Yi Myo-muk, matched the
profile to a tee. He attended missionary-run schools in Pyongyang and graduated from Chosŏn Christian College in 1921. After graduation, he studied
abroad with the support of the Korean Methodist Church Conference. He
went on to receive a master's degree at Harvard and a doctorate in history
from Boston University in 1931. He returned to Korea several years later and
eventually became Dean of Yŏnhŭi College (which would later become Yonsei

Cho Pyŏngok in his customary bow tie.
Margaret Bourke-White / The LIFE Picture Collection / Shutterstock

University, today one of South Korea's leading universities). During the Second World War, Yi promoted Japanese war propaganda and recruited Korean student volunteers for the war effort.[27]

As Hodge's Korean interpreter, Yi had the general's ear, which gave him enormous influence over key personnel decisions concerning the bureaucracy and the police. He persuaded Hodge and his advisers to install close ally and a founding member of the KDP, Cho Pyŏngok, as chief of the Korean National Police.[28] Like Yi, Cho was a scion of a prominent Christian family and was sent to the United States for his education. He went to high school in Kingston, Pennsylvania, before attending Columbia University in New York City, where he earned a doctorate in economics in 1925. He returned to Korea shortly after completing his degree, bringing back with him a fondness for bowties. Unlike some of his fellow party members, Cho had a record of resisting the Japanese and spent time in prison to show for it.[29] Yet when Cho became director of the Korean National Police, he rehired over 80 percent of the Korean force who had formerly worked for the Japanese.[30] Why would someone who opposed the Japanese retain the former colonial police? In his mind, now that the Japanese were gone, communism loomed as the larger threat.

His decision led to stunning reversals in which former colonial policemen who had been run out of town only a few weeks earlier were back at their old posts, able to exact revenge on the shocked villagers. In most cases, however, the former colonial police dared not return to their hometowns. Ch'oe Nŭngjin, head of the Detective Bureau, a division within the KNP, wrote: "I have discovered that most of the policemen Dr. Cho calls 'new' are newly hired by the Military Government, but actually they are bad Japanese-trained police who ran away from their homes in North and South Korea." He added matter-of-factly, "The Police Department is the refugee home for Japanese trained police and traitors."[31] It is worth noting that Ch'oe was a KDP supporter (he came from a wealthy Christian land-owning family and was educated in the United States) and on friendly terms with Cho, though maybe not after this memo.

Hodge's closest advisers knew exactly what they were getting with Cho. A US intelligence assessment described Cho as a "monarchist" and "traditionalist" who believes in the "firm rule of the people by an enlightened authority, in which category he places himself."[32] They may not have liked all of Cho's methods but, as far as they were concerned, he was better than the alternative. "There has never been the slightest danger that American military officials would support any except rightists in the key posts of the police," is how one government adviser put it.[33]

The police were to Hodge what the emperor was to MacArthur: nonnegotiable. MacArthur preserved the imperial system in Japan, despite overwhelming evidence that implicated the emperor in Japan's wartime aggression.[34] Maintaining the throne was the centerpiece of MacArthur's plans to reconstruct Japan, and he would cover up the emperor's war record to do so.[35] Hodge basically did the same for the Korean police. For him, they were the only thing standing in the way of a communist takeover of the peninsula. He would keep the hated colonial institution at all costs, with a few superficial changes.

The decision to retain the Korean colonial police had enormous ramifications. If the police would not be held accountable for collaborating with the Japanese, who could be? This did not necessarily mean that all police were collaborators. But any reckoning with the colonial past surely required a thorough investigation into one of its most foremost institutions, of which half was comprised by Koreans, including my grandfather, who told me he joined the police during World War II to avoid military conscription.[36]

The policy to restore the colonial system led to a showdown between Hodge and Pak Hŏnyŏng. At their first meeting in late October, Hodge demanded Pak give up his dream of creating a "communist paradise" in Korea and invited him to work with other Korean leaders to form a coalition government. Hodge warned Pak that following his communist vision would only lead Korea down the path of authoritarianism. (He was not the only one wary of Pak's rigid commitment to communism; Yŏ split from the KPR over ideological differences, starting the People's Party in November 1945.)

Pak fired back at Hodge, insisting that the goals of the Communist Party reflected the aspirations of the Korean people, which included eliminating the remnants of Japanese colonialism. He could not understand why Americans refused to join him in this effort. Didn't the United States just fight a war to defeat Japanese fascism? an exasperated Pak asked. He also saw Hodge's offer to join a coalition government as not genuine, given a government stacked with collaborators. He warned Hodge that if occupation officials did not remove pro-Japanese collaborators from the government, the Communist Party would fight the Americans as if they were the Japanese imperialists.[37] And with those defiant words, the meeting came to an abrupt end. They skipped the traditional photograph—Hodge normally took pictures with Korean leaders after their meetings—and there would be no serious talks between the two men after this.

Not long after his meeting with Pak, Hodge had the KPR and local people's committees dissolved. He also ordered military government teams to disband the workers' control committees in the factories and reappropriate the lands that had been seized by Korean peasants in the countryside. It was almost as if Hodge was trying put Korea's Asian Spring back into the bottle.

The military government teams replaced the workers' committees with American advisers, who quickly turned over operations to Korean managers who had served under the Japanese. The managers started with the factories in and around Seoul (the men and women workers at the Kyŏngsŏng Textile Factory, who had wrested control of the company from their president, Kim Yŏnsu, never got a chance to prove their managerial chops). The teams then fanned out south and west to factories in Kwangju and Busan. The process of replacing workers' self-management committees took weeks and, in some cases, months. They had taken over more than seven hundred factories.

Occupation officials pointed to the poor, chaotic conditions in the factories to justify the purge. "Korean labor, at the time of Japan's surrender, appears to have reacted in an undisciplined manner, which created serious difficulties in maintaining production," one adviser noted disapprovingly. "Korean management and labor were completely unready to assume their respective roles."[38] Hodge announced a state of emergency in the factories on October 30, 1945, declaring, "The policy of the Military Government is to let nothing stand in the way of revival of production and trade."[39] The "nothing" included work stoppages and strikes.

Yet the system of American advisers and Korean managers that replaced the workers' committees fared no better, if not considerably worse. According to the official history of the American military government's Department of Labor, "there was no maintenance of existing plants and equipment, no replacement of parts and a great dissipation of existing stockpiles." Korean managers also failed to enforce standards regarding discipline, hiring and firing, and scheduling. Worst of all, they engaged in rampant corruption and graft, selling raw materials, machinery, and finished products on the black market. Their negligence and malfeasance hampered industrial production and demoralized workers.[40]

Hodge's conservative advisers defended their policy, arguing that the loss of Japanese managers and technical experts left them with few options. This was, of course, the rationale for US occupation policy writ large. The labor adviser to the military government, Stewart Meacham, wasn't buying it: "It may very well be that we have permitted the loss of Japanese technicians to loom larger in our minds as a deterrent to industrial rehabilitation than it will prove to be the fact." His own investigations showed that "Koreans are not sitting on their hands waiting for something to be done for them."

Meacham had spent the previous ten years working for the National Labor Relations Board in Los Angeles. Born in Birmingham, Alabama, he attended Davidson College, where he roomed with Dean Rusk, the US army officer who recommended dividing Korea at the 38th parallel and who would later become secretary of state. (The two men were extremely close in college, according to Rusk—"about as close as two people could be." But Meacham would later become a thorn in the side of his former college roommate, as a prominent leader of the antiwar movement in the 1960s.) After college, Meacham went on to Union Theological Seminary in New York City, earning a master's degree in 1934 before returning to Birmingham to serve as a presbyterian minister. His ministry included organizing black and white workers in the Jim Crow South.[41]

Drawing from this experience, Meacham used a racial analogy to challenge the notion that Korean laborers were unready for expanded roles in the rehabilitation of their economy: "In our country where it is not uncommon to exclude Negroes from the more highly-skilled positions in industry, it is by no means rare to find a Negro helper 'breaking in' his white boss. The know-how is there, but the opportunity is denied. There is real reason to believe that something of the same thing will prove true of the Koreans."[42] Meacham's comparison to Black Americans pointed to the assumptions about colonized people that shaped American policy in Korea. Imperial habits of the mind die hard, if they ever do.

Meacham cited Korean railway workers, who kept train service running smoothly after liberation, as an example of what Korean labor could do if only given the chance: "Most of the locomotive engineers were Japanese before liberation. Koreans have moved into their places and are performing with responsibility and skill."[43]

But there was no chance Hodge would cede managerial responsibilities to the workers, even with American advisers overseeing them. It smacked of communism and violated his core political values. Hodge was for the free market, private property rights, freedom of choice and association, and a minimal state (with the exception of preserving law and order). He was not about to support a proletarian revolution. One of his advisers stated Hodge's position on the matter: "Labor's attitude is that all Japanese properties should be taken over by labor. AMG [American military government] has taken steps to disabuse this idea. Korean labor states the case deceptively, saying they want management of industry. In fact, what seems to be wanted is ownership with rights to all profits."[44] The latter was a big red flag for Hodge.

Hodge and his senior staff thought they had secured workers' rights when the military government passed Ordinance 19, which enshrined "the right of any individual or group of individuals to accept employment and to work unmolested." With this stroke of the pen, Hodge believed he had emancipated Korean laborers from the tyranny of Japanese colonialism and democratized labor relations in southern Korea. But the right to choose where and when to work—the right of "free labor"—was hardly a new freedom. As Meacham pointed out, "Korean labor had enjoyed this 'right' during the entire Japanese regime."[45]

For Korean workers, the colonial status quo was not good enough—they wanted more from liberation. At the Kyŏngsŏng Textile Factory in Seoul, laborers refused to work if the factory was returned to its former president, Kim Yŏnsu. They vehemently opposed a pro-Japanese industrialist profiting off their labor now that Korea was free. They were willing to accept "conscientious" Korean capitalists and technicians. Similarly, at the Yangnim Silk Factory in Kwangju and the Undershirt Factory in Taegu, workers staged a protest when US military advisers appointed pro-Japanese executives to manage the factories.[46]

Free labor was also not enough for the workers at the Seoul Electric Company. They organized a union to bargain collectively with the military government's appointed American supervisor. Their representatives submitted a long list of demands, including a living allowance, union recognition, and worker input on the selection of department managers. When the onsite US labor adviser rejected the demands, the workers—5,300 strong—went out on strike.[47] Their demands and actions looked like a classic case of trade unionism. What happened to workers' self-management of the factories?

As it turns out, workers had mixed feelings about becoming owners. The lack of capital and managerial experience gave them pause, especially with the economy suffering from soaring inflation and supply shortages. (As their final parting gift, the Japanese colonial government had printed millions of yen.) Under these conditions, having the US military government as a potential backstop didn't sound like the worst idea as long as pro-Japanese managers were expelled and workers could unionize and bargain collectively.

Just as important, the military government had signaled its hostility to workers' control of the factory floor. Most workers thought that control was not worth fighting for, given some of their reservations. They turned to trade unionism instead. Almost all of them became affiliated with the National Council of Korean Labor Unions, which brought together workers' groups from different factories into a loosely organized federation. The Chŏnp'yŏng, as it was known in Korean, was formed by longtime labor activists with unimpeachable nationalist credentials. Both the chairman, Hŏ Sŏngt'aek, and the vice chairman, Pak Seyŏng, had been jailed for union organizing and anti-Japanese activity during the colonial era.[48]

The socialist and communist activists, who led the takeovers in some factories, didn't put up much of a fight either. They thought it best to avoid open confrontation with the Americans, at least for now. Some of them also genuinely believed they could work with US occupation officials to enact reforms on behalf of the laboring classes.[49] It was not an unreasonable expectation. MacArthur's reformers had pressured the Japanese parliament to pass the Trade Union Law in December 1945, which guaranteed workers the right to organize, strike, and bargain collectively.[50] If this law could be enacted in Japan, why not in Korea? In fact, Captain Owen Jones, director of the Commerce Department, proposed basically the same law. For Jones, a New Dealer, it was the best way to safeguard workers' rights without going "red."[51] A middle ground between workers' self-management and Hodge's "free labor" seemed distinctly possible.

In the countryside, peasants held rallies to protest the military government's decision to reappropriate former Japanese lands. But when American forces came to take the lands into custody, the peasants did not try to stop them. During the second week of the occupation, American troops had shot and killed three Koreans at a rice warehouse, southeast of Seoul, where a "near-riot" had supposedly occurred.[52] Resistance seemed foolhardy, given that the Americans had the guns and the peasants did not. All told, the military government repossessed nearly 875,000 acres of land.

"We cannot let every Korean take property," Military Governor Arnold explained at a press conference in October 1945. "In order that all may be well done according to democratic principles, this property must be sold by the Japanese to the Koreans." When a Korean reporter asked why Koreans had to buy Japanese properties that originally belonged to Koreans, Arnold answered, "They must buy it. There must be an honest transaction for a fair price."[53] This thinking also led the military government to establish a free market in rice in southern Korea. Previously, the Japanese colonial government had instituted a system of rationing and price controls. Archer considered any control on the "free play of supply and demand" contrary to freedom and democracy.[54] "What could more directly show the Koreans they were now liberated than to sweep away these requirements completely?" is how one military government report put it.[55] The free market, Hodge and Archer believed, would make Koreans free.

The flip side of this was that almost anything else was communism or a trojan horse for it. As legal adviser Roger N. Baldwin wrote, "If you are a liberal who feels that the pro-Japanese collaborators must be purged, that the police must be gotten out of politics, that suppression of the left only breeds Communists, [that] the unions should have freedom to strike, and that North and South Korea must be reconciled—you are a Communist."[56] The agrarian reformer Arthur Bunce quipped that Hodge's definition of communism was anything "an inch left of center."[57]

Yet to ease the loss from the repossession of Japanese lands, the military government passed Ordinance 9, which restricted landlords from charging tenants more than 30 percent of their annual yield for rent. This regulation was the brainchild of Yi Hun'gu. In the 1920s, Yi had studied at the University of Wisconsin under pioneering agricultural economist Benjamin Hibbard, whose students included future US vice president Henry A. Wallace. The Wisconsin School, as it was better known, was on the cutting edge of progressive reform, incubating ideas for future New Deal policies. (One of its students would draft the Social Security Act, passed in 1935.)

In the field of agriculture, Hibbard and his colleagues sought to reinvigorate the small farm ideal—akin to Thomas Jefferson's yeoman farmer—through a combination of modernizing reforms and government regulations. As a student, Yi learned about agricultural science, cooperative farming, land regulations, and tenancy laws. After graduating with distinction, he went on to work for the US Department of Agriculture. He was recruited by fellow Wisconsin alumnus L. C. Gray, the first head of the newly created Division of Land Economics, who was best known as author of the landmark two-volume *History of Agriculture in the Southern United States*. Yi returned to Korea in 1931 to become head of the Agriculture Department at Sungsil Junior College in Pyongyang. George S. McCune, who later became head of the Korea desk at the State Department and developed the McCune-Reischauer romanization system, recommended him for the post.

Yi found conditions in the countryside worse than when he had left Korea, which he described as the most tenant-ridden country in the world. Yet he believed the system could be reformed by regulating what landlords could charge for rent. He thought capping farm rent at one-third of a tenant's yield would level the playing field and create a path for tenants to become independent farmers. The problem, as he saw it, wasn't capitalism; it was landlord monopoly. Yi, in short, was no revolutionary—he joined the KDP after liberation. As a liberal, Christian nationalist, he wanted to reform, not overturn, the private land system, in essence to save rural capitalism from itself. Yi finally got a chance to apply his theories when he was appointed head of the Department of Agriculture by the US military government in September 1945.[58]

Ordinance 9 provided considerable relief, slashing rent by as much as 50 percent in some cases. It was exactly the kind of tenancy law peasants had fought for during the colonial period.[59] Kim Chŏlhwan, who came from a poor farming family in Kyŏnggi province, remembered being elated when the rent regulation was announced (interestingly enough, he credited Yŏ Unhyŏng, not the military government, for it). Kim and his two younger brothers had struggled to make rent and pay the bills since their father had passed away. During the evenings, Kim collected night soil—human excrement used as fertilizer—to make ends meet.[60]

For others, however, the rent regulation was a letdown. The peasants who had already negotiated lower rents with their landlords found little use for Ordinance 9. The peasants who already had taken possession of Japanese lands had now owned the land for more than a month, long enough to feel like it was theirs. So, when the Americans reappropriated the lands, it felt like a dream ripped from them. Han Saengwŏn, who had relished getting his land back from the Japanese, saying at the time, "There could be nothing in this world so wonderful and rare," now complained bitterly: "We're independent they say, then they take the people's land . . . you call that independence?"[61] Lower rent aside, it would seem impossible to go back to being a tenant. Land ownership was not solely about livelihood for peasants; it was also about a sense of self-sufficiency and dignity that money couldn't buy.

The landowning classes were not exactly thrilled with the rent regulation, but if it meant staving off expropriation of their lands, they grudgingly accepted it. After venting about Ordinance 9, Yi Sŏndal, the wealthy landowner in An Hoenam's "The Sorrows of Peasants," tells his tenant farmer, "Land reform, land reform, people say, land reform is done now," while contentedly smoking his long pipe.[62] Landlords felt even better about their outlook after the military governor told reporters that any transfer of property had to abide by free market principles.[63]

Some occupation reformers recognized the limited scope of Ordinance 9, understanding that it would not alone fulfill the aspirations of Korean farmers. Wolf Ladejinsky, the roving agrarian reformer who was in Korea on loan from SCAP headquarters after helping to design land reform in Japan, wrote, "The Military Government is well aware that this regulation is only one step on the road towards the creation of an economically better-off peasantry, and that the full realization of the objective calls for the shifting of farmers from a tenant to an owner basis." He added, "The Military Government is in a position to begin the implementation of such a program because it has taken title to approximately 875,000 acres of agricultural lands in Korea that were formerly owned by the Japanese."[64]

Sensing an opportunity, socialist and communist activists, once associated with the now defunct KPR and allied people's committees, seized on the issue of land reform to mobilize peasants. In November 1945, they formed the National Federation of Peasant Unions (NFPU), which called for the confiscation of lands owned by the Japanese, national traitors, and Korean landowners with extensive holdings to redistribute them to poor peasants. Simultaneously, they criticized Ordinance 9 as a cynical ploy by the military government to stall "momentum for resolving the land problem."[65]

The activists' message resonated. The NFPU organized close to two hundred peasant unions, boasting two million members, in less than two months.[66] In addition to advocating for land reform, the organization pushed peasants to form agricultural cooperatives. By establishing consumer, marketing, and credit associations through their pooled resources, peasants would be able to bypass usurious middlemen, negotiate lower prices for equipment and supplies, and share distribution channels and marketing costs. NFPU activists promoted cooperatives to encourage peasants to imagine themselves as part of a collective project. The ultimate goal of land reform was not making peasants into yeoman farmers; instead, they viewed private land ownership as a transitional step toward a collective system in which land would be held by a union or the state.[67]

American occupying forces faced a curious situation in Naju. Instead of disgruntled peasants, they encountered a welcoming group calling itself the Kungsam-myŏn Tenants Committee, with paperwork in hand. Na Chaegi, flanked by other committee members, calmly presented American officers with legal documents showing their families' and villages' ownership of lands in Naju. The thorough records, they believed, would distinguish their claims from those of other peasants by showing without a shadow of a doubt that theirs were not "enemy property"—that is, Japanese lands. Their almost six-decade quest for justice seemed finally in reach.

After barely glancing at the paperwork, American officers declared the lands in question "enemy property," owing to the fact that they were held by the Oriental Development Company at the time of liberation. Na and the committee protested furiously, insisting their case was different from the others, and offering to show more records. But to no avail—their lands were taken into custody along with the rest. Na then convened a meeting of the Kungsam-myŏn Peasant Union several days later to figure out what to do next. The thousands of members who gathered at the local elementary school affirmed their commitment to recover their ancestral farmlands. Na drew up a petition demanding the return of their family and village lands, insisting they were "definitively not enemy property"; and the return of all rental payments made to the Oriental Development Company, which had unjustly charged rent on lands that were theirs. Na also went to the Naju County executive, the highest-ranking Korean official in the region, to ask him to write a letter confirming that "Kungsam-myŏn lands are not enemy lands."[68] Na and the committee then submitted the letter, along with the petition, to the provincial military governor. After several days passed without an answer, the committee resubmitted the package.

When the second attempt failed to get a response, union representatives traveled to Seoul to appeal directly to the leaders of the US military government. They stayed in Seoul from late November to early December 1945 in hopes of meeting with General Hodge or Director Yi Hun'gu. If they got one of them in a room, they believed they could—with such comprehensive records—convince the Americans of their case. During their three weeks in the capital, they handed out their petition on the streets and posted copies in government offices, party headquarters, media organizations, and community centers.[69] Their efforts to raise awareness of their cause seemed to pay off when a member of Hodge's staff assured them that the petition would be relayed to senior advisers. Union representatives returned home optimistic that the military government would rule in their favor; at least that is what they told members in a post-trip meeting.

Behind the scenes, however, Hodge and Arnold viewed the petition suspiciously, believing the group behind it to be communist led. Apparently, several members of the union leadership were active in the Naju's People's Committee before the military government closed it down. Just a hint of red, in the eyes of the military government, made everybody red. The Americans also considered the group's demand for land without payment a tell-tale sign of communism. The high command seemed unable or unwilling to separate the union's petition for recovery of lands that were legally theirs from the wider movement for land redistribution. It was all the same to them.

Not long after the union representatives returned home, US military teams raided their offices, searching for evidence tying them to the Communist Party. Despite not finding anything, they shut down the union and ordered members to cease all activities. Union leaders scheduled an emergency meeting, where members angrily denounced the occupation government and accused American officials of being no different than their former colonial overlords. As one peasant put it: "Just as [Korean] people believe the colors green and blue to be [shades of] the same color, the United States and Japan have different names but are ultimately the same."[70] With the union shutdown and their petition ignored, members were at a loss as to what to do next. The meeting ended without a clear path forward.

5 False Starts and Missed Opportunities

Three months into the occupation, Hodge knew things were not going well in Korea. In his December 1945 cable to the Supreme Commander of the Allied Powers (SCAP), he reported, "In South Korea the US is blamed for the partition and there is growing resentment against all Americans in the area, including passive resistance to constructive efforts we make here." He cited the lack of essential supplies, high inflation, and political schisms as reasons for America's waning popularity. These problems, he contended, stemmed from a single root. "The dual occupation," he wrote, "imposes an impossible condition upon our occupation's missions of establishing a sound economy and preparing Korea for future independence." Hodge viewed the arbitrary division of the country at the 38th parallel as the original sin from which all other troubles followed. And as long as the partition remained, he saw no way of turning things around in Korea, posing a no-win situation for his military government.

Koreans had also grown restless over the lack of progress on reunification and independence. "The Koreans want their independence more than any one thing and want it now," Hodge explained in his cable. "This stems from the Allied promise of freedom and independence which is well known by every Korean without the qualifying phrase 'in due course.'" He thought by "occidental standards" that Koreans were not ready for independence. But he also thought that their capacity for self-government would not improve under the current conditions. In Hodge's judgment, the United States was "surely drifting to the edge of a political-economic abyss from which it can never be retrieved with any credit to U.S. prestige in the Far East." Seeing a near hopeless situation in Korea, he made a stunning policy suggestion: "Under present conditions I would go so far as to recommend both the United States and Russia withdraw from Korea simultaneously and leave Korea to its own devices and an inevitable internal upheaval for its self-purification."[1] Hodge wanted the United States to cut bait in Korea before it was too late.

Officials in Washington did not take the general's recommendation seriously even though he was the on-site commanding officer. The State Department thought that if Hodge had spent more time working on solutions and less time cozying up to reactionary right-wingers, southern Korea would be in better shape. "In a situation crying out for boldness and spectacular reform," one adviser from the State Department wrote, "the American command adopted a policy of trying to establish order with as little reform as possible."[2]

More than that, Washington wanted to stick to the original plan of establishing an international trusteeship in Korea. In mid-December 1945, American and Soviet foreign ministers met at the Moscow Conference to negotiate the terms of trusteeship in Korea, among other issues. (They also discussed the political fates of Eastern European countries—Poland, Romania, Bulgaria—and the occupation of Japan.) The American delegation, led by Secretary of State James Byrnes, proposed a four-power trusteeship to administer Korea for a period of five years, which could be extended for up to another five years, if deemed necessary. This plan would cut roughly thirty years from FDR's proposed timeline, but conditions in Korea and around the world had changed dramatically since Yalta.

The Soviet delegation, led by foreign minister Vyacheslav Molotov, countered with a hard cap of five years. They didn't think Koreans would tolerate anything longer. In their estimation, five years would be more than enough time to eradicate the vestiges of Japanese colonialism, rebuild the Korean economy, and prepare Koreans for independence.[3] The Soviet draft called for the creation of a Joint Commission, which would consist of representatives from the American and Soviet military commands in Korea who would consult with Korean political parties and social organizations to form a Provisional Korean Government. After its establishment, the four powers would jointly *consider* "working out an agreement concerning a

four-power trusteeship of Korea for up to five years." The vague wording left
room for interpretation as to whether trusteeship would be necessary at all.
Byrnes accepted the Soviet counterproposal almost verbatim. Americans
did not want to be held responsible for the permanent division of the country, and the Soviet proposal provided a reasonable roadmap to unite Korea.[4]
It appeared trusteeship was back on track.

The Moscow Conference was hailed as a success in the United States. The
front-page headline of the *New York Times* on December 28 flashed: "Big
Three Re-Establish Unity with Wide Accord." Calling it a new start for
peace, the editorial board wrote breathlessly, "The final communiqué issued
by the Moscow Conference is by all odds the most hopeful document that
has been presented to the world since Germany and Japan surrendered."[5] At
the White House, however, Truman was not pleased with the concessions
made by Byrnes. The president thought Byrnes gave the Soviets too much
control over the fate of Eastern Europe. Truman vented that he was "tired of
babying the Soviets" and resolved to get tougher with them. The Moscow
Conference was a turning point in US-Soviet relations but not in the way
imagined by the press.[6]

Halfway around the world, the Moscow communiqué provoked a furious reaction. Angry Koreans in the South erupted in protest, with thousands of
people taking to the streets on the day of the announcement. The crowds,
by and large, demonstrated peacefully, but there were incidences of Koreans
hurling stones at American soldiers and tearing down American flags from
military government buildings.

At a press conference the next day, Hodge did his best to allay Korean
concerns. "I disagree entirely," Hodge declared to the press, "with the use of
the word 'trusteeship.' I object strenuously to the use of that word in this
connection, and nothing can make me believe that the Allied powers have
established any such institution over the Korean people." He insisted that
his own reading of the document indicated a "speedy independence" for
Korea. But Hodge's explanation failed to satisfy the Korean press corps. Reporters returned time and again to the question of whether Korea would be
placed under trusteeship, for which the general had no straight answer.
Hodge's press conference did little to assuage their worries or those of the
Korean public. "The Korean press this morning had dealt with yesterday's
incomplete and contradictory accounts of the decision as a lethal blow to

the independence hopes of Korea," wrote *New York Times* reporter Richard Johnston.[7]

Kim Ku, leader of the Korean Provisional Government (not to be confused with the Provisional Korean Government to be established as per the Moscow communiqué), seized the moment to rally Koreans behind him.[8] A longtime nationalist, Kim vehemently opposed trusteeship and demanded immediate independence for Korea. He formed the Committee of National Mobilization for Anti-Trusteeship, which claimed that Koreans "already have an independent country and government established by Korean blood."[9] Kim blamed traitorous pro-Japanese collaborators for trusteeship. His accusations may have sounded odd coming from the balcony of a villa donated to him by Ch'oe Ch'anghak, who hoped to receive a pardon from Kim when he became president.[10] As a goldmining mogul who got rich collaborating with the Japanese, Ch'oe was exactly the kind of figure Kim would have targeted for assassination during the colonial period. Kim had directed the Patriotic Corps during the 1930s, a secret group of Korean patriots—or terrorists, depending on one's viewpoint—who targeted high-ranking Japanese officials and wealthy pro-Japanese Koreans for assassination.[11] (The 2015 South Korean film *Assassination* portrays Kim Ku, based in Shanghai, orchestrating the assassination of wealthy, pro-Japanese businessman, Kang In'guk, who could have easily been Ch'oe Ch'anghak.)

Yet even the longtime leader of the independence movement needed benefactors. Fighting for independence was going to take money. Kim's horse-betting habit, as well as his coterie of concubines, also required financing from time to time. He was a regular at the Sinsŏl-dong racetrack, easily spotted in his bright white *hanbok* (traditional Korean garb).[12]

Kim called for a nationwide strike, urged government employees to follow his orders, and demanded the government be turned over to the KPG—some might say he was staging a coup. His campaign culminated in a New Year's Eve rally at Tongdaemun Stadium in Seoul, the same venue where a ceremony to celebrate his return to Korea was held two months earlier.[13] The anti-trusteeship rally drew tens of thousands of protesters, including storeowners who shut down their businesses and police chiefs who resigned their positions in opposition to the Moscow decision.

Rebellion seemed to be in the air. Song Chinu, leader of the KDP, had been assassinated the day before, presumably for his refusal to support the anti-trusteeship movement. Seoul's chief of police believed that Kim Ku and

Kim Ku (right), in front of his villa, talks to longtime ally Cho Wanku.
John Florea / The LIFE Picture Collection / Shutterstock

his associates were behind the killing, though the evidence was circumstan-
tial. Two days before Song's death, Kim had said ominously on a radio
broadcast: "We must purify corrupt politicians, pro-Japanese elements, and
national traitors."[14] Fearing more trouble, US military authorities imposed
an 8:00 pm curfew and placed American forces on high alert. Hodge also
ordered GIs to bring Kim to the general's office at once. Kim's attempt to
take over the government infuriated Hodge, who considered throwing him

and his entire KPG bunch into the POW internment camp in Inch'ŏn. If he wanted to exact maximal punishment, imprisoning Kim among Japanese prisoners of war would do it.[15]

When Kim was brought before Hodge on New Year's Day, Hodge tore into him for inciting an insurrection and threatened to kill him if he "double-crossed" him again. (The KPG leader had signed a pledge to respect the authority of the military government upon his return to Korea.)[16] Kim responded dramatically by offering to kill himself right then and there.[17] Cooler heads eventually prevailed. A contrite Kim promised to protest peacefully and never again challenge the authority of the occupation government. That was enough for Hodge, who chose not to punish Kim for the attempted coup. (It is doubtful he would have let Pak Hŏnyŏng or any other leftist off so easy.) Kim did, however, lose his status as favored conservative nationalist with the military command, and with it, any chance of leading Korea. That mantle now belonged to Syngman Rhee, who channeled public anger against trusteeship to the Soviet Union.

Newspapers in Seoul planted the seed when they first broke the news about the results of the Moscow Conference. Multiple outlets had erroneously reported that Americans wanted immediate independence for Korea but the Soviets had insisted on trusteeship. Seoul residents woke up the next morning to giant posters throughout the city condemning the Communist Party for the trusteeship plan.

The Communist Party's shifting positions on the Moscow agreement didn't help their cause. Pak had initially joined Koreans across the political spectrum in opposing trusteeship, in a rare moment of national unity. In fact, he and other KPR leaders had engaged Kim Ku in talks about forming a coalition to oppose trusteeship before Kim was hauled into Hodge's office.[18]

However, on January 3, the Communist Party abruptly reversed position, declaring its support for the Moscow agreement. The announcement came on the heels of Pak's visit to Pyongyang, where Soviet officials pressured him to fall in line. They had already placed the prominent nationalist Cho Mansik under house arrest for refusing to support the decision. Known as the "Gandhi of Korea," for his nonviolent resistance against the Japanese, Cho was one of the most revered figures in the North (a kind of center-right version of Yŏ Unhyŏng).[19] He also happened to be the most prominent

Christian nationalist Cho Mansik.
Archive PL / Alamy Stock Photo

Christian nationalist in the most Christian city in East Asia. Pyongyang was known as the "Jerusalem of the East."

Owing to his public stature, Soviet officials allowed Cho to maintain his position as chairman of the South P'yŏngan People's Committee, despite his conservative leanings. The Soviets were also not initially impressed with the communist alternative. "The reestablished Communist organizations turned out to have neither the proper leaders nor a clear and specific platform" is what a 1945 Soviet report on communists in Korea said.[20] As a result, Cho was the odds-on favorite to become the leader of north Korea at the start of the occupation.[21]

But just like Kim Ku, Cho lost his front-runner status (and more) because of his vehement opposition to trusteeship. And by now, Soviet officials had identified a possible replacement in a former anti-Japanese guerrilla fighter, Kim Il Sung, whose popularity had grown rapidly since returning to north Korea in October 1945. (Before the fallout from trusteeship, Cho Mansik and Kim Il Sung had discussed forming a new party, a united national front.) This is not to say that Kim Il Sung was a handpicked puppet of the Soviets. But having someone else to possibly back did make it easier for Soviet officials to take a hard line with Cho over his opposition to trusteeship.[22]

Pak's flip-flopping on the Moscow decision made him appear as a puppet on the string of the Soviet Union. Back in Seoul, Syngman Rhee pounced, accusing Pak and the Communist Party of selling out the country to yet another foreign power. Their support for trusteeship, he alleged, was a plot to subjugate all of Korea to the Soviet "motherland." (Rhee's ghostwriter, Robert Oliver, a speech professor at Pennsylvania State University, whom he had met in the United States while in exile, provided much of the language and metaphors for his anti-communist speeches.[23]) The KDP aided Rhee's campaign by circulating a pamphlet, "Down with Pak," which denounced the Communist Party leader as a "country-selling Soviet stooge."

Up to this point, Syngman Rhee had not gotten much traction, despite his nationalist credentials. He had spent most of his life fighting for Korean independence in exile, mainly in the United States. While abroad, he obtained a master's degree at Harvard University and a doctorate at Princeton University.[24] But this also meant he had been away from Korea for over thirty years. Returning with a non-Korean wife—the Austrian-born Francesca Donner—and speaking what one reporter called a "Hawaiian brand of pidgin Korean" did not help his cause.[25]

The trusteeship imbroglio gave Rhee a chance to reboot. As he railed against trusteeship and communism, his popularity surged with Koreans who felt betrayed by the Moscow agreement. In addition, the affair left his main rivals badly damaged. When Hodge's advisers created the Representative Democratic Council (RDC) several weeks later, they selected Syngman Rhee as president and Kim Ku as vice president to reflect the new pecking order. (With the RDC, Hodge's advisers sought to revive the advisory council that was abandoned after Yŏ refused to participate.) Flexing his newfound political muscle, Rhee incorporated Kim's Committee of National Mobilization for Anti-Trusteeship into his newly formed National Society for Rapid Realization of Korean Independence (NSRRKI) in February 1946.

The Soviets were none too happy with what was transpiring in the South. In Moscow, Stalin confronted the US ambassador, Averell Harriman, with intelligence that showed southern newspapers falsely reporting that it was the Soviets, not the Americans, that had insisted on a trusteeship. These reports also indicated that "US representatives there were advocating that the decision to set up a trusteeship be abrogated."[26] Not only had Hodge done little to clear up falsehoods around the Moscow decision, but he supported opposition to it behind closed doors, though he wanted it to be peaceful. He thought trusteeship was the half-baked idea of "pinkos"—communist sympathizers—in the State Department that had no chance of succeeding.

"I do not know who have been the experts on Korea who have advised and guided the State Department in their disregard of my recommendations," Hodge wrote angrily. "Here we are not dealing with wealthy, US-educated Koreans but with poorly trained, and poorly educated Orientals strongly affected by 40 years of Jap control, who are definitely influenced by direct propaganda and with whom it is almost impossible to reason."[27] (Koreans would say Hodge had not developed *chŏng*—positive feelings or attachments—for them.)

Hodge offered his resignation on January 28, in an acknowledgment that he may have overstepped his bounds by encouraging opposition to trusteeship. Whatever actions he took, he was adamant that they were in the interest of Korean independence. "In my opinion, Koreans do not want communism, but the unsettled conditions, the lack of clear cut policies for the future and lack of hope for early national sovereignty may easily push those in the US zone to radical leftism, if not raw communism."[28] Officials in Washington convinced Hodge to stay on. Replacing the leader of the occupation on the eve of the Joint Commission would have been risky.[29]

In the meantime, General Terentii F. Shtykov, the Soviet occupation leader in the North, issued a play-by-play of the Moscow decision to set the record straight. His statement, which was published by the Soviet news agency Tass, pointed out that it was the Americans who reproposed the idea of a four-power trusteeship at Moscow. He also noted that the American proposal did not provide for the creation of a Provisional Korean Government; the Soviets had added that provision. Finally, he emphasized how the Soviets capped the period of trusteeship to five years, while the initial American draft allowed for a period of up to ten years.[30]

Hodge feared this disclosure would ignite another round of upheaval in the South: "As the significance of the Tass statement recently released by

General Shtykov sinks in, the Korean people are feeling that the United States has again sold 'them down the river' this time to the Russians instead of the Japanese."[31] None of this boded well for the Joint Commission, which was set to kick off in March 1946.

The State Department dispatched advisers to Korea in hopes of jump-starting reform ahead of the opening of the Joint Commission. One of them was former missionary Arthur Bunce, who made his way back to Korea after being away for more than a decade. Between 1928 and 1934, he had set up a dozen YMCA schools in northern Korea to teach peasants cooperative farming. He had drawn inspiration from the Danish cooperatives he believed had helped establish a model social democracy there. He had noticed "very few rich people and practically no poor" on a visit to the Scandinavian country in 1928.[32]

Arthur C. Bunce in South Korea, circa 1950.
John Florea / The LIFE Picture Collection / Shutterstock

One of Bunce's fondest memories of his work in Korea was teaching apple farmers how to get the highest return on their products, even in a down market. "The prices fell to just about half of what it was last year," he recalled. "The farmers were in a quandary and I felt here was an opportunity to prove some of the theories I had been teaching." He convinced the apple growers to form a cooperative, which would allow them to bypass middlemen eating at their profits. Bunce and his Korean assistant then traveled to Japan to identify wholesale agents to whom the farmers could sell their apples directly. The project was a resounding success. "The Korean farmers have learned to cooperate together," Bunce wrote triumphantly. "They have found out they were not in the grip of insoluble hostile forces; they have obtained about double the local price for their apples; and they have realised anew the reality of international Christian cooperation and friendship."[33]

Such stories of hope and uplift were rare. Instead, what Bunce mostly witnessed was the crushing effects of rural poverty. "On a four-acre farm where 50% of the crop goes to the land owner it is impossible for a tenant farmer to live and save money to buy his own land, and thus virtual serfdom is imposed," he wrote to the YMCA's head office in 1933. "The conditions are so serious that in the winter and spring, whole communities of peasants are reduced to eating roots and bark to keep alive."[34] In his most pessimistic moments, he suggested darkly "that a sane program of eugenics is the most needed thing in all the Orient."[35]

Yet Bunce kept the faith, believing that "the greatest need of Korea today is a vision of a world of social justice which will be linked up to their religious hopes." He spent many a service at the pulpit defending his social gospel against communists attending the weekly meetings. Hamgyŏng was a hotbed for red peasant activism, and his work among local farmers piqued their interest. "When I preached on Wednesday evenings every one of them turned up to hear me discuss the question 'What is the best Religion in the World,'" he wrote. "My answer was that the religion which could remake men and the social order was the best and if Communism could do that better than Christianity then Christianity must go."[36] He would then pull out the Denmark example—his go-to argument—for the win, or so he thought.

As a self-described Christian socialist, Bunce sympathized with the communists' vision for economic equality, but he thought there was more to life than the material world, including what he called the "inner core of personality making a joyous free individual." He also disapproved of their use of violence to enact political change: "The self-styled communists terrorize the farmers by murder and incendiarism. They ordered farmers not to sell any grain and not to pay any rent, then punished those who disobeyed by burning their crops and deeds of tenancy and, upon the slightest provocation, shooting the farmer."[37] Bunce's work among the Korean peasantry eventually caught the attention of Japanese authorities. In 1933, he reported to his supervisors: "The increased watchfulness of the Japanese police and the growth of militaristic nationalism have affected our work a good deal."[38] A year later, colonial officials shut down his schools and expelled him from Korea.

Bunce returned to the United States and enrolled at the University of Wisconsin to study with Benjamin Hibbard (essentially trading places with Yi Hun'gu). From there, he went on to work for the US Department of Agriculture, for which the Wisconsin School served as a pipeline, before returning to Korea in January 1946. Bunce was the rare American expert who spoke the language and had prior experience in the country. "He is the first man I have met here who speaks with genuine affection of the Koreans," wrote the journalist Mark Gayn. "He is also the first to lay emphasis on social reform, and not on the Soviet menace."[39]

Bunce received a chilly reception from the high command during his second time in Korea. When he and his team arrived in late January 1946, they were taken from the airport directly to the offices of the new military governor, Major General Archer Lerch. Hodge had hand-selected Lerch to succeed Major General Archibald Arnold, who became head of the American delegation to the Joint Commission. Lerch was as, perhaps even more, opposed to reform than his predecessor. Gayn reported this exchange between the new military governor and Bunce:

Lerch: "You're not welcome here. We don't need any advice."
Bunce: "General, we don't accept your ultimatum."
Lerch (retreating): "What I mean is that you'll be part of our organization, and we'll call on you when needed."
Bunce: "General, I repeat, we don't accept your ultimatum. My staff and I will consider it, and will let you know our decision tomorrow."[40]

Lerch had only contempt for the reformers. He told one US labor adviser, who approached him about passing child labor laws in the South: "As long as I am Military Governor, we change nothing." This anti-reformist attitude prompted Gayn to write, "The men in command here neither have a constructive program of action nor are they willing to accept one."[41]

A few days later, Bunce informed Lerch that his State Department team would be staying in Korea and would start drafting a land reform program. His team spent the month of February hammering out the details. Their initial draft called for the redistribution of Japanese-owned lands and large Korean estates to poor farmers. But in a strategic concession to the military command, Bunce quickly dropped the second part of his plan, despite the prevailing belief among SCAP reformers that "the objective will fall short of fulfillment if agrarian reform is restricted only to Japanese-owned lands."[42] He knew they had to compromise if they were going to get anything passed. Half a loaf was better than nothing.

After heated debate, Bunce and his staff also agreed that peasants should pay for land. Under their proposal, poor farmers would make fixed annual payments of 30 percent of the harvest for fifteen years. Bunce pointed out that the payments were less than tenant farmers had paid for rent, and after fifteen years, the land would be theirs. The truth was, he would have distributed the land for free if it had been up to him. But again, Bunce had to consider how to get the high command's approval. He thought requiring payment would do the trick. His plan mirrored the land reform proposal in the KDP platform (every other political party in Korea called for land redistribution "without compensation").[43]

News from the North gave their work a renewed sense of urgency. In March 1946, the North Korean Provisional People's Committee (NKPPC) announced it would redistribute former Japanese lands and those owned by wealthy Korean landlords to impoverished farmers. Landlords were allowed to keep their homes and about twelve acres of land, which was not nothing but was substantially less than their holdings. "For the first time in my life," one former landlord remembered, "we had to do some work. . . . That is the first time I ever put my right foot into the rice beds."[44] This was not what the NKPPC had originally planned. Their initial proposal had limited the expropriation to lands owned by the Japanese and pro-Japanese collaborators. But pressure from peasants who demanded the inclusion of all large estates forced their hand. On the anniversary of the March First

Movement, over a million peasants had gathered all over the North to call for comprehensive land redistribution.[45]

The NKPPC, led by Kim Il Sung—grandfather of the current North Korean leader, Kim Jong Un—delivered on its promise in just under three weeks. "The North Korean land reform," as one historian put it, "was one of the most rapid and thoroughgoing land redistribution efforts in history, and took place with very little violence."[46] This was because most northern landowners fled south shortly after the announcement. (While the landowners were leaving the North, Left-leaning artists and writers were coming up from the South. One of them was writer Pak T'aewŏn, who left behind his daughter in Seoul. His grandson, whom he would never meet, is Bong Joon-ho, the award-winning director of *Parasite*.)[47]

My grandparents, along with their one-year-old daughter (my aunt), were among the fifty thousand Koreans who escaped to the South that spring.[48] After talking it over with his parents, my grandfather decided to pay an operator of a gas-powered boat to take him, his wife, and their daughter south across the 38th parallel. Little did he know this would be the last time he would see or speak to his parents. My grandparents were part of the more than 100,000 Koreans who were separated permanently from their families as result of the division. Sailing late at night, the boat driver dropped them off the coast a little south of the line. Once ashore, they made their way to Seoul by foot, where they lived for the next four decades before immigrating to the United States.

Shortly before my grandfather passed, I asked him why he left Pyongyang, since he wasn't a landlord. Using a metaphor from his favorite sport, baseball (he wore Aaron Judge's Yankee jersey at his hundredth birthday party), he explained to me that he had three strikes against him. He was from a wealthy landowning family, he was a Christian, and perhaps worst of all, he was once a member of the colonial police. I was tempted to ask him what kind of policeman he was, but rather than complicating things, I just wanted to remember him as he was.

The significance of land reform in the North was not lost on American officials: "By this one stroke, half the population of north Korea was given a tangible stake in the regime and at the same time the north Korean government gained an important propaganda weapon in its campaign against the south."[49] Political groups, including the Communist Party and the National Federation of Peasant Unions, put out statements calling on the US military government to implement north Korean–style land reform. These events alarmed large southern landowners, triggering another round of land sell-off in the spring of 1946.[50]

In addition to redistributing land, the North enacted new labor laws that established an eight-hour work day, paid vacation, daily rations, and the right to bargain collectively. The NKPPC also passed gender equality laws that gave women the right to vote and access to education and economic opportunities. They also made polygamy and the trafficking of women and concubines illegal—a major reform, as patriarchy ran deep in Korea.

The principal author of the women's rights laws was none other than the feminist socialist Hŏ Chŏngsuk, who had managed to survive Japanese persecution and reappeared in the North, where she became the minister of culture and the highest-ranking woman official. She later went on to become the chief justice of the Supreme Court. But her political ascent was not without controversy. To maintain her prominent standing within the North Korean government, Hŏ denounced her husband for disloyalty to the state in 1958, resulting in his execution.[51]

It seemed the perfect time to enact Bunce's plan. His proposal would match the land reform that had been implemented in the North. The NKPPC's plan, while touted as "free" land redistribution, required farmers to pay 30 percent of their harvest as an in-kind tax to the state, which was similar to the payments that peasants in the South were expected to make under Bunce's plan. Now, of course, the regime in the North confiscated and redistributed *all* lands, including the ones owned by big Korean landlords.

But if we recall that more than half of tenanted lands held by Korean landlords were sold off by this time, there was considerably less Korean-owned land available for redistribution in the South. "The limitation placed on rentals has resulted in making the status of the landlords less profitable, and there is a large and growing volume of private sales to tenants," one US official explained. "Thrifty peasants make private purchase of land, and pay for it, in a minute fraction of the time and labor formerly required."[52]

The two plans were more alike than either side cared to admit. Liberals, communists, and socialists, almost unanimously, saw land reform as a tool to break up the feudal tenancy system and replace the inert landlord with a dynamic class of small owner-cultivators. The small farmer was universally idealized as an "economic man," someone who would invigorate agricultural production by pursuing his self-interest, so he had every reason to innovate and improve. But the newly minted Korean yeoman, they all agreed, would have to be guided from above, taught in the ways of scientific farming—including the use of chemical fertilizers and new seed varieties—to increase agricultural output. Socialist and liberal reformers believed collective scientific farming could overcome the economy of scale problems of small, individual family farms: everybody was an agricultural modernist.

But instead of rushing to implement Bunce's proposal, the military government announced it would conduct a public poll on land reform and treat it as a quasi-plebiscite. Determining policy based on public opinion was decidedly out of step with how Hodge governed in the South; he had not gauged public opinion before enacting earlier policies, and would not do so with those that came after.

The polls were conducted by Korean interpreters with close ties to the landlord class, and the results came back showing opposition to a land reform led by the military government. A majority of Koreans wanted reform to be carried out by the Korean provisional government once it was established.[53] The results also indicated that Koreans were evenly split over the question of whether landlords (or the government in the case of former Japanese lands) should receive compensation for the lands being confiscated and redistributed. The high command cited these results to justify its decision not to pursue land reform at this time.

Mark Gayn panned the polls as a "neat device to kill what was called 'Bunce's Folly.'"[54] The agrarian reformer Wolf Ladejinsky came to the same conclusion: "General Lerch is motivated solely by the opposition of the South Korean as expressed in the public polls conducted by the Military Government. But in the opinion of this observer, in this instance the results of the public polls serve only as a convenient pretext for inaction." His own observations indicated "favorable conditions as evidenced by the eagerness of tenants to buy the land and by the support of such a scheme to which all the political parties of South Korea are pledged."[55]

Then what was the issue? "The clear-cut impression," Ladejinsky wrote in his report to SCAP, "is that to General Lerch the very word 'reform' is suspect; that reform partakes of communism, and that those who advocate land reform are not altogether free of communism."[56] He thought the charge was ridiculous, especially given the SCAP-led land reform program in Japan. Did Lerch think General MacArthur was a communist? As a Jew who had fled communist Russia in 1921, Ladejinsky took the accusation personally.

The clash over land reform exposed deep divisions over how best to meet the communist challenge in Korea. Hodge and Lerch viewed the landed elite as a bulwark against revolutionary socialism and, thus, preserving its position was critical. Working through the native elite also followed the textbook strategy for foreign rule—it was exactly what the Japanese had done in Korea. For reformers, maintaining the interests of the few over the many made little sense. The better strategy to fight communism was to fulfill the hopes and expectations of the great majority. As they saw it, there was no greater weapon than land reform—80 percent of Koreans lived off the land.

In his scathing report to SCAP, Ladejinsky wrote the "do nothing" attitude of the military government toward South Korea's land reform was wrongheaded because it would demoralize peasants, leaving them vulnerable to communist suasion. "They are not even permitted to buy Japanese owned lands at a fair price. Such inactivity on the part of the Military Government will provide fertile ground for extremists." He wrote forcefully: "The time for change and for the setting of the pattern of the change is now." Inaction on land reform, he continued, "would bring in its wake unrest and political embarrassment to the American occupation forces in South Korea."[57] His warning failed to persuade the high command, which decided to shelve land reform indefinitely, thereby ending what Gayn called "the only major reform drafted by an American in the past fourteen months."[58] General MacArthur received Ladejinsky's report but did nothing about it, mostly because he didn't care. His messianic fervor extended only to Japan, and even there it lasted for just a little over a year.[59]

Gayn was wrong about Bunce's plan being the only major reform proposed by Americans. Captain Owen Jones had recommended a raft of labor reforms in the spring of 1946, including the right to strike and bargain collectively—about 20 percent of Koreans were working for wages at that time. He also insisted police reform had to be part of any labor reform package. To guarantee workers' rights, he felt that ending the colonial practice of police acting as strikebreakers was needed. Some of these ideas probably came out of conversations with his roommate and labor adviser, Stewart Meacham, for whom Jones had enormous respect.

The military government approved a new labor policy that affirmed the workers' right to form and join democratic labor unions "without interference from employers or their agents." It sounded good on paper, but without the reforms Jones had sought, it lacked teeth. Workers were still expected to negotiate with employers without recourse to strikes or other interruptions to production. Jones also argued that without police reform, the workers' right to unionize was a dead letter. His objections to the "new" labor policy, which he called old wine in a new bottle, led to his ouster as director of the Commerce Department.[60]

As Jones predicted, the "new" labor policy did little to improve the situation of Korean workers. For one thing, occupation officials never struck a balance between workers' rights and industrial growth, as promised. As the official history of the Labor Department tells it, "Labor officers and other officers of the Bureau of Commerce assigned as production managers of individual industries emphasized uninterrupted production at all costs, and not only condoned but participated in the use of police force to prevent organized efforts of laborers to bring and seek redress of grievances."[61] Stewart Meacham recounted the story of how one army officer dealt with workers who attempted to organize. When the officer heard that the Korean employees in his department were planning to form a union, he invited them to a meeting to discuss the matter. When they showed up, they were seized by the police and dragged away from the premises. "That," he said with pride, "is how we handle labor problems in my department."[62]

By calling on the police to silence discontent, American advisers reproduced a colonial pattern all too familiar to Korean workers. "In the face of this situation," the director of the newly formed Labor Department wrote, "attempts at collective bargaining were meaningless and it was equally meaningless to encourage the formation, let alone require the registration, of democratic labor unions which were prohibited by Ordinance interpretation from using the recognized methods of trade unionism."[63] The Labor Department director later admitted that the promise of worker emancipation was "never quite realized" and their efforts were of "limited effectiveness in convincing labor in South Korea that the policy of the Military Governor represented any significant change from that existing under the Japanese Governor General."[64]

Some American advisers who wanted the police reined in tried to do something about it. But they needed evidence. In 1946, Lieutenant Colonel Rankin Roberts and Captain Richard Robinson investigated allegations of police misconduct in the east coast provinces of Kangwŏn and North and South Kyŏngsang (they brought several English-speaking journalists with them). Their investigation was initially stymied: "Police intimidation of the local populace," they explained, "was such that people were afraid to talk to Americans."

However, as the two officers toured the region, they uncovered a number of abuses. A village elder was held in prison without ever being charged with a crime. The elder had led the local people's committee after liberation, which made him suspect in the eyes of the local police. But since he wasn't leading it now, it wasn't a crime. They detained him for two months anyway. "The police," as Roberts and Robinson wrote, "were trying to find some reason for keeping these people in jail regardless of the lack of evidence." In the working-class city of Samchŏk, the police raided unions and farm organizations, arresting twenty-six officials. Finding no evidence of wrongdoing, the police arrested them for gathering for May Day celebrations. Why was this a crime? A law on the books, a holdover from the colonial era, prohibited public meetings without prior permission from local authorities. Police officials were convinced that leftists "should be restrained whether there is reason for it or not."

Roberts and Robinson cited these examples in a report they wrote for the military command. In the most damning part of their account, they witnessed a Korean prisoner "kicked and beaten, and his wrists tied to the back of his neck, and a stick thrust through the crook of his elbows." The victim was then placed on his back and subjected to the water cure—an interrogation method similar to waterboarding that had been favored by the Japanese colonial police. (In addition to the water cure, colonial police used electric shock, whipping, and sexual torture as interrogation methods.)[65] The water cure involved pouring water over the mouth and nose while the subject was bound. To avoid drowning, the prisoner would be forced to swallow the water until he vomited or passed out. The interrogator repeated the process until the subject had confessed to the charges made against him. Robinson arrested the torturers on the spot.

Occupation officials later learned that this was not an isolated case. The US provost marshal confirmed that "scores of prisoners in Busan had been tortured into confession."[66] These reports of police brutality and abuse went nowhere with the occupation's high command. In fact, Robinson's intervention—arresting the torturers—"very nearly netted me a court-martial."[67] As a Justice Department adviser recalled, "The Military Governor ordered

American advisers in the Department of Justice not to interfere."[68] The use of colonial police methods was regarded as a necessary evil in the struggle against communism: "Though much of the police methods of crime detection and law is still of Jap vintage, out of necessity, they must be used."[69] Right around this time, the Tokyo War Crimes Tribunal, formed by General MacArthur, charged high-ranking Japanese military leaders with various war crimes. One of the charges was torturing Allied military servicemen with the water cure. "We cannot do this with Jap-trained men," an exasperated Ch'oe Nŭngjin wrote to his superiors. "These men are against the independence movement. They do not wish liberation of Korea." He warned that "80% of the Koreans will turn Communist if this condition persists."[70] But as with the other reformers, his words fell on deaf ears.

Needless to say, the Joint Commission did not begin under the most ideal conditions. An attempted assassination of Kim Il Sung on March 1, 1946, heightened tensions right before the commission was set to open. Right-wing terrorists associated with Kim Ku lobbed a grenade at the North Korean leader while he was speaking at a ceremony commemorating the March First Movement in Pyongyang. He was saved by the quick actions of a Soviet Army lieutenant, Yakov Novichenko, who grabbed the grenade midair before it reached the podium where Kim was standing. It exploded in his hand, blowing off his arm and damaging his eyes. (The two men went on to become lifelong friends.)[71]

On March 20, 1946, the Soviet delegation, led by General Shtykov, arrived in Seoul. Americans did what they could to arrange a warm welcome. The Soviet caravan drove through streets lined with throngs of Koreans and passed "through aisles of colorfully uniformed Korean mounted police and U.S. Army honor guards." And when they reached Tŏksu Palace, the site of the opening ceremony, they were serenaded by the US Army band.[72] During the ceremony, speakers took pain to strike an optimistic tone. "Our Joint Commission representing the American and Soviet commands is called upon to carry out the historic decisions of the Moscow Conference," Shtykov declared. "These decisions express the good will and the wishes of the great Allied powers to assist by all means in the rehabilitation of an independent Korea." He reminded the Korean audience that it was the "great armies" of the United States and Soviet Union that "have forever eliminated Japanese domination in Korea."[73]

Hodge echoed similar sentiments in his speech: "This is a day to which all Koreans have looked forward with great hope for the future of their nation, and should be a day Koreans will celebrate in the future as a start of a new era in Korean history." He stated confidently: "This commission will prove the ability of two great nations of the world to cooperate fully . . . to restore a less fortunate, long oppressed nation to an independent, sovereign status among the family of free nations."[74] It was easier said than done. Just a few days into the conference, negotiators ran into an impasse. Shtykov had hinted at the issue in his speech when he said, "In the way of gradual democratization, there stand serious difficulties, brought about by the furious resistance of reactionary and anti-democratic groups, whose object is to undermine the work of creating and firmly establishing a democratic system in Korea."[75] It wasn't hard to figure out who the Soviet commander was talking about.

Soviet negotiators made it clear they wanted all individuals and groups who opposed trusteeship to be disqualified from the process of forming the Provisional Korean Government. This would have meant the exclusion of almost all rightists, most prominently, Kim Ku and Syngman Rhee. Their reasoning was seemingly straightforward: How could people who actively opposed the agreement be trusted to carry it out? How did they know these people wouldn't pull the same stunt after the Moscow Conference?

Americans balked at the Soviet demand, believing it a ploy to exclude rightist parties from the Provisional Korean Government. They feared, with good reason, it would be dominated by the communists if Kim and Rhee's groups were barred from being consulted. (One is left to wonder if American negotiators would've been more amenable if Cho Mansik was still in the picture.) But instead of saying this outright—and perhaps he couldn't— Hodge argued that in opposing trusteeship the groups were merely exercising the right to protest, and to exclude them now would be a violation of their freedom of speech. "These freedoms," Hodge admonished, "are not mere words to be used to gain political favor."

Internally, some American officials found the argument wanting. "Somehow, by a strange quirk of reasoning, the American position became a defense of free speech. Clearly it was a false issue manufactured for the occasion to cloud the real issues and discredit the Russians," Richard Robinson wrote. "Perhaps ours was a necessary maneuver to prevent Russian domination of all of Korea, but let us not delude ourselves by insisting that our position was logically sound."[76] To break the deadlock, American delegates floated the idea of requiring participating parties to publicly endorse the Moscow agreement. The proposal seemed to address Soviet concerns while giving rightist parties a chance to support and join the process. But it was rejected by Soviet delegates, who were not in a compromising mood.

The fact was that the two sides had a hard time agreeing on anything. It started with rice. Soviet officials had asked for rice in exchange for coal and electricity to alleviate chronic food shortages in the North. (By colonial design, the South was the "rice bowl," while the North was the industrial base, supplying most of the country's manufactured goods and services.) American negotiators told the Soviets that they didn't have any surplus rice to share and that they were dealing with their own shortfalls. Soviet negotiators were incredulous. Everyone knew about the famous bumper crop from the most recent harvest. "The Russians," one US official wrote, "thought that the Americans were lying through their teeth."[77] What had happened to all that rice?

After the US military government instituted a free market system, "the people went hog wild" and "per capita consumption of rice went up by leaps and bounds," according to one report.[78] American officials thought Koreans would act "rationally" and reinvest profits to increase domestic rice production. This assumption turned out to be utterly wrong. Korean farmers, accustomed to living hand to mouth, took the opportunity to eat more and work less. Wealthy landlords and corrupt officials (especially the police) smuggled rice to Japan, where they made a killing on the black market. According to one estimate, a quarter of the fall 1945 rice harvest was smuggled out of Korea.[79]

The free market policy resulted in overconsumption and speculation that turned a bumper crop into a severe shortage. American officials had to import tens of thousands of tons of grain from the United States to avert starvation. Grant Meade called the American military government's rice policy "the height of stupidity." The military government, he noted, "disregarded the fact that these same Koreans lacked the knowledge and experience to operate within an uncontrolled, capitalistic economy."[80] The rice shortage led to a surge in inflation that crippled the economy. Over the first year of the occupation, the cost of basic food rose far faster than wages, as much as ten times faster.[81] Earnings failed to keep up with rising prices because the military government, in an effort to slow inflation, imposed strict controls on salaries and wages.[82] The free market rice policy was universally opposed by Koreans, including the conservative KDP. It was one of a handful of issues that unified Koreans.

The occupation government was forced to revert to the Japanese system of rationing and price controls in January 1946, just three months after the free market policy had been first implemented. US officials also cut back daily rice rations by half. As one Chŏnp'yŏng official wrote, "The problem of rice was a problem for all people, except for the big capitalists, landowners, dishonest merchants, and brokers."[83] American officials were not lying about the rice shortage. But the Soviets, understandably, had a hard time believing them. Agreement was elusive in an atmosphere of mistrust.

After six weeks of negotiations that went nowhere, the two sides agreed to adjourn on May 16, 1946. No one had any idea when, or if, talks would resume. The outgoing political adviser to Hodge, Colonel Preston Goodfellow, told reporters ominously "that if the Soviet delegation did not return to the deliberations here soon the Americans should go ahead with the job of setting up a separate government in Southern Korea."[84]

Nothing seemed to be going right in the South. Labor adviser Stewart Meacham summed up the situation:

Korean confidence in the United States has been badly shaken. Her hope for early unity and independence has almost disappeared. Her landless farmers are still without land they can call their own. The Japanese police are gone but their despised Korean colleagues whom they trained still run the National Police. Industrial workers still do not have the opportunity to choose freely their own representatives. While those who grew rich under the Japanese have retained and even enlarged their riches, those who work on the land and in the factories suffer from an inflation-produced poverty of fantastic proportions. Organized political terrorism stalks the streets in broad daylight. The night is filled with murmurings of disaffection and plots of revolt.[85]

South Korea was simmering with discontent.

6 Rising Up

The summer of 1946 gave rise to an unexpected and peculiar scene: peasants setting their rice crops on fire. The homes of village elders and town officials were also set ablaze. These scenes could have been taken from An Hoenam's "Fire," the story of rebirth and starting over, but this was not anything like playing *pul nori*. This was about protest and resistance.[1]

The spring had come and gone without land reform. And now, on top of that, the US military government wanted to go back to the old, colonial system of rice collection. American officials established the New Korea Company to oversee the collection process. Farmers seethed at the return of the rice collector and the policeman, whom they remembered as the hated twin faces of Japanese colonial rule. And because the occupation government maintained much of the colonial force, the faces were literally the same in some cases. The former police who had been reinstated were taking "August 15th revenge" on the locals who had ousted them.[2]

Indeed, the police had quickly gone back to their old ways: beating peasants on a whim, setting higher than the required quotas to skim off the top, and illegally arresting and torturing those who failed to comply. As a result, farmers came to see the New Korea Company as the Oriental Development Company by another name. "Things remained the same as before," lamented a peasant farmer, Han Saengwŏn, from Ch'ae Mansik's "Once Upon a Rice Paddy." "Whether Korea was independent or not, it was all the same."[3] The electrifying sense of possibility of a year ago had given way to anger and disillusionment. Enraged peasants torched their harvest and the houses of those responsible for rice collection, physically attacked rice collectors and the police who showed up at their doorstep, and stormed government rice storages.

A Korean crowd breaks into a rice distribution center in Busan.
National Archives (111-SC-303036)

The authorities responded to the spike in protests by stepping up enforcement, including mass seizures, searches, and arrests. The police threw over a thousand farmers in jail during the summer for resisting grain collection. The offenses ranged from refusing to farm to hiding crops to lighting the harvest on fire.[4] Once in prison, peasants were often extorted: "Farmers who refused to give up their rice were taken to police headquarters and kept in jail with no food except that bought from the police at exorbitant prices." Other peasants were flogged or imprisoned because they didn't have enough grain to turn over at collection time. More often than not, it wasn't their fault. As one investigation revealed, "Frequently the amount of rice demanded was unreasonable and there was very good reason to believe that some of the grain collected was not turned over to the proper authorities."[5] Many farmers purchased rice at inflated prices on the black market to meet their quota. Going into debt was better than being beaten or jailed. "Farmers complained that the rice was taken away much in the same manner as under the Japanese," wrote Captain Robinson in his report on police abuse, "but that the treatment received was much worse as no ordinary patrolman under the Japanese would have dared to do such things."[6]

To make matters worse, the New Korea Company mandated the collection of wheat and barley in addition to rice. The summertime grains were staples in the Korean peasant diet; even the Japanese authorities had left these crops alone. In some places, farmers put up greater resistance to the collection of wheat and barley, which was of lower value, than to rice. However much they hated it, at least there was precedent with rice collection. American officials knew that collecting the summer grains was a departure from colonial-era policy but given food shortages, they did not think they had much choice. By the summer of 1946, the average Korean was eating fewer than eight hundred calories a day. The press reported stories of Koreans committing suicide out of hunger. Hugh Borton, director of the State Department's Korea Desk, wrote, "What evidence we have seems to indicate that the Russians are doing a better job of feeding the Koreans in their zone than we are in ours."[7]

Mistake was compounded by mistake.

Local farmers' associations offered an alternative to the military government's collection method. Calling for the "democratic management of food," they proposed the establishment of local cooperatives to manage grain collection. Their plan would have removed the hated police from the process and allowed local farming communities to assume responsibility for the necessary, but highly charged, task.[8] The two agricultural experts, Arthur Bunce and Yi Hun'gu, championed cooperatives as a middle solution that was neither communism nor capitalism. They were both longtime admirers of the Danish system, believing it to be a model for the developing world (the two men had visited Denmark separately in the 1930s).[9] General Hodge and Archer Lerch, however, refused to cede control to local groups, in part because they did not trust them to collect the rice efficiently, though it is hard to imagine them doing worse than the American military government, which collected less than 13 percent of the targeted goal in 1946. They also feared that the cooperatives would be infiltrated and used by communists for subversive purposes.[10]

With support from the authorities, the police raided local farmers' groups throughout the countryside. According to the official history, the Korean police "retained the Japanese police idea that all farmers' and laborers' organizations were communist."[11] In Taegu, they searched the NFPU offices for evidence linking them to the peasant unrest in the region. They found in-

structions on what farmers should do in case the police made unfair demands—ask for official documentation was the advice—but nothing indicating an organized conspiracy. The organizations' leaders were beaten and
apprehended anyway. The police chief who ordered the sweep declared,
"The Farmers' Association has no right to represent the farmers," even in an
advisory capacity.[12]

In Naju, American troops stormed the offices of the Kungsam-myŏn peasant
union. They seized union files and arrested its leaders, including Na Chaegi,
for illegally distributing "enemy property." Defying earlier government orders,
the union had continued to operate, supporting the Kungsam-myŏn peasants in their effort to get back their ancestral lands.[13] "Big nose Americans
ordered us to raise our hand," one person on the scene remembered. He recalled yelling back, "This is my land and I will do what I want!" After the government interpreter translated what he said, "one of the big noses suddenly
pulled out his gun and pointed it at my head."[14]

State repression goaded peasants into taking more militant actions, including assaults on police stations and government offices. The peasants cut
power lines, destroyed bridges, and set up obstacles to isolate their targets.
The police, backed by the military government, would then cite the violent
turn to justify further suppression in a vicious cycle. Hodge accused communists of fomenting the disturbances in the Korean countryside but almost no one believed this. The resistance to grain collection in the summer
of 1946 was almost entirely spontaneous, stoked by mounting anger over
unjust rice quotas, the collection of summer crops, and police brutality.[15]

Hwang Sunwŏn's coming-of-age story, "Bulls," published in 1946, provides a
visceral sense of the despair and rage that drove peasants to rebellion that
summer. In the winter before liberation, Pau, the story's young protagonist,
sees his father lying on the ground, blood gushing from his mouth and nose
after a savage beating from the Japanese police for failing to meet his rice
quota. His father, who had prided himself as the village wrestling champ,
couldn't even get up on his own. When it was over, the constable dragged
his father off to the police station in Ch'ungju.[16] The memory of that day
haunts Pau: "What a fool I was! All I did was tremble and watch." He vows
it will be different this time—it is a year later and he is a man now.

Pau suspects something is up that morning when he hears his normally
good-natured father angrily muttering to himself: "Even worms will squirm

if you step on them." Pau isn't sure what it means, but he is convinced something is going to happen to his father that night. His suspicions are confirmed when he comes home after dark and sees him among a group of village men speaking in a low voice in the front yard.

After they finish talking, the group heads off in the direction of the farm fields. Pau secretly tails them. He assumes that they are out to catch the thief who has been stealing their crops, but when they pass the farm fields, he now thinks they are going to fight the villagers in Hŭin Pawi Hollow, where each year fights break out over water during the irrigation season. He sees that he is wrong again, when instead of taking the road to Hŭin Pawi Hollow, the group turns down the road to Ch'ungju. *Of course, Ch'ungju.* He remembers his father's words: "Even worms squirm if you step on them." He has a vision of his father and the other villagers squirming on the floor and crying out:

> If you keep this up, we'll starve! We're not asking to get rid of the grain quotas, we just want it to be fair! Why do you let people fill up their sacks in the granary and sell on the sly in Japan or God knows where else? Why do you let them do that? Why do you harass the needy night and day—what will you get out of them? If things don't change, we'll starve.

Pau now knows why they're in Ch'ungju. Thinking about it makes his heart race. He tries to steady himself by telling himself that he will stay by his father's side no matter what. Suddenly the streets go dark: "The next moment all the villagers stood up, as if they'd been waiting for this signal. Before Pau knew it, he was standing too, a stick in hand. And the next thing you know, they were rushing downhill, like bulls in fury."

Pau has a hard time keeping up with his father and the other men. He stumbles and falls and can't see where they went. When he looks up, he's blinded by a bright light coming from what he thinks is a car headlight. Before he can be sure, he hears gunshots, and a second or two later, the sounds of people crying out. "Oh my God, oh my God. Why couldn't you catch up with the grown-ups? You idiot, you idiot!" he chides himself.

Suddenly, flames shoot through the darkness and upon seeing them, Pau feels "as if those flames were flaring up inside him—the outcries from the people were sounding inside him as well, his father's voice distinct among them." He realizes, then, that they were actual voices he was hearing, and they were coming from where the flames were rising. As he staggers toward the fire, Pau hears a voice saying, "I can't believe those sons of bitches set fire to the police station!" It's the big landlord, Old Kim Long Pipe, with a candlelight in hand. "Come on boys, hurry up!" His voice gets louder and more desperate. There are big men carrying sacks of rice. One of them stops to tell Old Kim alarming news: "We're in big trouble—they just raided Chief Yi's home." Old Kim's hands begin to tremble: he knows he's next.

He doesn't know what to do with the candle. But then an idea comes to him: he brings the candle close to his mouth and blows it out. When the flame disappears, "the trembling hand and the ever-so-large pipe were no more."

Even worms squirm if you step on them.

It was also a summer of unrest in the city. Rampant inflation, declining real wages, and the lack of goods and services made life miserable for urban dwellers, especially for the working class. The price of rice and barley had jumped 700 percent and 400 percent, respectively, between February and August 1946, while wages remained largely flat.[17] In addition, working hours grew longer and more intense under the military government, which let "nothing stand in the way of a revival of production."[18] It also didn't help that it was the hottest summer in recent memory—with temperatures routinely soaring to 90 degrees Fahrenheit or more, accompanied by stifling humidity.

Feeling the squeeze and the heat, rank-and-file workers across the South revolted against management and occupation policies. In a wave of strikes and protests, they demanded higher wages, rice rations, better working conditions, and the right to collective bargaining.[19] This struggle for labor rights had a transformative effect on Yi Ilchae. The timid young man who had reported for his draft assignment and stood guard at the Taegu railroad station for two days after Japan's surrender was now leading May Day protests at almost the same spot six months later. Perhaps he always had it in him, but it was this experience of being part of something bigger than himself, fighting for a just cause, that brought it out.[20]

Protesting workers often acted without union consent or support. As was often the case in the first year of the occupation, the working masses ran ahead of the leadership. In fact, the Chŏnp'yŏng had pledged not to strike. Work stoppages—strikes, sit-ins, and sabotage—were prohibited by the military government, and union leadership was leery of starting a confrontation that would give the Americans a reason to shut them down. The Labor Department also offered a carrot for keeping labor peace. In return for not striking, US advisers to the department promised to recognize the Chŏnp'yŏng as the official union of Korean labor.[21]

Beginning in March, a new group, calling itself the National Federation of Korean Unions (Taehan Noch'ong) began to appear on factory floors. "This organization from the start was scarcely designed to protect and advance the interest of industrial workers," according to Stewart Meacham. "It was an appendage to a political party backed by large Korean landowners and others who had managed to make not only their peace but their fortune under the Japanese."[22] To be more precise, it was bankrolled by businessmen with close ties to Syngman Rhee and Kim Ku. The new union, at least initially, held little appeal for Korean workers, who overwhelmingly supported the Chŏnp'yŏng. By now, the Chŏnp'yŏng had grown to over a half a million members, a quarter of whom were women, organized in more than two hundred branches, making it by far the largest labor organization in the South.[23] It still wasn't a bad idea to gain the military government's recognition. The Chŏnp'yŏng, therefore, remained on the sidelines even as rank-and-file protest surged in the late spring and early summer. In fact, it sent out orders admonishing workers not to strike, though they were encouraged to use other methods that remained unspecified.[24]

The deal, however, quickly fell apart. In May, the Korean National Police raided the Communist Party headquarters in Central Seoul to break up an alleged counterfeiting ring. The authorities seized metal plates and nearly three million yen in counterfeit bills and arrested a dozen people, including the party's finance manager, Yi Kwansu. Officials from the Communist Party vehemently denied the charges, claiming they had been framed. (Pak Hŏnyŏng later admitted to the counterfeiting but argued it was justified because the right wing was being backed by wealthy collaborators.)[25]

The government crackdown divided the Chŏnp'yŏng leadership. A number of them wanted to abandon the strategy of accommodation with the American military government. It had not yielded any tangible benefit to the union or the workers they represented, and now their comrades were sitting in jail—they argued they were being strung along. But the head of the secretariat of the Chŏnp'yŏng, Han Chŏl, held fast to the deal he had made with US labor advisers, imploring rank-and-file workers, as late as July 14, not to strike. Han Yangsŏp, the Korean director of the Labor Department, later testified that their promise to recognize the Chŏnp'yŏng was genuine.

By August, however, most of the Chŏnp'yŏng had run out of patience. The union's Standing Committee sent a call to action to the south Korean laboring masses, contravening the earlier no-strike order:

Comrades! Militant workers!
Our working class is the only true democratic and patriotic force.
We are the only vanguard that can rescue the nation from starvation and terror, and from darkness and despair.
Focus your main force on crucial key industries such as railways, telecommunications, and electricity!
Organize a tempest-like struggle by raising the banner of "give rice, work, and home" in all the areas where the working masses are concentrated![26]

The Chŏnp'yŏng moved quickly to organize the swelling discontent in the factories, railway yards, and construction sites throughout the South. At the Kyŏngsŏng Textile Factory outside of Seoul, the Chŏnp'yŏng made demands for higher wages and cloth distribution (given high inflation, the products the workers made were more valuable than any increase in their wages). When management refused to negotiate, workers—mainly girls and young women—walked off the job and shut down the plant.

Management did what it always did in these situations; it called in the police. But first it needed the plant back up and running. The factory manager told union leaders that if they formed a committee to represent the workers, he would meet with them—on the condition that they all return to work. They agreed to the terms, and the next day workers were back at their jobs. But right before the committee was scheduled to meet management, the police descended on the factory to arrest workers on trumped-up charges. Trying to justify his deception, the manager railed, "Under Chŏnp'yŏng there was too much liberation." "Stories of this sort," Stewart Meacham reported with disgust, "were freely told by the factory managers" in the plants he visited. "In no instance was it claimed that Chŏnp'yŏng had been doing anything more than attempting to get wage conditions improved or some other working conditions better."[27]

The female workers at the Oriental Spinning Company in Inchŏn, one of the largest textile factories in the South, went on strike in early August. The on-site Korean manager, Ch'oe Nam, a former department store owner who had been accused of being a Japanese collaborator, had treated the women workers with contempt, calling them prostitutes and telling them to join the Taehan Noch'ong if they knew what was good for them. The American head of the Textile Section of the Commerce Department retaliated by evicting the striking workers from the factory dormitory. According to Meacham, Chŏnp'yŏng organizers took the three hundred girls and women to Seoul, about thirty miles away, where they were provided with temporary shelter in union offices.[28]

It should be noted that Meacham had a tendency to depict women workers as passive or as victims who needed the support of male organizers, even though they made up a quarter of the union membership and had initiated a number of strikes and other collective actions. He had a hard time seeing women workers as equal to male workers. Indeed, not a single woman was mentioned by name in his sixty-page *Korean Labor Report*. Meacham was a champion for the working class and later a committed peace activist but it seemed he had a blind spot. "Stewart tried real hard to be a good feminist," his wife, Charlotte, a housing and justice activist in her own right, said about her husband of forty-seven years in an interview in 1985. "But he *had* been brought up as a good ole Southern boy and sometimes it was hard."[29]

The Department of Labor protested the evictions at the Oriental Spinning Company and demanded that the workers be allowed back into their dorms. Labor advisers eventually brokered a compromise: the Chŏnp'yŏng would end the strike and, in return, management would enter contract talks. The two sides agreed. An adviser from the Department of Labor personally escorted the young girls and women back to the factory from Seoul. But when they returned to work, Ch'oe Nam refused to recognize the Chŏnp'yŏng. He would only negotiate with the Taehan Noch'ong, which he claimed was the only legitimate union, even though it had no following in the factory. The promise to bargain was, therefore, never fulfilled.

Occupation authorities came down hard on the union for its activism. As one US labor adviser wrote, "The arrest of Chŏnp'yŏng leaders became widespread." The police, in early August, arrested five of the union's leaders at Tang Yank Textile Mill. "This ended Chŏnp'yŏng's open existence in that plant," according to the same adviser. On August 16, the authorities went straight to the source, raiding the main headquarters of the Chŏnp'yŏng in Seoul and seizing membership records and accounting books, among other files.[30] The raid was part of a larger crackdown on the Left. In the first week of September, Hodge issued arrest warrants for Pak and several other communist leaders, charging them with endangering the lives of American soldiers. Pak went underground to avoid arrest. He complained bitterly that the military government's persecution of him "exceeded that of medieval witch-hunts."[31]

In early August, Yu Pyŏnghwa—the labor activist whose father had read him the *Communist Manifesto* as a child—received a visit from members of a railroad union affiliated with the Chŏnp'yŏng. Yu, who was working as a locomotive engineer at the time, was surprised to see them and even more surprised to hear about the existence of the union—it was the first time he had heard of it. They invited Yu to join them and asked for his help in organizing a branch in Taegu. He agreed and several weeks later held an inaugural meeting with about ten people.

Yu began visiting the railway yards in Taegu to recruit new members for the union. He didn't find it difficult: discontent was running high among railway workers, who faced punishing twenty-four-hour shifts, dangerous work conditions, and stagnant wages. "Conditions," according to Yu, "became worse than during the colonial era." In the past, "working during the night shift included a packed meal, and in the spring and autumn they provided a set of clothes," he recalled. "After August 15 there was nothing and those who had served as petty intelligence agents fawning over the Japanese were promoted to railroad police chiefs bullying the workers."[32]

Several weeks into the organizing drive, Yu received a message from the union higher-ups to be prepared for a general strike in the fall. It seems they had chosen the railways to make their stand. Not everyone was thrilled with this decision. Kim Samsun, who, like Yu, was a locomotive engineer, had a bad feeling about the plan. Fearing a strike could put them on a collision course with American forces, he resigned his position as union representative of his section and went home, twenty-five miles outside of Seoul, hiding out there until the strike was over.

On September 15, the Southern Korean Railway Workers' Union in Busan submitted a list of demands to the Department of Transportation. The list was mostly boilerplate, including demands for wage increases, rice rations, improved working conditions, and the right to strike and bargain collectively. But further down the list appeared some less traditional union demands: freedom of press, speech, and assembly; the release of political prisoners; and worker managerial control of the railroads.[33]

Their demands were met with silence. When almost a week passed without a response, the union petitioned the military governor, Archer Lerch, to intervene and mediate. After this appeal was also ignored, the union authorized a strike. On September 23, between seven thousand and eight thousand railway workers in Busan walked off their jobs. The next morning, the entire membership of the Railway Workers Union—thirty-six thousand workers spread across the South—joined them, bringing railroad service to a complete standstill. Yu Pyŏnghwa set up a picket line to stop employees from coming to work.

The next morning, Lerch took to the airwaves to declare the strikes illegal. The military government, he stated, owned the railroads, and therefore railway workers were government employees and as such were prohibited from striking. Lerch warned the striking workers that they would be arrested if they did not immediately return to work. Despite his threats, the strikes quickly spread to other cities and industries, growing to three hundred thousand protesters. The strikers included members of the Taehan Nochʻong. One US official wrote, "It is interesting to note that in all instances both the Left and Right wing labor unions have cooperated to this strike, and that they are in accord on their demands."[34]

Yet Hodge was convinced that communist agitators were behind the labor unrest. In a cable to his superiors, he requested permission to create a "Rightist Youth Army" to defend against what he called communist infiltration from the North.[35] The State Department doubted the charges made by Hodge: "The situation described by General Hodge, alarming as it might be, did not form a basis for Government accusations of the Russians." Officials also thought it was "entirely inappropriate" to organize a paramilitary youth group. But they did suggest "that General Hodge might achieve the ends he desired by increasing the strength of the Korean police and constabulary."[36]

Taking this as a green light, Hodge authorized the military and police to quash the strikes. Cho Pyŏngok and Chang T'aeksang, Seoul's chief of police, in turn, took the opportunity to arm thousands of rightist youths with guns and grenades, thereby creating their own paramilitary forces.[37] The campaign began in Busan, where seventy police, with the support of American tactical troops, arrested union leaders and forced railway employees back to work. Several days later, an armed force of two thousand police and rightist youth, accompanied by American MPs, rushed into the Yongsan railway yards in Seoul and violently broke up the strike there. Workers tried to fight back but were quickly overwhelmed by the show of force. By the end of the day, one striker had been killed, another forty were injured, and seventeen hundred had been arrested. "We went into that situation just like we would go into battle," the director of the Department of Transportation described as the strategy. "We were out to break that thing up and we didn't have time to worry too much if a few innocent people got hurt. It was war and that is the way we fought it."[38]

In Taegu, the police apprehended and tortured Yu Pyŏnghwa for leading the strike there. Yu recalled, "At the time the railroad offices were Japanese-style buildings made with wood. Behind the office there was a rope hanging from the main pillar in the corner." The police tied him up, and while his body dangled in the air like a piñata, took turns beating him. He was hospitalized for a week, and when he was discharged, he was handed over to the police again.[39]

Facing the threat of imprisonment and blacklisting, about half of the striking railway workers, after promising to sever ties with the Chŏnp'yŏng, returned to their jobs by the first week of October. When the workers returned to the railway yards, they found that the Taehan Noch'ong had taken the place of the Chŏnp'yŏng. "While the police were busy arresting strikers a typical early-1930s American back-to-work movement was launched," Meacham wrote. "The [Taehan] Noch'ong moved in and assembled a committee of 'loyal employees' who could speak for those workers who 'wanted to return to their jobs.'"[40]

Despite his best attempts to avoid being linked to the strikes, the police arrested Kim Samsun at the Seoul railway yards a few days after he returned to work. An American provost judge found him guilty of engaging in an illegal strike. When he asked what he was guilty of, the court interpreter told him that he "would be better off if he went quietly." Kim spent almost two months in jail. When he went back to work upon his release, the manager informed him that the railroad would not hire back anyone who had been found guilty of involvement in the strikes.[41]

The Korean police had revived colonial tactics to put down the labor unrest. They used Ordinance 72, which prohibited public gatherings without permission from authorities, to stamp out labor and peasant organizing in Samch'ŏk. Ordinance 72 was one of the many colonial laws the occupation government chose not to repeal. Others included Ordinances 2 and 34, which prohibited acts that disturbed public peace and order; and Ordinance 55, which required that groups of three or more who engaged in "political activities" register with the military government.

The Korean police utilized the entire slate of colonial ordinances in their fall campaign. (It was Cho Pyŏngok who convinced occupation authorities to allow the police to go back to Japanese methods.) Every one of the seventeen hundred workers arrested at the Seoul railway yards was charged with one or more of these offenses. According to one American provost judge "practically all of those tried were found guilty of illegal meeting, illegal assembly."[42]

The arrest and conviction of Oh Pyŏngmo shows how the police exploited the colonial ordinances to systematically dismantle the Chŏnp'yŏng. Oh was arrested on October 12 at the Chŏnp'yŏng headquarters in Seoul. He was charged with disturbing the peace (Ordinance 2) and with illegal assembly (Ordinances 34 and 55). The state's witness, a Korean police sergeant, testified that

1. Mr. Oh Pyŏngmo had made an encouraging speech to the railway operators at the front of the Ryongsan Railway Station about the strike that was going on at that time.
2. Mr. Oh Pyŏngmo had held illegal assembly at the office room in the Chŏnp'yŏng building about the plans propelling the railway strike.
3. He had handed the written declaration of strike to Mr. Min-Oh Sik, the adviser to the director of Department of Transportation.

Oh's lawyer argued that his client did not slander the military government (a crime) and that he was organizing workers peaceably with his speech in front of the Yongsan Railway Station in Seoul. He also argued that the meetings Oh attended were part of the Standing Committee of the Chŏnp'yŏng, and legal, since the union had formally registered with the military government. Nevertheless, the court found Oh guilty on all counts and sentenced him to five years in prison.[43]

These practices became standard police procedure with the full blessing of the military high command. Roger Nash Baldwin, director of the American Civil Liberties Union (ACLU), was appalled by what he saw on his visit to Korea in the spring of 1947. He had been in Japan the previous month and raved at what General MacArthur was doing for civil liberties and democracy there.[44] He severely criticized Hodge: "We hold in the prisons thousands of men convicted for offences against the occupation such as 'attending, organizing or acting as an officer at an unauthorized meeting; uttering speech or words or singing a song hostile to the United States.'" He found that 70 percent of the prisoners were held for labor protest of some kind. "These are," Baldwin wrote, "offences taken from the [colonial] manual—and in a liberated country." He did concede, however, that Hodge faced a more challenging situation in Korea than MacArthur did in Japan.[45]

Labor protesters, however, were not the only ones taken into custody. The police also arrested a number of Korean lawyers attempting to organize a civil liberties union in Seoul. They were imprisoned for a week until the local bar association intervened. The arrests had a chilling effect. As Baldwin reported, "They dare not go ahead now and [they] suggested that they might be arrested after I leave just for meeting me."[46]

Hodge justified the heavy-handed response by insisting that the strikes were of a "purely political character," the work of "dangerous anarchists." "There is absolutely no reason," he declared sternly, "for disorders in connection with legitimate labor disputes."[47] He then drew on his own background to make it seem like he knew what the workers were going through:

> I have been a worker myself and have known the pinch of real poverty. As a boy and a young man, I have performed manual labor on the farm and [in] industry in order to get funds to live and to get an education. In fact, I once worked several months as a railway employee. Hence, no man can say that I do not know personally of [a] worker's life and his hardships. This is all the more reason that I regret to see the worker misled into blind alleys by those who make great promises of something for nothing.[48]

Korean workers disputed Hodge's characterization of the labor protests. "Despite General Hodge's attempts to blame these revolts on a 'small agitator group,'" one worker wrote, "the real reasons for the uprisings are clear: Our struggle for good wages, our struggle against 'rice collection,' our peaceful people's demonstrations have been suppressed."[49] Meacham believed the strikes were initiated reluctantly and as a last resort:

The war of attrition that the factory managers, police, and Americans were carrying on against the organization had reached a point where [the organization's] life was at stake. It decided to attempt to mount a counterattack. This decision grew out of a series of rebuffs it encountered in trying to get the American director of the Department of Transportation to sit down with the Chŏnp'yŏng committee and negotiate regarding such matters as a larger rice ration, wage increase, etc. When these demands were met with a casualness that amounted to open contempt it was decided to call a strike.

"If Korea becomes bound by the Soviet straight-jacket," Meacham wrote caustically, "one of the big reasons will be the stupid labor policies followed in South Korea."[50]

Hodge fired back at Meacham, calling his reporting naive, "resulting from an idealistic humanitarian approach to the problem and failure to learn and understand basic underlying conditions affecting the situation pertaining to labor in Korea." Defending his actions to his superiors, he wrote, "Meacham shows no understanding of Communism in the raw, as we have faced it here since arrival, with the Russians guiding it directly." He added, "His acceptance in his report of the most potent Communist tool, the Chŏnp'yŏng as a legal bona fide labor union shows either an utter lack of reality or a complete surrender to the Communist line."[51]

There were certainly communists among the Chŏnp'yŏng. The chairman, Hŏ Sŏngt'aek, fled the South a year later and went on to become North Korea's first minister of labor in 1948 (he was purged and executed in 1954). But the Chŏnp'yŏng was far from a monolithic bloc. As one Korean labor activist interviewed by Roger Baldwin explained, "We do not support the Communist Party dictatorship." But he also added that the unions could not get anywhere with the US occupation government. "All our activities are suspected as Communist. The army stops our strikes. Our demonstrations of protest at public meetings are regarded as riots and our leaders are arrested," despaired one activist. "Any meeting they don't approve is illegal. Any speech they think is anti-American is illegal. You can't criticize a thing the army does without going to jail. The Korean police work hand in glove with them."

Baldwin's own investigations confirmed most of what the leftist said. He found that "the actual Communists among them who want a single-party Communist state allied with the Soviets are comparatively few. But the military

officials are making more of them daily by their policies of suppression."[52]
Hodge's hard line, in other words, was creating a self-fulfilling prophecy.

Just as it appeared that the authorities had a handle on the situation, the
southeast suddenly erupted into violence. Events started off innocuously
enough. On October 1, several hundred women and children marched
through the streets of Taegu demanding rice rations. The area had suffered
from terrible food shortages resulting from a cholera outbreak in the late
spring that had claimed over ten thousand lives. American authorities had
imposed a weeks-long lockdown to contain the epidemic. Pak Hŭimyŏng,
who treated hundreds of cholera patients as a physician at the Taegu Hospital, remembered the outbreak "causing severe shortage of daily necessities
and food, especially rice."[53]

As women and children marched through the city, they picked up protesters along the way, including Yi Ilchae. When the demonstrators reached
city hall, the mayor came out to address them. Yi recalled him patronizingly
asking, "What are you so-called household-managing women doing here?
Shouldn't you be preparing food?" He tossed several soap bars into the crowd,
to which the women protesters quipped acidly, "Do you eat laundry soap in
your house?"[54]

The police were called in and proceeded to fire on the crowd, killing one
demonstrator. The peaceful protest for food burst into a conflagration. The
reaction was months in the making, as mounting anger over food shortages, police brutality, and summer grain collection had turned Taegu into a
powder keg. The killing of the unarmed demonstrator lit the fuse. The next
morning, protesters carried the dead body to the Taegu police station. Soon
after laying the body on the front steps, the incensed crowd, carrying clubs,
knives, and cudgels, stormed the station causing the police to flee in all directions. The mob caught fifty policemen and murdered most of them over
the next few days.[55] Historian Bruce Cumings writes that "they were tortured to death, burned at the stake, skinned alive. And once dead, their
homes and families became objects of attack. Rioters sacked the homes of
Korean officials all over Taegu, including that of the provincial governor;
they looted their belongings, beat their families, attempted to stamp out
every trace of their existence."[56]

The protests spread like wildfire, sweeping through North and South
Kyŏngsang and South Chŏlla Province. In Yŏngchŏn, the mob burned the

police station and post office to the ground, then threw the police chief into a roaring fire, burning him alive. Thirty miles due east from Yŏngchŏn, in Waegwan, protesters beat their police chief with a big rock until they smashed his face to pieces. They tied up his mutilated corpse and dragged it around the town before dumping the body in the Naktong River. Sŏ Chŏngju, the principal of Waegwan Elementary School, remembered thinking, "One can't be human to do something like that."[57] To that, Pau's father in "Bulls" might have replied that "even worms squirm if you step on them." Political demands were thrown into the mix. Some rioters demanded the government be returned to the KPR and the people's committees. Others called for North Korean–style land and labor reforms. School children in Waegwan could be heard singing: "Raise high, the red flag. Underneath it, solemnly swear."[58]

Nearly a third of all the counties in south Korea were touched by peasant uprisings.[59] One of these places was Naju, where the Kungsam-myŏn peasants, who had gone to great lengths to distinguish their claims from those of other peasants, joined the wider insurgency. In a coordinated ambush, the Kungsam-myŏn peasants staged attacks on six different police substations on the evening of October 31. These clashes left thirteen protesters and two police dead, with scores injured and arrested.[60]

The military authorities scrambled to quell the escalating unrest. On October 2, American officials declared martial law in Taegu and dispatched several hundred provincial police, along with US tactical troops and armored military vehicles, to secure order in the city that started it all. Despite facing a ragtag army of lightly armed peasants—wielding clubs, sticks, and swords—the initial force was overmatched by thousands of rioters. The high command was forced to send in reinforcements from Seoul by the trainful (getting the railways back up and running was essential to US counterinsurgency efforts).

The government crackdown on the protesters was brutal. In Taegu, armed police in teams of five went door-to-door searching for rioters. As witnesses observed, "Young adult and middle-aged men were indiscriminately and forcibly taken and held at police stations or schools, and those who refused to comply were killed on the spot." On October 4, a police battalion surrounded a village in Ch'ilgok, several miles outside of Taegu. The men of the village ran to the rice paddies to hide, while the women, children, and the elderly holed up in their homes. The police encircled the rice field and announced to the men they would not kill them if they gave themselves up. When eleven men did exactly that, they were immediately gunned down; the men who remained hiding survived.[61]

In the nearby village of Taejae, young and middle-aged men escaped to the mountains. Pak Yonggyu and Pang Talto made the mistake of fleeing to the mountain behind Taeji-ri instead of Songch'in Mountain, where everyone else was hiding. The police tracked them down and shot Pak. Pang believed he was spared because he was short and looked like a schoolboy. Once the coast was clear, he attended to Pak's wounds. As he recalled, "[Pak's] face blackened and his intestines came out of his body like a pig's gall bladder. I was too young to know what to do so I tried to sweep his intestines together and put them back into his body, but the amount was too much to put back in." Pak died soon after.

The police did not distinguish "rioters" from civilians. In the case of Ha Manju, a family servant under police interrogation falsely accused Ha of forcing him to join the uprising in Taegu. Ha was arrested and taken to Yŏngch'ŏn Police Station, where he was tortured and where he then died of his injuries. Kwŏn Oyong, the San'gol village representative, was also killed while in police custody. He also did not participate in the October protests, but when the police arrived in San'gol, his position as village representative made him a suspect (he was selected because he was one of the few villagers with a formal education). The police hauled him off to the precinct station, where his family later recovered his body.

One enlisted US soldier was so disturbed by police atrocities that he wrote President Harry Truman. "My name is Sergeant Harry Savage," he wrote. "I have just been discharged from the army after spending some ten months in the Occupation Forces in Korea. I am writing this now while I have it fresh in mind and while I am eager to do something about it." His unit was deployed to put down the uprising in Masan on October 7. Facing thousands of protesters, the soldiers fired indiscriminately into the crowd. "Our entire Battalion," he recalled, "patrolled that town all day with dead bodies lying all over the streets, and we kept our machine guns ablazing." There he "saw atrocities that I have never seen before, but now I know how it must have been to live under the Nazis." The Masan police had herded several hundred people to the front of the police station and had them kneel for hours. "Every now and then they would take a few of them inside and the torture would begin," Savage wrote. "Many times people would come running out to us and beg us to kill them, shoot them, anything to end this torture."[62]

Some American soldiers were angry over the torture and started to beat the offending police. But the commanding officers, according to Savage, ordered them not to intervene. He knew exactly why: "Our Division Artillery sent a letter to our Battalion to the effect not to criticize what the police were doing." This was, of course, the military government's policy writ large. Savage wrote angrily, "I did not go to Korea with democracy in mind and with the thought that I was there to help the Korean people, to sit idly by and watch these things without wanting to do something about it."

Savage's letter to the president received no attention from the media, and the Autumn Uprising barely made headlines back in the United States. *The Stars and Stripes* had reported that there were "riots" in Masan but that American forces "had restored law and order without firing a shot."[63] Hardly—it took far more than a few shots, and several months, to quell the uprisings. As security forces suppressed insurrection in one place, another would pop up somewhere else, as if it were a game of whack-a-mole. But, by the end of 1946, the police, with the support of the US military, had contained the most serious protests. When it was over, more than 100 police officers and 500 civilians were dead, close to 7,500 were injured, and over 2,500 were imprisoned.[64]

The high command pinned the insurrections on outside agitators. Major General Archibald Arnold claimed, "Evidence has been plentiful showing that the disturbances are well planned and organized by a small, but extremely active group of Koreans, who receive their direction from north Korea." Who was this group exactly? US officials believed that hundreds of communist infiltrators from the North, led by Pak Hŏnyŏng, had directed the uprisings.[65]

Hodge blamed Koreans for allowing themselves to be deceived by interlopers. "The American command," he lectured, "is doing everything it can to improve the condition of the worker and farmer." But Americans "cannot do these things alone," he chided the Koreans. "Each and every one of you has a definite personal responsibility to add his patriotic efforts to improve conditions, and to prevent agitators from putting your peaceful country in bloody turmoil."[66]

The evidence that a cabal from the North plotted the rebellions was thin. "Among the thousands of arrests made during the strike not one individual was found who was other than a bona fide resident of South Korea," Richard Robinson reported. "General Hodge's oft-repeated charge that North Korean agitators engineered the whole thing seemed to be unfounded."[67] In his investigation in November 1946, the head of the Detective Bureau, Ch'oe Nŭngjin, found that police abuse, especially in rice collection, was the main cause of the uprisings. Ch'oe blamed the police department's policy of retaining former colonial personnel for the tensions that flared in Taegu and elsewhere and demanded their immediate dismissal. Angered by his criticisms and diagnosis of the uprisings, police chiefs Cho and Chang had Ch'oe ousted from the police department in December 1946.[68]

This did not stop socialist activists from trying to make revolutionary myth out of the Autumn Uprising. The brilliant socialist composer Kim Sunnam wrote "Song of the People's Resistance," using lyrics from the equally distinguished poet Im Hwa to memorialize the Taegu Uprising as a revolutionary moment. (Both men eventually left for the North.) The lyrics describe the August uprisings as a solemn and defiant struggle against oppression. They speak about fallen comrades who "spilled hot blood" to "cover the flag, the red flag," which symbolizes revolutionary freedom. The song is a rallying cry for those battling "white terror," and a commitment to defeat those who threaten Korean independence. It ends with the exhortation, "Let's go and defeat them, Guerrilla Unit of the People's Children." Leftists in the South sang the song as an act of resistance, and many Koreans in the North adopted it as their national anthem, until "Aegukka" was made the official state anthem in 1947.[69]

In reality, the people's uprising in Taegu was less about starting a revolution (almost no attack was made on US military government installations or personnel) and more about festering grievances over bread-and-butter issues. A post-analysis of the uprisings put it plainly: "Grain collection and the brutal methods employed by the police in carrying out the collection program were basic factors."[70] What happened in Taegu (and elsewhere) was no doubt protest and resistance, but it was not inspired, for the most part, by "comrades" and "red flags."

7 Taking a Shot at the Middle

The Autumn upheavals complicated the military government's plan to create a centrist coalition in the South. In the summer of 1946, the occupation government initiated talks with moderate rightists and leftists to create a "true coalition of democratic parties." Why the sudden change of course? Didn't Hodge still view an "inch left of center" as communism? The general remained an anti-communist stalwart but he was not blind to the deteriorating conditions in the South. "The general morale of Koreans is at a low ebb," he wrote to Douglas MacArthur that summer. "Their outstanding point of judgment is that Americans have been here one year and the physical benefits from there do not yet equal those under Japanese rule." A poll taken by the Department of Public Information captured the steep decline in American prestige, showing that half the Korean respondents preferred Japanese colonial rule to US occupation. This was a shocking reversal for a group that less than a year earlier was hailed as liberators.[1]

Hodge blamed the Koreans directly for what ailed them. "In all consideration of Korean problems, the character, psychology and temperament of these people is a vital factor. . . . All are individualists of a high order[,] . . . are highly volatile and excitable over trifles and can easily reach such a point of frenzy over real or fancied wrongs that they do not listen to reason. They are opportunists of a high order, with a low degree of personal integrity."[2]

Koreans, in a seeming rebuttal to Hodge's confidential assertions, rejected the notion that they were to blame for the country's problems. An editorial published in the *Chosŏn ilbo*, the largest-circulation newspaper in the South, asked the general to consider "the present situation in Korea," where the "Korean people are now suffering more than they ever did under Japanese rule." It placed the responsibility squarely on the Americans. "We believe that the Military Government in Korea has not been successful in its efforts, and that this failure is due to your country's lack of understanding concerning Korea, the interpreters' administration, the permission of free economy without any preparation and to your wavering policy."[3] While they could not agree on who was to blame, everyone agreed the situation in the South was growing dire. Something had to change.

Complicating the situation, the high command's favorite sons, Kim Ku and Syngman Rhee, proved to be unreliable allies. Kim had tried to organize a coup after the Moscow decision. Rhee spent his time as president of the RDC calling for a separate government in the South and the expulsion of the Soviets from Korea—in the middle of the Joint Commission discussions, no less, which embarrassed US officials to no end. In March 1946, the State Department, according to Richard Robinson, had advised Hodge to "stay clear of Dr. Rhee and Kim, that negotiations which the Department had had with them over the past few years had been 'unsatisfactory,' and that it would be highly desirable to give support to younger and more liberal elements who were more closely in touch with the desires of the Korean people."[4] It is unclear why the State Department waited six months into the occupation to provide Hodge with this vital piece of information.

Hodge met with Rhee several times to try to get him to tone it down. After one stormy session, Hodge told a confidant that he now knew what it must have felt like to be the angel wrestling Jacob in the Old Testament story.[5] A later CIA analysis would describe Rhee as a genuine patriot, but added, "He has also been unscrupulous in his attempts to thrust aside any person or group he felt to be in his way." The report continued: "Rhee's vanity had made him highly susceptible to the contrived flattery of self-seeking interests in the US and in Korea. His intellect is a shallow one, and his behavior is often irrational and literally childish."[6] Not exactly a ringing endorsement.

The current course was untenable. So when the State Department pushed the idea of a centrist coalition, Hodge decided to get behind it, even though he was not particularly enthusiastic. A part of him continued to see a strongman as the only answer to the communist threat in Korea. But given the state of affairs, Hodge was willing to give the plan a go. He put a young lieutenant, Leonard M. Bertsch, in charge of assembling the coalition. The cherubic-faced Bertsch held a doctorate from the College of the Holy Cross and a law degree from Harvard University. He was among hundreds of civ-

il affairs officers who had been trained for the occupation of Japan but ended up in Korea instead. "I am by profession a lawyer, by preference a student
of history, and by accident a solider and politician," is how he described
himself and his unlikely path to Korean politics.[7]

Bertsch's first order of business was to split off moderate leftists and dis-
sident communists from the Communist Party, starting with Yŏ Unhyŏng,
whom he saw as the linchpin to the whole project. Along with Arthur Bunce
and Stewart Meacham, Bertsch saw Yŏ as the hope of Korea. But not all the
liberal advisers were as enamored with Yŏ. "I found him one of the most
charming men that we had met here in the Far East," Owen Jones wrote in
his diary, "but had reservations on his capacity to lead us out of this crisis
because of his rather weak face and his vacillations."[8]

Yŏ initially resisted Bertsch's overtures because he would be required to
leave his People's Party. But a short time later, he approached US officials for
help in his ongoing fight with Pak Hŏnyŏng, hinting that "it was essential to
the success of the American program that Pak be dealt with drastically at
this juncture, perhaps jailed by some juggling of the counterfeit trial due
July 29." When American officials asked him why he did not expose the
communist plans to sabotage the unity efforts himself, Yŏ replied that "large
labor, farmers and youth elements in southern Korea divide their allegiance
between him and Pak, that if an open break between him and Pak came
now it would harm the unity movement." Yŏ suggested that "if Pak could be
made to lose face at this moment," he might be able to "win a considerable
portion of these elements over to his, and, therefore, our side."

Yŏ's reluctance to call out Pak publicly alarmed Bertsch. He had heard
rumors that Yŏ had "maintained highly secretive relations with a number of
very highly-placed Japanese officials throughout the war." He was afraid the
communists were holding compromising information on him. At Bertsch's
urging, the military government sent Major Charles O'Riordan to Japan to
interrogate former colonial officials, including the governor-general of Korea, Abe Noboyuki, about their past dealings with Yŏ. They needed to know
Yŏ was "clean" before going all in on him.[9] Meanwhile, occupation officials
rebuffed Yŏ's appeal, at least according to what political adviser William
Langdon told Secretary of State James F. Byrnes: "We made it plain to Yŏ
that we have no intention of abusing the counterfeit trial for political persecution and that he must fight his own battles."[10] Yet a few weeks later in the
summer of 1946, the military government issued a warrant for Pak's arrest

and raided the homes of his closest allies. Yŏ left the People's Party right around the time the warrant was issued.

All Bertsch needed now was a moderate rightist to pair with the leftist. Yŏ recommended his longtime friend Kim Kyusik. The two had met in China while establishing Korea's government in exile with other nationalists. Yŏ couldn't stand most of the other members (he threw a chair at Kim Ku at one meeting), but he found Kim Kyusik earnest and profoundly decent. They remained close even after Yŏ left the KPG. It was Yŏ who encouraged Kim to attend the Paris Peace Conference in 1919 to petition for Korean independence. (Like so many nationalists from the colonized world, Kim had been bitterly disappointed with Woodrow Wilson's empty promise of self-determination.) Several years later, the two men attended the First Toilers Congress together in Moscow, where they dabbled in socialist politics. Both men eventually became disillusioned with communism, Kim more so than Yŏ.

Born to an impoverished family in Busan, Kim Kyusik was orphaned at an early age. He was adopted by Horace Underwood, one of the earliest and most prominent American missionaries in Korea. (Underwood founded the school that would eventually become Yonsei University, today one of South Korea's leading universities.) With Underwood's support, Kim attended Roanoke College, a liberal arts school in Virginia, where he was a standout student studying philosophy and history.

Kim returned to Korea following graduation and worked as a teacher at the YMCA School and then as dean at the Underwood School. After Japan annexed Korea in 1910, he joined the overseas independence movement in China, where he met Yŏ. Unlike his friend, Kim Kyusik remained with the KPG, serving as its foreign minister, and worked closely with Kim Ku, which gave him a certain amount of credibility with the Right.

When Kim Kyusik came back to Korea in November 1945, along with the rest of the provisional government, he studiously avoided the spotlight, in sharp contrast to Kim Ku, who had a celebratory welcome in front of thousands of cheering supporters in Seoul. Kim Kyusik made very few public appearances, and refused to answer the pressing questions of the day. For example, he did not take a position on trusteeship. The truth was that being a politician never came naturally to him. Kim Kyusik was at heart a teacher and a scholar. He moonlighted at some of the most elite universities in China, teaching English literature during his three decades

Kim Kyusik, chairman of the Interim Legislative Assembly and
co-leader of the Centrist Coalition, speaking in 1947.
National Archives (111-SC-291202)

in exile.[11] Could a scholar who was more comfortable in a library navigate
the treacherous waters of Korean politics? "Kimm Kiu Sic [Kim Kyusik] is
a good man," explained one Korean labor leader, "but he doesn't know what
the common people want, and the common people don't know what he
stands for."[12]

American reformers knew Kim didn't have the name recognition or cha-
risma of some of the other leaders but they thought he had other strengths
that complemented Yŏ's. "With full awareness of his defects," Bertsch wrote
to Hodge, "it remains true that he is fundamentally decent, and that he

comprehends at least the nature of the democratic process," adding that "these comments cannot be made of most of his opponents." The Yŏ-Kim pairing, Bertsch believed, offered the best chance for a centrist coalition in the South.

The Left-Right Coalition Committee, as it was called, consisted of ten members divided equally between the two sides, a far more equitable distribution than earlier coalition efforts. (The Advisory Council and the Representative Democratic Council had a 9:1 rightist to leftist ratio.) Yŏ chose Hŏ Hŏn, a wealthy communist and father of socialist feminist Hŏ Chŏngsuk, who stayed behind in the South, to be one of the Left's five representatives. Starting in June 1946, the committee met at the Tŏksu Palace in Seoul every Monday and Friday afternoon to negotiate a program for a centrist government. In keeping with the spirit of the coalition, Kim and Yŏ alternated chairing the meetings.

On June 30, Hodge publicly endorsed the Coalition Committee. The extreme Left and Right—Pak, Rhee, and Kim Ku—were now all officially outside looking in, and not happy about it. Pak had warned Yŏ not to "play the American game," when he found out about the plans to form a coalition government. When that failed to sway Yŏ, Pak tried to rally leftists against it. That, too, failed, suggesting that there was genuine interest in compromise among the Left.[13]

Rhee took a different tack. In fact, he donated funds to the coalition efforts as a show of support. But this was faux support. During the spring, Rhee had campaigned in the countryside to extend his political reach outside of Seoul. He was a gifted retail politician who knew how to organize his supporters. Police assistance, of course, helped. He and his allies, as journalist Mark Gayn reported, "set up a mass network of organizations, from women's clubs to terrorist bands."[14] Rhee's political machine soon became the dominant organization in some provinces, replacing leftist ones.

Rhee did not do all this only to play second fiddle, and Kim was all too aware of it. He was overheard telling Rhee, his senior by six years, "Older brother now you put me high up on the tree, but later you are going to shake me down."[15] True to form, Rhee set up an opposing organization, "The General Headquarters of Korean Unification," in August and denounced Kim Kyusik as a traitor for leading the Coalition Committee.[16]

After months of negotiating, the Coalition Committee reached an agreement on a seven-point framework. The highlights included the following: supporting the Moscow decision and reconvening the Joint Commission; redistributing land with little or no compensation to the big landowners; punishing collaborators based on a criterion determined by the committee; releasing political prisoners; and guaranteeing freedom of speech, press, and assembly. This is what the political center looked like in the South.

The KDP came out hard against the platform, especially the provisions on land reform and purging collaborators. Their constituency of wealthy landowners and businessmen would have seen both proposals as a threat to their interests. KDP members, most prominently Cho Pyŏngok, worked behind the scenes to malign committee members as "opportunists" and "wobblers."[17]

Given the rightist opposition, one would think the Communist Party would have supported the platform, but that was not the case. Pak and his allies wanted the military government to transfer powers to the people's committees immediately. Everyone knew this was a nonstarter with the American military government (as well as the Right-leaning members of the committee). Was Pak trying to sabotage the coalition efforts with the demand? He had met with North Korean leader Kim Il Sung in the summer to talk strategy, although the exact details of their conversation are unknown.

On the other hand, military government reformers were pleasantly surprised with the Coalition Committee's platform. They had feared that the centrist coalition would be all symbol and no substance. Arthur Bunce, who had grown pessimistic about prospects for reunification, thought that a Left-Right government enacting genuine reforms in the South would bring the Soviets and the North back to the negotiating table. With the centrist coalition and platform in place, American officials planned to hold elections in November 1946. This would be a first for most Koreans in the South. (Only a small number of Korean landlords and other wealthy taxpayers had been allowed to participate in local elections under the Japanese.) Not to be outdone, the North announced its own elections shortly thereafter.

Occupation officials saw the elections as an opportunity to introduce Koreans to representative politics and to boost America's flagging support in south Korea. This would, however, be democracy with training wheels. The South Korean Interim Legislative Assembly (SKILA) would consist of ninety members, but only half would be elected by the Korean people. The other half would be appointed by General Hodge in consultation with the Coalition Committee. The same logic applied to SKILA, which was vested with lawmaking authority, but the military governor held the veto pen, which could not be overridden. Koreans would be given a chance to practice democracy but it would be under American tutelage.

Nevertheless, reformers believed things were finally moving in the right direction. "Present political conditions are more hopeful," Bunce reported to the secretary of state in August 1946. "Lyuh Woon Hyung [Yŏ Unhyŏng] has split from the Communists and has agreed to join the coalition of Rightists and Leftists."[18] In another good sign, the Coalition Committee had come up with a standard to define "collaborators," to exclude them from running for office. They also made plans to ensure a free and fair election, including secret ballots and election monitoring.

Koreans were all set to go to the polls in November. But then the uprisings and police repression transpired. Members of the Coalition Committee begged General Hodge to postpone the elections. "Can we have a democratic election," Hŏ Hŏn asked, "when thousands of leftists are in jail? Can we have an election when labor unions are in jail? Can we have an election when labor unions are barred from politics, and the police terror is at its height? Can the coalition of Kimm Kiu Sic and Lyuh Woon Hyung be taken seriously when Lyuh Woon Hyung's entire People's Party is in jail or hiding?"[19]

They seemed valid questions, but Hodge was determined to push forward with the elections. He told Bertsch he would not be cowed by communist machinations. Richard Robinson believed that the rush to hold elections was about tilting the field in favor of the Right. If this was the case, it worked a little too well. Forty of the forty-five candidates who won a seat in the Interim Assembly were from Rhee's party. Even Yŏ had lost the election in his district in Seoul. Leftist candidates won only two seats, both in Jeju Island, which managed to escape the Autumn upheavals and conduct peaceful elections under the watch of the People's Committee. Mun Tobae, one of the leaders of the Jeju's People's Committee who had a sterling record of anti-Japanese resistance, was one of the two elected representatives. The election, Bertsch insisted, "was so rigged as to elect fascists."[20] He was speaking about the police intimidation and voter fraud, which were widespread on election day. Military Governor Lerch had refused to put in any of the safeguards—including secret ballots and election monitors—recommended by Kim and Yŏ.

George McCune, head of the State Department's Korea Desk, noted similarities between the elections in the South and the North, which took place roughly at the same time, explaining how they established "two puppet states" on the peninsula. "The carefully regulated elections in the Soviet zone, modeled after elections in the Soviet Union, resulted, as had been anticipated, in a sweeping endorsement of candidates chosen by the single party." In the South, he wrote, "a sweeping conservative victory took place at the polls" that "even the middle-of-the-road Korean leaders declared to have been fraudulent."[21]

Kim Kyusik rushed off a letter to Hodge questioning the legitimacy of the elections: "The election of so many pro-Japs and the members of the extreme Right Parties tend to give the impression that this election has not been conducted according to democratic principles and therefore does not voice the real sentiment of the people."[22] Kim asked the general to nullify the election results and allow the Coalition Committee to select the ninety members. He and Yŏ also requested the removal of former Japanese collaborators from the police and bureaucracy, the release of all political prisoners, the reopening of all newspapers that had been shut down by the military government, and the end of the rice collection program.[23]

Hodge made several concessions but stopped short of meeting their demands. He ordered new elections in Seoul and Kangwŏn province, which amounted to six seats, where election irregularities were thought to be most widespread. Hodge also promised to appoint the other forty-five members based on the recommendations made by the Coalition Committee, on which he largely followed through on. At Yŏ's request, Hodge made Kim Kyusik chairman of the interim assembly.[24]

But now the Right erupted in protest. They accused Hodge of thwarting the will of the Korean people and blasted him for appeasing the communists. Conservative members threatened to boycott the opening session of the interim assembly if Hodge did not reverse his decision on holding new elections in Seoul and Kangwŏn province. The general refused to back down. He announced the legislature would open as scheduled on December 12, and he had the minimum for quorum changed from three quarters to one half of the members to neutralize their threat. He also formally dissolved the Representative Democratic Council (RDC).

In December, Rhee flew to Washington, DC, to make his case against the coalition efforts and reconvening the Joint Commission. His allies in Washington had pleaded with him to stay in Korea, believing the trip would do more harm than good, but he went anyway. Upon landing, Rhee tried to get meetings with Secretary of State Byrnes and other high-ranking American officials, but they all refused to see him. Hodge had forewarned them of the visit. Rhee told any who would listen that General Hodge was a communist and called for his ouster. He also demanded elections be held immediately in the South to establish a separate government, with him as president.

Why did Rhee opt for such a desperate move? William Langdon thought that "the coalition compact of Right and Left and Gen. Hodge's support of the Coalition Committee's efforts, as well as Rhee's final realization that we mean to go ahead with the Moscow decision which in the nature of things ruins his chances of being first president, crystallized his decision to fight the Moscow decision."[25] Rhee also feared that Kim Il Sung and his Communist Party was consolidating power in the North and he was falling behind. He was not wrong; Kim's party had redistributed lands, passed labor reforms and women's rights, nationalized large industries and businesses, and formed a nucleus for a North Korean state by the end of 1946. Rhee's political instincts were almost always spot on, and he possessed a supernatural talent for pushing his agenda to the very edge without falling over. He was the king of brinkmanship.[26]

Almost everyone acknowledged Rhee as a true patriot. He had spent nearly four decades away from his homeland fighting for Korean independence. But at some point, Rhee couldn't differentiate his own interests from those of the country. "He tends," a CIA analysis concluded, "to regard the best interests of Korea as being synonymous with his own. It is as if he, in his own mind at least, were Korea."[27] C. L. Sulzberger, the *New York Times* lead foreign correspondent, later described Rhee as a "great patriot but, philosophically, qualified for charter membership in the John Birch Society."[28]

US intelligence indicated that Rhee was directing his followers in the South to start "mass demonstrations in protest against delays in Korean independence and against the Moscow decision, which may include violence and sit-down strikes, to show the Americans that they are helpless without cooperation of his group." It was the anti-trusteeship movement all over again, except this time it was Rhee, not Kim Ku, spearheading it. "Rhee is a nuisance in that he wants everything done his own impractical ways and wants to head separate Govt of South Korea," Hodge wrote the secretary of state on New Year's Eve. "However, we cannot and must not overlook his potential to do irreparable damage unless carefully handled."[29] On more than one occasion, Hodge, enraged by Rhee's latest antics, sent orders to his MPs to throw him in jail, only to take them back at the last minute.[30]

Rhee was not Hodge's only problem. Yŏ Unhyŏng failed to show at the opening session of SKILA. Hodge wrote scathingly to Yŏ: "I regret that you don't find it convenient to perform your duty as a loyal Korean citizen by serving your country in the Legislative Assembly."[31] Hodge told him that he would appoint a successor if he did not assume his seat within the week. What had happened to Yŏ? The Pak wing of the Communist Party had ratcheted up pressure on him to resign from the coalition. On the morning of October 7, 1946, he was abducted by members of the "extreme wing" of the Communist Party and taken to an undisclosed location in the redlight district in Seoul, where he was held for thirty-six hours without sleep. After being released, he was taken to Seoul University Hospital. Exactly what was said or done to him is unclear; Yŏ refused to provide any details. Bertsch suspected it was Pak who had orchestrated the kidnapping. The reason, he believed, that Yŏ had been tight-lipped about the affair was because he was holding out "the unreasonable hope that he might induce Pak Heung Young [Pak Hŏnyŏng] by persuasion to change his course."[32]

The right-wing sweep and the election of collaborators made convincing the Left much harder. Desperate to show something for his coalition efforts, Yŏ called for the removal of the two police chiefs, but his demand was met with silence. Many leftists began to suspect Pak was right about the Coalition Committee.[33] "He secretly told me he must resign his position," a close ally of Yŏ wrote to Major General Albert E. Brown, who was overseeing the coalition efforts along with Bertsch. "His chief reason is that the leftists won't believe in him, because what Mr. Lyuh Woon Hyung once asserted that the police headmen should resign their posts, has not yet been realized. They strongly persuade him to withdraw from the coalition committee, saying that he will be fooled by the American Military Government."[34]

Trying to do damage control and buy themselves time, the Coalition Committee came out with a cryptic statement that Yŏ would continue to fight for reunification, the reconvening of the Joint Commission, land and labor reforms, release of political prisoners, and the elimination of terrorism—the CC's platform, in essence—without saying whether he would ever take his seat in the assembly.

As his first act as chairman, Kim Kyusik formed a special committee to draft legislation to prosecute collaborators. The nine-member committee was chaired by Chŏng Ihyŏng, a former guerrilla fighter who spent close to two decades in prison under Japanese rule. For nearly two months, the committee debated how to define collaboration and what the punishment should be. They came up with several categories. The first was "national traitors," defined as people who actively assisted Japan in colonizing Korea. This included Koreans who had negotiated and signed the initial annexation treaty, had assumed high positions in the colonial government, police, and military, or had persecuted and murdered the resistance (the inclusion of this last one must have been especially important to Chŏng). The second was "war criminals," which included Koreans who had supported Japan's wartime aims by spreading wartime propaganda, donating funds, or providing munitions. Village elders who recruited young Korean men and women for the draft fell into this category.

The first two crimes applied mostly to Koreans in positions of authority and carried the stiffest penalties, including long-term imprisonment or execution. The more power, the more responsibility seemed to be the thinking. For the third and largest category, "collaborators," the committee adopted a broad definition that encompassed "working against the interests of the nation by compromising themselves in sinister activities, utilizing themselves of the Japanese influence during the Japanese domination over Korea." This category included more ordinary acts, from working in the colonial government to volunteering for the colonial army to speaking Japanese in everyday conversation.[35]

The committee estimated that 100,000 to 200,000 Koreans would be convicted for collaboration, about 1 percent of the population in the South. That number, if correct, was roughly in line with Western European countries. (The Netherlands, for instance, indicted 200,000 out of a population of nine and half million for wartime collaboration.)[36] The committee was not looking to be punitive with this group. There would be no prison time or death penalty. Instead, collaborators would be barred from voting or holding office for up to ten years. Those who collaborated would not be allowed to participate in the initial rebuilding of the nation, but after a period of time they would be welcomed back as full citizens. The goal, as one member put it, was to establish "correct national spirit" while leaving room for personal redemption and national healing.[37]

In the middle of the committee's deliberations, a high-ranking police official, Yi Haegin, published a blistering letter in a local newspaper, denouncing the draft bill. He defended those who had been accused of collaboration, arguing that they did so against their will (perhaps he was speaking about himself). He slammed the committee for sowing division when they should be unifying the country and called for their immediate impeachment. SKILA members protested, with one assemblyman calling the letter a "declaration of war against the Assembly."[38]

This was not the first time the police had tried to intimidate lawmakers. The Seoul chief of police, Chang T'aeksang, had attended the legislative session back on January 20, to whip up support for a motion opposing trusteeship. He was seen with a large contingent of KDP members cheering on the speeches of the anti-trusteeship politicians. In a room outside the chamber, rightist youth members could be heard shouting "They should be killed" and "Death to the traitors" at the assemblymen who opposed the motion.[39]

By the spring of 1947, the police state was in full force. The new powers and personnel it amassed during the Autumn Uprising had supercharged it. As Roger Baldwin, the SCAP legal adviser who was in Korea at the invitation of General MacArthur, explained, "Our zone of Korea, it must be admitted, is, like the Russian zone, a police state, run in the interests of the political Right. Gangster methods against the Communists are not only tolerated, but the police are allied with the gangsters; and the American occupation is allied with the police." People's committees, farmers' cooperatives, and labor unions suffered virtual extinction, their leaders either in prison or underground. The police even jailed the lawyers who tried to defend them in court (they were released only after the entire bar association protested).

Indeed, the authorities stopped bothering to hide their partisanship. Baldwin, in one of his strolls through Seoul, observed a huge sign reading "Kill the Reds and the Pinks" hanging from a building occupied by a right-wing organization. "Nobody among Korean or our own authorities apparently thought it improper," he wrote. He was sure that if the sign had read "Kill the Fascists and Reactionaries," it would "have come down in a hurry." Baldwin wrote, "The left is insecure, hunted, driven out," while the Right went "unmolested."[40]

The youth groups under the police became unhinged. In the spring of 1947, American agents raided the headquarters of the Korean Democratic Youth Alliance, where they came upon a grisly scene that resembled a medieval torture chamber. They saw exotic instruments and spilled blood everywhere. They found several victims tied up, their bodies mutilated. One man had his genitals electrocuted and cut off. Somehow, he miraculously survived. The group (and the torture) was led by a vicious gangster named Kim Tuhan. Orphaned at a young age—his father was an independence fighter who was killed in Manchuria—Kim had grown up on the streets of Seoul. By the time he was a teenager, he was an underworld boss. Kim would later portray himself as a noble gangster who defended poor Korean shopkeepers from the Japanese colonial police. (Korean street gangs typically made money offering "protection" to local merchants in the areas they controlled.)

After liberation, Kim was in and out of jail, apparently for dealing drugs. Sometime that fall, he joined a communist youth auxiliary—the Left also had youth groups—headed by a childhood friend. Kim brought his former gang members over with him and was quickly promoted to captain. In April 1946, he and his crew suddenly left the group to merge with a new right-wing youth group, the Korean Democratic Youth Alliance. According to one American source, "These quasi-criminal organizations take advantage of the displaced youth, organize them into black market and extortion groups, and proceed to do business under the color of patriotism."[41]

Kim Tuhan later claimed he switched parties only after learning his father was killed by a communist. But it was more likely that he saw the political wind shifting and changed accordingly. If the streets had taught him anything, it was to seize an opportunity when he saw one. Rhee and Kim Ku were the group's honorary chairmen, and Cho and Chang were its patron saints. The two police chiefs supported rightist youth groups with arms, food, and other supplies, which their leaders in turn used to recruit members, especially targeting refugees from the North (about a million people eventually fled from the North).[42]

Kim Tuhan became an overnight hero to the Right in October 1946, when he led several hundred youth members (with arms provided by Cho) into the teeth of the railroad strikes in Seoul. When the American director of transportation talked about going "into the situation as if it was a war," it was Kim Tuhan leading the charge, seeming to relish the role. He and his men sent dozens of strikers to the hospital.[43] He used his newfound status to terrorize civilians who showed even a hint of supporting the Left. The conductor of the Korean Symphony Orchestra told Baldwin that he could not play "Left" music without Kim's gang threatening him and his musicians.

Kim Tuhan's actions were not entirely out of step with the military high command, which had issued an arrest warrant for socialist musician Kim Sunnam for composing "Song of the People's Resistance" after the Taegu uprising. The order outraged Ely Haimowitz, the American military government's chief cultural adviser and a classically trained pianist, who viewed it as censorship, plain and simple. He also considered Kim Sunnam a friend and a singular musical talent. Haimowitz was working with Kim and other Korean musicians to revive traditional Korean music, which had been banned under the Japanese. What Haimowitz decided to do next was the stuff of a Hollywood movie or a K-drama. He got into his car and raced to find Kim, and he helped hide him from the American authorities, risking insubordination. He later arranged a scholarship for Kim at the Music Academy of the West in Santa Barbara, California, but because of the arrest warrant, Kim was unable to leave Korea to accept it.[44] Eventually, Kim fled for the North, where he became director of the composition department at the Pyongyang National Music School. His musical career was cut short when he was purged in the mid-1950s and sentenced to a lifetime of hard labor. He was last seen thawing resin at a shipyard in Sinp'o off the coast of South Hamgyŏng Province.[45] The artist could not find a home in the North or the South.

After Kim Tuhan was taken into custody for murder and torture, Bertsch confronted Rhee about his association with him: "When I protested to Dr. Rhee over the fact that his agents, a group of political murderers and extortionists working in Taehan Noch'ong had committed a series of torture murders in their private dungeons in the name of loyalty to his principles, Dr. Rhee replied to me, 'What would you have me do? Should I stop their patriotism? The people they killed were leftists.'" Bertsch found out that "many of the people killed, and the overwhelming majority of those who suffered from extortion, were not leftists." In other words, Kim's "patriotic" fight against communism was mostly cover for an extortion racket.[46]

Major Richardson reported that Kim was treated with "exceeding deference by the police," while in their custody. The case against him was dropped a few days after he was arrested. Bertsch could do nothing but watch. He and other American officials were still under strict orders not to interfere with the Korean police. Kim was arrested again a few months later for threatening the president of the Seoul Electric Company, a conservative, after he was told his "protection" services would no longer be needed at the plant. "In 60 days, Dr. Rhee and I will be in power," he yelled at the president. "When we are, I will return and kill you with my own hands."[47]

Rhee's youth reminded Captain Richard Robinson of the Nazis. "Dr. Rhee should be stripped of every shred of prestige which the American

Command has ever bestowed upon him," Robinson wrote. "His record shows clearly that he is anything but a democrat. In fact, his record shows a striking similarity to the activities of one Adolph Hitler during the embryonic days of the Third Reich—and just as ruthless."[48]

Kim was not the only one in the extortion business. Law enforcement higher-ups coerced wealthy Koreans to bankroll Rhee and Kim Ku's political operations. In the spring of 1946, a committee of Korean millionaires, organized by former political adviser Preston Goodfellow, donated ten million yen to Rhee. (Goodfellow was called back to Washington after it was reported he had an under-the-table deal with Rhee for Korean gold mines.)[49] Several months later, Rhee went back to the same group for another round of donations for "patriotic purposes." When the money didn't roll in, a top Justice Department official, Kim Hongsŏp, ordered the police to arrest three committee members: Pak Kiho, Chun Yong-sun, and Cho Chunho.

When they appeared before him, Kim demanded to know why they had not provided the additional funds. They told him they were following the orders of the military government. (It seems that Hodge had instructed the committee to cut off Rhee, who was becoming a nuisance.) Kim responded by accusing the men of engaging in black market activities. He hinted that they would be prosecuted and then left the room, presumably to allow the threat to sink in. An hour later they were released. Pak later told Bertsch that "he and the rest of the committee feared that there would be prosecution against them on some fictitious basis unless they capitulated to the demands of Dr. Rhee." Bertsch intervened so no money was exchanged. As for Kim Hongsŏp, he faced no disciplinary action. His father-in-law was a prominent member of the KDP.[50]

Despite this setback, money continued to flow into police coffers and the war chests of Rhee and Kim Ku. According to Bertsch, Cho Pyŏngok visited Rhee in July 1947 to make him a huge offer. Cho would support him with seventy million yen from funds "raised" for the police department if Rhee agreed to take him into his party. Where did he get this huge sum of money? It is hard to know exactly. But in the spring, the Benevolent Society for the Police organized a drive to raise thirty million yen "to help poor police." Solicitation letters were mailed to businesses in Seoul, arriving with a "recommended" donation amount. Cho's wealthy patrons probably made up the difference.[51]

Right before liberation, Cho's family had fallen on hard times. But it seems that a year and half as chief of the National Police had fixed that.

Rightist groups stepped up their campaign to intimidate Kim Kyusik and Yŏ Unhyŏng. Posters, handbills, and banners calling for their elimination appeared throughout Seoul. A police official told Bertsch he could "prove the direct complicity of the police in all of the above, but that he would be unwilling to have his name used, in fear for his life." When a local newspaper published an article criticizing the police for permitting the threats on the two coalition leaders, they arrested its editor.[52]

In May 1947, Kim Kyusik took refuge in a hospital ten miles outside of Seoul. He told General Brown, who visited a few days later, that he was "unable to continue in political life and that he had prepared his resignation as Chairman of the Interim Legislative Assembly." When Brown asked why, he stated that "there existed four or five organizations of young ruffians who claimed to be affiliated with the right who were led by Chang Taik Sang [Chang T'aeksang], Chief of the Seoul Police Force, who threatened him and other members of the Coalition Committee." Chief Chang held Kim Kyusik (and other members of the independence movement) responsible for the death of his father.[53] Chang's family had a history of collaborating with the Japanese, and his father was killed by an independence activist for refusing to support the KPG. Kim Kyusik told Brown he didn't feel safe anywhere and "that he could no longer live or operate under these conditions."[54]

The same went for Yŏ. When Roger Baldwin asked to meet him, he could not invite him to his home or office because he had no fixed location. Fearing for his life, Yŏ slept in a different bed every night. He held the unenviable title of "the most shot at man in South Korea." He hired bodyguards but they were arrested by the police. Not long after, his home was bombed in a failed assassination attempt—three of the four walls of the house were destroyed. The perpetrator was never identified, if any effort at all was made to find him.[55]

Back at the hospital, Kim Kyusik told General Brown that Hodge would have to choose: him and Yŏ or the police chiefs. As Brown saw it, the Americans had three options: rightist political groups that "desire nothing short of an independent government for South Korea led by Syngman Rhee"; an extreme Left group that "desire[s] nothing short of a Russian controlled government"; or a center group that "refuse[s] to cooperate unless the Commissioner of Police and the Chief of Area 'A' are dismissed."[56]

For the reformers, the choice was an easy one. They thought the removal of the two police chiefs was long overdue, given their long record of abuse and corruption. "Mr. P. [an American adviser] said he took part in an investigation of Messrs. Chough [Cho] and Chang, in which enough evidence was gathered to hang 20 men, after which he and his partner in the investigation were called off," wrote American police adviser William L. Patterson."[57] Richard Robinson thought, "The police situation has become progressively worse, and will continue to be so until Dr. Chough [Cho] and Chief Chang are removed from office and replaced by men with some conception of liberalism." He predicted that "if the present situation is allowed to remain indefinitely, Dr. Kim Kyu Sik and Lyuh Woon Hyung will be forced to align themselves more closely with the Korean Communist Party." In Bertsch's opinion, Kim's request was "the absolute minimum of concession which would enable them to carry forward their program and [win] public support."[58]

The findings of Major Charles O'Riordan, who had returned from Japan after interrogating former top colonial officials, gave team Kim-Yŏ a boost. His report concluded emphatically "that there is absolutely no evidence that Lyuh Woon Hyung ever cooperated with the Japanese in any way that was inconsistent with his professed devotion to the cause of absolute independence for Korea." In fact, the Japanese "offered him every bribe in their power, but could not make him compromise his insistence on absolute independence." They told O'Riordan that any Korean government formed without him "would have difficulty in finding wide popular support." The sum total of their opinion, he wrote, "adds up to an impressive tribute to the man, his character and his patriotism—a sincere tribute in the mind of this investigating officer."[59]

A draft statement in Bertsch's personal papers suggests Hodge came tantalizingly close to firing Cho and Chang:

There was no phase of the Japanese tyranny in Korea which so directly and so bitterly affected the lives of so many of the Korean people as did the police force. While it is necessary to recognize the fact there were those in the police force who tried to do their best to protect their people, the overwhelming fact is that the great majority of the Koreans who served in the Japanese police force have won for themselves the proper hatred of their people.

It is desirable that the old enmity should be forgotten and that Koreans should advance as a united people into the new day. But this

cannot be done while the rankling sense of injustice yet remains unful-
filled.

Ever since liberation, Koreans have been hoping and expecting that
the police forces would be cleansed of those who betrayed their people
to the Japanese invaders. With the passing months it has become sadly
apparent that it was the intention of those in control of the police force
not to remove, but rather to strengthen, the influence of those who had
betrayed their own people.

For this reason, using the power that has been vested in me, I am
hereby removing Chough Pyung Ok from his office as Director of the
Department of Police, effective immediately; and I am removing,
Chang Taik Sang from his office as Chief of Division "A' of the National Police, effective immediately.

It is to be hoped that their successors will recognize more clearly
their duty to the Korean people and will proceed with due diligence
and efficiency to remove from the police force, completely and within
the minimum possible time, all who have served under the Japanese
police force or related organizations.

When the people's sense of justice shall have been satisfied by the
removal from influence of all those who used their influence against
the people, then we shall be able to lay the foundations of true Korean
unity and harmony.

I call upon the officials of other departments of government to observe this action and to take due recognition of its meaning; and I call
upon the thousands of loyal members of the Korean police force to
recognize the fact that they are not agents of political controversy but
servants of the people, to obey promptly and completely their new superiors and to carry out the law without fear or favor and without partisanship, to the greater glory and stability of the Korean people and
state.[60]

It never happened. Hodge could not bring himself to remove Cho and
Chang. Maybe it was his knee-jerk anti-communism, maybe the Autumn
uprisings spooked him, or maybe he just did not believe that a centrist government would work out in the South, especially after the announcement in
March 1947 of the Truman Doctrine, in which America pledged support to
countries resisting communism. (Hodge would later say the Truman Doc-

trine "came at just the right time for us. It stopped the drift to the left and made the right secure.")[61] Whatever his reasons, the unsigned statement remained a draft, yet another reminder of the roads not taken in south Korea.

Despite his earlier ultimatum, Kim stayed on as chairman of the Interim Assembly. His sense of duty probably got the better of him. But his efforts to pass the coalition agenda ran into rightist obstruction. Conservative lawmakers absconded anytime a bill they did not like came up for a vote, leaving the assembly short of quorum.

They did this time and time again with land reform. In February 1947, Bunce teamed up with Yi Hun'gu to revive land reform in the South. The two men were kindred spirits: both were inspired by their Christian faith; both were disciples of the Wisconsin School (and thus steeped in agricultural science); and both were committed to remaking the Korean countryside through reform. If there was any daylight between them, it was in their views of capitalism. Bunce was a socialist critic of the system, whereas Yi believed its excesses could be regulated through incremental reform. Bunce supported redistribution without compensation to the landowners, while Yi wanted to see landlords paid for confiscated lands. They agreed that large Korean land holdings, as well as those formerly owned by the Japanese, should be included in the program.[62]

Bunce and Yi worked with the relevant committees in the assembly to draft a land reform bill. After months of wrangling, lawmakers emerged with a proposal that paid Korean landowners for confiscated lands and required poor farmers to pay for the lands they received. Some American advisers agreed that landowners should not be left empty-handed, as the advisers envisioned them playing an important role in modernizing Korea by converting landed wealth into factories and industries. In fact, a number of large landowners started to make the transition soon after liberation, the most notable being Ku Inhoe, who sold his vast landholdings in South Kyŏngsang to start the Lak-Hui Chemical-Industrial Corporation, which went on to become the present-day electronics giant LG.[63]

The NFPU decried the compromise legislation as a "KDP bill," viewing it as a giveaway to wealthy landowners. But the reformers did not object too strenuously since it closely resembled Bunce's earlier plan and the goal was to pass some form of land reform—the details were less important. "If we are to erect a strong foundation upon which a government can evolve into a democracy," Bertsch wrote, "a concrete program of land reform is a necessary part of our program."[64] Yet despite the concessions, the bill continued to stall in the Assembly owing to rightist obstruction. "The present legislature is," Roger Baldwin wrote, "too closely allied to landlords and pro-Japanese to pass bills with teeth."[65]

But the assembly was able to break the gridlock to pass anti-collaborator legislation. The rightist faction could have sunk the bill by denying quorum, which is, of course, what they did with land reform. Yet it passed, with revisions, on July 2. Conservative lawmakers could not just ignore the public outcry for justice. Koreans in the South wanted pro-Japanese collaborators punished. So they passed a watered-down bill. "The Rightists, comprising all the elected and several of the appointed members who had been largely men of substance under the Japanese," one US official wrote, "strove to draft a law in such broad terms that only notorious collaborators no longer living or, if living hiding in shame, would be affected."[66]

Kim Kyusik thought very few people would be convicted under the law and acknowledged it was "purely to save national face."[67] Would symbolism be enough for Koreans? Probably not, although some might argue that, while not exactly the same thing, the war crimes trials in Germany and Japan, where a small number of leaders (minus the Japanese emperor) were convicted, were just that. But at this point, symbolism was the best they would be able to manage given the rightist tilt of the assembly.

Yet even this law proved too much for the police. They issued a statement demanding General Hodge veto the legislation or else—threatening the commanding general was a new level of brazenness. Threats were also made against Major General Brown, who was slated to head the American team on the Joint Commission when it reconvened. Maybe Hodge lost his nerve, because the military government vetoed the bill. Kim Kyusik was told the language in the bill defining collaboration was too broad and therefore ripe for abuse. Officials claimed they wanted to avoid the widespread score settling that had led to a bloodbath in Europe. They also questioned whether an interim assembly was the appropriate body to pass such a sweeping law.

These arguments made little sense to Kim Kyusik, who defended the bill: "This law defines clearly the limit and extent of its application and it will be applied only when necessary evidence is obtained by the courts." He wanted to know what the point of creating SKILA was, if they were not going to be allowed to pass a law on a core issue like collaboration—it was a plank in the Coalition Committee's platform, after all. And why wait until now to let them know? American officials knew they had been working on the bill for months. Kim viewed the rejection as a no-confidence vote in SKILA and in the centrist coalition project more broadly.[68] To try to appease Kim, occupation officials promised to study the bill and return it with recommendations. It never came back.

The death knell for the centrist coalition came in the form of an assassin's bullet. Yŏ was gunned down on a sweltering summer afternoon in late July 1947, less than a hundred meters from a Seoul police station. According to American investigators, the police made no effort to apprehend the assailant. Yŏ was on his way to meet a US official from the Economic Cooperation Administration when he was shot dead. The assassin was a right-wing fanatic by the name of Han Chigŭn, who recently came from Pyongyang. He plotted to assassinate Kim Il Sung before coming to Seoul. No one believed he acted on his own. When Han was captured, he was at the same home as Kim Tuhan. American officials believed the order came from Kim Ku, Rhee, the police, or some combination of all three. Yet no one but Han Chigŭn was arrested.[69]

Bruce Cumings called Yŏ "a man for many seasons but not for the season of divided Korea and the Manichean world that eventually destroyed him."[70] This was undoubtedly true but it does not entirely explain why Yŏ wasn't *ever* able to find a political home. This was his perennial Achilles heel—he was a man without a party. Whether it was the KPG, the Communist Party, or Chiang Kai-shek's Nationalist Party, they would all disappoint, fail to live up to his ideals, and he would eventually leave. He always stayed above the fray, which contributed to his immense popularity, but politics sometimes required getting messy and working through conflict. For all of Yŏ's virtues, he was not a necessarily a fighter. Yŏ's biographer attributes his aversion for conflict to the childhood trauma of seeing his parents fight violently. According to Kim Samung, it was why he "took compromise and reconciliation as creed," though this might be a little too much armchair psychology.[71]

Tributes to the slain Korean leader came pouring in. Leonard Bertsch's in memoriam to Yŏ was published in *The Stars and Stripes*.

He harmed no one. Yet, he was coldly murdered by fiends who crave power for themselves rather than the freedom of their country. He

A mourner holds a portrait of Yŏ Unhyŏng at his funeral ceremony in August 1947.

Mongyang Memorial Museum

fought for his country and died for it. Let us hope that his blood will not have been spent in vain. He dared the Japanese oppressor. He was not deterred by imprisonment. The enemy feared and respected him. He loved the young people and he loved the poor. His heart was warm and he held no enmity toward his adversaries. His kindness never failed to shine in his expression. He sought no wealth, no comfort, no position, and died a poor man. To him, no one was too great and no one was too lowly. Everyone was his friend. He did not try to dominate the people. He loved them. He did not act great, but he was the greatest leader in modern Korea.[72]

The Coalition Committee called it quits in December 1947. The writing had been on the wall for months. Kim Kyusik formally dissolved the committee in a letter to General Hodge: "The reason for this decision was because we considered that since the death of Mr. Woon-hyung Lyuh who was really the initiator of the coalition movement, and with further changes of the political atmosphere internally and internationally, there seems to be no possibility of fully realizing the original aim of the committee."[73]

The reformers couldn't blame him. "We have played consistently into the hands of the rightists by our vacillating policies and our fear of disorder from labor and the left," Roger Baldwin explained. "We have muffed every opportunity to develop a democratic middle."[74]

8 Searching for a Way Out

Several months before Yŏ Unhyŏng's assassination, US Secretary of State George Marshall sent a private note to Soviet Foreign Minister Vyacheslav Molotov requesting the resumption of the Joint Commission. There had been few talks between the two sides since it had adjourned almost a year ago, but they were now all together in Moscow for a meeting of the foreign ministers. "The Government of the United States desires to further the work of establishing a free and independent Korea without additional delay," Marshall wrote to his Soviet counterpart. "I ask that you recommend to your Government to agree with the United States to reconvene the Joint Commission as soon as possible."[1]

At the suggestion of his undersecretary, Dean Acheson, Marshall blamed the Soviets for having failed to reach an agreement up to this point. "The Soviet commander has insisted on a formula which would result in eliminating the majority of representative Korean leaders from consultation," he wrote. "It has therefore been impossible to agree upon a basis for reconvening the Commission."[2]

Marshall's letter drew a testy response from Molotov: "The work of the Joint Soviet-American Commission . . . was suspended as a result of the fact that the American delegation took a stand contrary to the Moscow Agreement." He cited American support for "extremist groups" that violently opposed the Moscow decision. He then went on to discuss how the Soviets in the interim had been doing their part to democratize north Korea by supporting essential reforms, including land redistribution, universal suffrage, and women's and workers' rights. In a thinly veiled shot at the American military government, Molotov added that "such wide democratic reforms have been carried out in the North only."³ These sounded like fighting words. Still, at the end of his response, Molotov accepted Marshall's proposal to reconvene the Joint Commission. He even suggested the date and place: May 20, in Seoul.

The decision to reconvene the Joint Commission infuriated Syngman Rhee, who was back in Korea after spending three months in Washington, DC, lobbying for a separate government in the South. He and his allies sent off an angry letter to the US secretary of state, demanding an immediate withdrawal of occupation forces to make way for an interim southern government. "To us this is an indication that the Rhee-Kim Koo [Kim Ku] 'diehards' are preparing a last desperate effort to embarrass, if not sabotage, the work of the Joint Commission," William Langdon wrote to Marshall. He told the secretary to ignore the message: "Our impression is that the vast majority of the Korean people are jubilant over the news of the reconvening of the Joint Commission and prospect of a national provisional government."⁴ Rhee and his allies, however, refused to be ignored. Drawing from the playbook of Kim Ku, they tried to galvanize public opposition to reopening the commission by tying it to the dirtiest word in Korean politics. "The word trusteeship," Hodge wrote the State Department, "stands in the way of millions of Korean people who would otherwise support the Moscow decision."⁵

On May 18, General Albert Brown held a three-hour conference with rightist leaders to address their concerns. He tried to explain to them that the Joint Commission was being reconvened to expedite Korean independence. His assurances failed to persuade them—indeed, they threatened to boycott the Joint Commission. Langdon conceded that their actions were driven by "a real fear of the Russians." Hodge met the same group the next day, hoping that as commanding general he might be more persuasive, but the discussion went even worse. Rhee called Hodge a communist and accused him of using the Joint Commission to sell them out to the Soviets. "General Hodge sees little hope of getting needed cooperation of rightist groups with Joint Commission, and feels they will continue efforts to force the proceedings to break down in order that a separate government for South Korea may become an alternative," Langdon wrote to Marshall several days after the meeting.⁶

With the Right boycotting the Commission, the American delegation would only have leftist groups to choose from. Rhee did not believe for a

second that the Americans would allow a provisional government dominated by the communists to go forward. He was sure they would abandon the
Joint Commission before allowing that to happen. And, at this point, Americans would have no other choice but to back a separate government in the
South. Rhee's strategy required keeping the Right unified, but this was no
sure thing. KDP leaders, for one, feared being locked out of the commission
and unable to have a say in the future of their country. They also had reservations about Rhee becoming president, if the commission failed. "Rhee
would be a completely impossible president. Actually, you Americans have
never understood Dr. Rhee anymore than you have understood our Oriental
art," Police Chief Chang told Leonard Bertsch. "He is like a Buddha, only ad-
mirable when seen from a distance. Close up the defects are too noticeable."[7]

The partnership between Rhee and the KDP had always been a marriage
of convenience, held together by their shared hatred and fear of the Left.
The KDP provided Rhee with a political base and resources after he came
back to Korea nearly penniless. In return, Rhee provided a party of landed
and business elites, struggling with its collaborationist past, nationalist cover.[8] But cracks in the relationship began to appear in the summer of 1947.
And they were not just over the Joint Commission. "It cannot have escaped
Dr. Rhee's knowledge that Kim Sung Soo [Kim Sŏngsu] and his party have
been drifting away from him," Leonard Bertsch said to Hodge.[9] With the
demise of the Left in the South, the KDP felt free to break with Rhee. The
second in command and the real brains behind the party, Chang Tŏksu, had
been urging members against blindly following Rhee and his policies. A
civil war was brewing within the Right.

It was déjà vu all over again when the Joint Commission reopened on May
21, 1947. The streets of Seoul were once again lined with Koreans and uniformed honor guards to welcome the Soviet delegation. They were serenaded by the same marching band when they reached Tŏksu Palace. Even the
speeches sounded the same.[10] But there was an omission in the head delegate's remarks that gave US officials a glimmer of hope: "[The] State Department no doubt noted in Shtykov's bland address the absence of fulmina-
tions against reactionaries or other name-calling characteristics of last
year's address."[11]

There were other encouraging signs. American officials thought they had
clinched an agreement with the Soviets on the thorniest issue when Molo-

From left to right: Hŏ Hŏn; General Terentii Shtykov, head of the Soviet delegation; unknown figure in black suit; Yi Myo-muk, Lieutenant General John Hodge's
personal translator; Kim Kyusik; and Yŏ Unhyŏng at a reception for the reopening
of the Joint Commission in late May 1947, held several weeks before Yŏ's assassination.

Mongyang Memorial Museum

tov accepted their proposal to allow any party or organization that publicly
endorsed the Moscow decision—even if they had opposed it earlier—to
participate in the formation of a provisional government.[12] Also, Hodge believed the Rhee-Kim Ku faction had been effectively isolated. "Although I
do not believe Rhee, Kim Koo and other principal exile figures will participate in consultation," Hodge wrote to General MacArthur in June, "it appears now that many or most rightist groups may pull away from them and
will cooperate." Hodge, who previously had expressed skepticism about reconvening the Joint Commission, told MacArthur that there was "an even
chance we get results."[13]

The promising developments turned out to be false starts. Several weeks
into the negotiations, the two sides were back bickering over which groups
would be eligible for consultation. Picking up exactly where it left off, the
Soviet delegation held firm that consultations should only include those
parties that unequivocally supported the Moscow accords, while the Amer-

From left to right: General Terentii Shtykov; Lieutenant General John Hodge; and
Major General Albert Brown, head of the US delegation, on May 24, 1947, ex-
pressing optimism after they agreed to a framework for negotiations at the Second
Joint Commission, which gave hope that a deal to unify Korea could be reached.
National Archives (111-SC-284518)

icans revived their free speech argument. What happened to the compromise allowing all groups to participate as long as they signed onto Commu-
nique No. 5, declaring their support for the Moscow decision? The Soviets
argued that any of the signatories could easily go back on their word following consultation. Past deeds, they insisted, were a better gauge of sincerity
to cooperate.

American officials believed that this was merely an excuse to exclude
rightist groups and stack the provisional government with communists.
They may very well have been right. But Rhee's actions didn't help their
case. He was claiming that when he was in Washington, the State Department had promised it would establish a separate southern government—
but no such promise was ever made. In addition, Rhee's allies in the press
were spreading rumors that Hodge was not carrying out his directives and
the policy of his government. Rhee then publicly broke with the American

A throng of Koreans, led by Kim Ku, storm the gates of Tŏksu Palace to protest against the Second Joint Commission.

National Archives (111-SC-288648)

commander on July 3, 1947. "I realized that it was hopeless to expect anything new of General Hodge and we could not support him any longer," he said in a released statement. "Mr. Kim Koo and I said that we would take our own free actions."[14] They believed time was on their side. The longer the negotiations dragged out, the more the opposition would intensify. They were right.

"Political unrest in Korea is growing and becoming more violent as the meeting of the Joint Commission goes on," Hodge wrote in July. "Threats and bold terrorism on the part of rightest groups are on the increase and the voice of anti-trusteeship grows bolder and more blatant under the leadership of the still powerful Syngman Rhee."[15] With each passing day, the Right unaligned with Rhee grew more skittish about supporting the work of the Commission. Hodge asked the State Department to issue a public statement refuting Rhee's baseless charges, but officials worried that doing so would only amplify his "fire-eating campaign," like adding oxygen to a flame. So, instead, they first tried to get Rhee's allies in Washington, including his speechwriter, Robert Oliver, to get him to stop. That worked for a short while, but a few weeks later, Rhee went right back to the inflammatory rhetoric.

Hodge and Joseph Jacobs met with Rhee privately to try to appeal to him directly. They found that there was no reasoning with him. "At times Rhee conversed in a rational manner but at other times he burst into irrational tirades, speaking rapidly and almost unintelligibly," Hodge reported.[16] Rhee exhibited the same wild behavior to KDP leaders when he did not get what he wanted. The erratic behavior was a deliberate strategy to throw his adversaries off balance. If Rhee was crazy, as Police Chief Chang insisted to Hodge, he was crazy like a fox.[17] Ultimately, Americans were unable to appease Rhee because they could not offer him the one thing he truly wanted: to be president of a separate government in the South. "Rhee made it completely clear that he and his party would not participate in the work of the Joint Commission and would not accept anything that the Commission did unless satisfactory to him and his party," Hodge reported glumly to Marshall.[18]

They really only had two choices at this point: lock Rhee up or give in to his demands. Hodge certainly contemplated the first option. When he heard that President Truman was sending General A. C. Wedemeyer to survey conditions in Korea, Hodge quipped: "Rhee may listen to him, if he is still out of jail."[19] But once again Hodge just could not bring himself to do it. He trusted the Soviets and the communists even less than Rhee, though it got close at the end.

Thinking a change of scenery might be helpful, the two delegations agreed to move the Joint Commission to Pyongyang in late June. Joseph Jacobs, who had replaced Langdon as political adviser to General Hodge, was not encouraged by what he saw there: "Photos of Stalin and Korean stooge Kim Il Sung everywhere; Soviet and Korean flags everywhere; book stores full of Communist literature in Korean language; purging of non-Communists from government agencies; youths sent away for training and indoctrination . . . and so on." By this time, the Workers' Party, led by Kim Il Sung, had established itself as the dominant political force in the North; criticism and dissent were increasingly silenced and suppressed by the party. Jacobs thought that even if the Joint Commission was successful, the "foregoing situation will present difficult problem in the integration of North and South Korea."[20]

It never got that far. The two sides refused to budge from their original positions after months of negotiating. Toward the end, they couldn't even agree on meeting notes so they started producing separate reports. As the summer wore on, Hodge suspected the Soviets of intentionally stalling, knowing how dire the situation was getting in the southern zone. "It is my personal belief that [the] Joint Commission has little chance of success on any basis acceptable to the United States," Hodge wrote to the secretary of state in July. "There is [a] growing trend of information from North Korea to the effect that the Russians do not expect or intend the Joint Commission to succeed."[21]

By the end of summer 1947, the Joint Commission was hopelessly dead-locked, Yŏ Unhyŏng was dead, and Syngman Rhee was daily maligning Hodge in the press. It was taking a toll on the commanding general. "The Hodge who stood before that crowd today was a tired old man with a hard-ened face that rather frightened me," Owen Jones wrote in late July 1947. Jones didn't think Hodge would make it to the fall.[22]

A palpable sense of gloom had settled over the American occupation, with one State Department official remarking that "whatever we do now in Korea is bound to be bad. Our only hope is not to do worse."[23] These bad and worse policy options were made stark in a top-secret State-War-Navy Department memo: "With the manifest failure of the Joint Commission to unify Korea under a provisional government, the United States is obliged to decide whether it will continue to occupy South Korea for an indefinite period, or whether it will withdraw and permit the Soviet Union to domi-nate the entire peninsula. . . . If the US determines that its interests will be better served by remaining in Korea, it will have to face up to the responsi-bility it is assuming in regard to the Korean people."[24]

Frustrated with the stalemate, US officials eyed an exit strategy. Back in April, the War Department had floated the idea of withdrawing troops from Korea. "I am convinced," the secretary of war wrote to Marshall, "that the United States should pursue forcefully a course of action whereby we get out of Korea at an early date and believe all our measures should have early withdrawal as their overriding objective."[25] With the virtual collapse of the Joint Commission in August, the War Department's proposal now gained steamed. Given the US's growing global commitments, military planners insisted policymakers had to choose where they would make a stand against the Soviets. In 1947, the United States pledged to support and defend Greece and Turkey as part of the "Truman Doctrine" and unveiled the Marshall

Plan, a multibillion-dollar aid program to Western Europe, to curb the spread of communism. US strategists were also growing concerned about the ongoing civil war in China, where the communists had made significant military gains. They couldn't fight communism everywhere. In their minds, Korea was not that place; it just did not hold enough strategic value; in fact, most of the military brass considered it a strategic liability. That being the case, they were prepared to withdraw and cede the peninsula to the Soviets.[26]

But now the State Department insisted on holding on to half the peninsula. They agreed with military planners that Korea was not important on its own. However, officials at State envisioned Korea as part of a grand regional strategy—what Dean Acheson would later call the "Great Crescent"—in which a rehabilitated Japan would assume a major role in US–East Asia security.[27] "Korea would be a military liability," and thus the United States had "little strategic interest in maintaining troops or bases in Korea." And yet, "control of all Korea by Soviet or Soviet-dominated forces . . . would constitute a strategic threat to U.S. interests in East Asia."[28]

The State argument won the day (and really the next half century). After two years of fighting over nearly every aspect of occupation policy, the high command and liberal advisers finally agreed on something: an exit strategy. The military government, with the support of the State Department, referred the question of Korean independence to the United Nations. Officials had a good idea of how the exit strategy would play out. They assumed that the United Nations would establish a separate government in the southern zone of Korea, leaving the country indefinitely divided. They also understood that an election held in the American zone would likely give Rhee and his rightist supporters the majority of the seats in the new assembly.[29] These outcomes, while clearly not good, were the best of bad options—a way out.

Some liberal advisers agonized over the decision. Captain Owen Jones, who had returned to Korea as part of an economic mission led by Arthur Bunce, went back and forth on the policy. "I'm not at all certain that history will be any more charitable to us than to the Russians," Jones recorded in his diary in July 1947. "Somehow I'm left with the feeling that had we not had such an overwhelming fear and distrust of the Russians, we might have fared better."[30] In the end, however, he joined his liberal colleagues in adopting the Cold War line, conceding that "the Russian advance must be stopped and Korea is just another of the many places where we have to draw a line and stop it."[31]

On September 16, the secretary of state wrote to the Soviet ambassador in Washington, DC, letting him know the United States would be introducing the problem of Korean independence at the next session of the UN General Assembly. He explained that there was no hope of reaching agreement through the Joint Commission. Korea remained divided and the promise of independence seemed no closer to being fulfilled. "The US Govt believes that this situation must not be permitted to continue indefinitely," he wrote.[32]

A week later, at one of the final meetings of the Joint Commission in Seoul, General Shtykov made a surprise counteroffer. "The Soviet delegation considers that it is possible to afford the Koreans an opportunity to form a government by themselves without the aid and participation of the Allies," he read from a statement. "If the American delegation would agree with a proposal for the withdrawal of all foreign troops during the beginning of 1948, the Soviet troops will be ready to evacuate Korea simultaneously with the American troops." He even offered to bring prominent Koreans from the North and South together to jump-start the process. General Brown was so flustered by Shtykov's proposal that he adjourned the meeting right then and there, saying he "was not authorized to discuss such a matter which was beyond the scope of the Moscow Agreement."[33]

The clever move put Americans in a bind. "If the Soviet proposal for mutual withdrawal is not accepted soon, we may next be confronted by a declaration on the part of the Soviets that they are withdrawing their troops regardless of whether we do or not," Jacobs wrote to the secretary of state. "This they can safely do, in view of the North Korean Army which they leave behind and the continued proximity of their own armed forces to Korea." If this were to happen, he worried, "we shall be left in the unenviable position both at the UN and here of continuing our military occupancy of South Korea."[34]

Rhee immediately put out a strongly worded statement opposing the Soviet proposal. But wasn't this what he had been calling for since coming back from Washington? He had been bluffing; Rhee knew very well that the North was in a stronger position militarily and that the withdrawal of foreign troops would result in the communist domination of the peninsula. He, therefore, added an addendum to his prior demand. "As we hold the US partly responsible for the division of our country, the US must not and cannot pull out until we have had time to evolve order and peace caused by foreign co-occupation," he contended. "We demand that the US maintain a small force of security in South Korea without interference in our sovereign rights until we organize our government according to the will of the people" and a "South Korean army is constituted."[35] Rhee did not want the Yankees to go home just yet.

The United States obliged, though not because of Rhee. Much of the American strategy for East Asia hinged on sticking to the original plan. The only question was what to do with the Soviet proposal to withdraw simultaneously so as not to look bad. Ultimately, the United States decided to include their offer as part of a package of proposals for the UN to consider. "With these proposals," the US representative at the UN wrote to Secretary General Trygve Lie, "it is hoped the General Assembly will be able to recommend measures for an orderly transition from the present systems of government in north and south Korea to an independent, united Korean government and the consequent speedy withdrawal of all occupying forces."[36]

The decision to refer the issue of Korean independence to the UN deepened the rift between Rhee and the KDP. At a November meeting, party leaders informed Rhee that they opposed his call for a separate election in the South. According to witnesses, Rhee went "into an ungovernable rage, stamping about the room and screaming at them, and had called them traitors."

Several days later, Leonard Bertsch met for lunch with KDP heads Kim Sŏngsu and Chang Tŏksu to discuss several matters. As they walked out of the restaurant, Chang pulled Bertsch aside to speak to him privately. He expressed concern for Kim's life, telling Bertsch that he "was being pursued by men who intended to kill him, and that he felt that Kim was not taking the matter sufficiently seriously." Chang should have been worried about his own safety: he was shot to death by two men in police uniforms outside his home less than thirty-six hours later.

Police Chief Chang, who was a close friend of Chang Tŏksu, believed that the assassins were "extreme rightists." He told Bertsch, "They acted under the direction of highly placed men and you know whom I mean." American intelligence indicated Rhee and Kim Ku had met a few nights before Chang's murder. While acknowledging he had no direct evidence, Bertsch believed "it to be probable that the current efforts to assassinate Kim Sung Soo [Kim Sŏngsu], and the successful effort to assassinate Chang Duk Soo [Chang Tŏksu] received the belated consent of Syngman Rhee at the meeting on November 30."

Syngman Rhee and his Austrian wife, Francesca Donner, attend the funeral of
Chang Tŏksu on December 8, 1947.
National Archives (111-SC-296459)

Kim Ku despised the whole KDP lot. He thought the entire party was
made up of feckless men who got rich staying home while he and the other
exiles sacrificed and toiled for Korean independence. But he harbored a
special hatred for Chang Tŏksu, whom he called "a running dog of the Japanese." The feeling went both ways. Chang considered Kim an uncouth,
revolutionary hothead who was "too stupid to deserve political influence."[37]
Kim knew Chang from the early days of the Korean independence movement, when Chang was the editor of the nationalist paper *Tonga ilbo* ("The
East Asian Daily"). By the 1930s, however, Chang was one of the loudest
supporters of Japanese assimilation policies. And during the Second World
War, he advised the Japanese Army in Seoul, recruited Korean youth for
military service, bought large amounts of war bonds, and even ran a "reed-
ucation camp" for political prisoners. Bertsch confirmed that Chang "coop-

erated heartily with the Japanese, spoke violently against American barbar-
ianism, and now cooperates heartily with the Americans and would in turn
cooperate heartily with the Russians."[38] Kim would have moved on Chang
Tŏksu sooner but he was restrained by Rhee, who insisted "that these people were useful to him and must be protected." But now that the KDP was
withholding support from Rhee, it appeared their usefulness had worn out.

The assassination of Chang threw Hodge into a rage. His initial instinct
was to lock up Kim and send Rhee into exile. But like so many times before with
the two leading rightists, he backed off. Instead, to humiliate him, Hodge
forced Kim to testify at Chang's murder trial in order to implicate his under-
lings. Two of Kim's associates were convicted for the murder, despite their
confessions to the police that it was Kim who ordered the hit. Ironically,
Chang's death—by the furor it ignited—probably saved Kim Sŏngsu's life.[39]

On November 14, the UN General Assembly adopted a resolution calling for
general elections in Korea no later than March 31, 1948. The resolution also
created the United Nations Temporary Commission on Korea (UNTCOK) to
oversee the elections. Comprised of representatives from Australia, Canada,
(Nationalist) China, El Salvador, France, India, Syria, and the Philippines, the
commission was given the mandate to "facilitate and expedite" the holding of
peninsula-wide elections to establish a National Government of Korea.[40]

Before the resolution passed, the Soviet Union and its allies tried to get
the General Assembly to consider their proposal to withdraw from Korea
simultaneously, but it didn't receive a vote. They called the UN body "a tool
of American imperialism," and vowed "to have nothing to do with the
Commission."[41] They pointed to the part of the resolution that assigned
seats in the Assembly according to population as being especially one-sid-
ed, since the South had almost double the number of people in the North.
(The North's strategy of "encouraging" southbound migration, especially
among its conservative elements, came back to haunt them, but even at the
start of the occupation, the South had about 50 percent more people.) The
UN had also invited the Ukrainian Soviet Socialist Republic to appoint a
representative to the commission, but they refused in protest.

American officials had to strong-arm some of its allies into participating.
The Canadian prime minister, Mackenzie King, had decided to withdraw
his country from the commission. He told his cabinet that he refused to be
used "as the cat's paw of United States policy." (Australia had similar misgiv-

ings.) For weeks, the US State Department, including Undersecretary of State Robert Lovett; Joseph Jacobs, who was back stateside; and Dean Rusk, now the director of the Office of Special Political Affairs, staged a full-court press on Canadian officials.

A few of their messages carried threatening overtones. "Should Canada on the eve of its taking its seat in the Security Council feel constrained to limit its responsibilities, I [feel] that this would be a very serious decision. It would undoubtedly give rise to speculation in Congress and in the press that Canada embarked on a new course of restricting its role in international affairs," Lovett explained to the Canadian envoy sent to Washington, DC. "If that were the case, its position as a member of the Security Council and its interests . . . would have to be regarded in an entirely new light."[42]

The pressure campaign worked to some extent. Prime Minister King agreed to participate in the commission but only if elections were held for the whole of Korea. He would withdraw his representative if the elections were held in the South only.[43] With Canada back in the fold, the UNTCOK team planned to depart for Seoul shortly after the new year.

Rhee responded coolly to the UN resolution. He did not want to wait for UNTCOK to hold elections. "As [a] first step toward a proper solution, South Korea should hold elections for congress without further delay, as promised [to me] by the United States State Dept and AMG [American military government] nearly a year ago," Rhee said a few days later, continuing the big lie. "This interim election will set up interim govt which will consult and cooperate with United Nations Commission when here." He claimed that a massive crowd of over a hundred thousand had gathered at Tongdaemun Stadium to support his call for immediate elections. Rhee insisted that the elections "will only take a few weeks as we are well prepared for it if General Hodge cooperates."

Conservative political adviser Joseph Jacobs doubted Rhee's numbers: "The estimates of our own agents who attended meeting and who are usually generous in their estimates were that only 25,000 attended." He also feared Rhee's intentions for the elections. Jacobs took his statement "we are well prepared" to mean that his "minions through intimidation and terrorism will control all votes." He continued, "This is one of the best indices of Rhee's concept of democracy, which so readily lends itself to Soviet charges that Rhee is reactionary, pro-Japanese and Fascist."[44]

Days before the UN Commission was supposed to arrive, Rhee huddled with top Korean police officials to tell them of his plans to oust Hodge. According to US intelligence, "Rhee intimated that he was considering, but had not decided upon, a policy of open disobedience and mass striking, which would probably force the American government to remove the Commanding General." Rhee wanted to know if he could "count upon the loyal support of the police" in such a scenario.[45]

Desperate for an alternative to the "old man," which was how Hodge referred to Rhee toward the end of the occupation, the general brought back Philip Jaisohn (Sŏ Chaep'il was his Korean name) to run for president whenever the elections were held. Jaisohn was a longtime independence activist who took refuge in the United States after being forced to flee Korea in 1898. Inspired by the First Continental Congress of the United States, Jaisohn organized the first Korean Congress in Philadelphia (1921), and was one of the biggest overseas donors to the Korean independence movement, which eventually forced him into bankruptcy. One of the people he supported was none another than an ambitious former student, Syngman Rhee.

Hodge had invited Jaisohn back to Korea to serve as a senior adviser to the military government in the summer of 1947, before he asked him to run for the presidency. Jaisohn only entertained the idea because he was disturbed by what his former pupil had become. But it was hard to see how this plan would work; Jaisohn was eighty-three and had been gone from Korea for over four decades. The attempt reeked of desperation. But before the general could even get to this part of the plan, he needed to make sure that the UN-sponsored elections would take place.

9   Fighting over Separate Elections

The UN commission arrived in Seoul on a bitterly cold evening in January 1948. Despite freezing temperatures, Koreans lined the streets for miles, waving Korean flags and holding signs that read "saviors of Korean independence," as the team's motorcade snaked through Seoul on its way from the airport to the hotel. Police estimates put the crowds at more than a quarter million. The assistant general secretary of the UN, Victor Hoo, who accompanied the team, was impressed with "the spontaneous welcome accorded to the United Nations Commission by the Korean people." He only regretted that he couldn't see more of the cheering throngs given the late hour.[1]

At a formal welcome at Tongdaemun Stadium on January 12, the temporary chair of UNTCOK, Indian delegate Kumara Menon, declared to the packed house that the sole goal of the commission was "the consummation of the independence of Korea." He called for national unity, insisting that without it there could be no independence. "As an Indian I can say this with feeling," Menon asserted. "Certain portions of India have formed themselves into separate states. This was a bitter blow to us who believed in national unity." (The summer prior, the Indian subcontinent had been divided into two nations: India, with a Hindu majority, and Pakistan, predominately Muslim.) He continued, "In India there was a plausible pretext for those who advocated partition. But in Korea there is not even this excuse. Nothing is more remarkable than the homogeneity of the Korean people." He called the 38th parallel an artificial separation that "was not meant to divide Korea forever."[2]

Menon's words would be tested a few days later when the commission learned that the Soviet Union had rejected its offer to oversee peninsu-

Delegates to the United Nations Temporary Commission on Korea are greeted by
Koreans bearing flowers upon their arrival on January 8, 1948. From left to right:
Yasin Mughir and Zeki Djabi of Syria, Kumara P. S. Menon of India, Liu Yuwan of
China, and Victor Hoo of China, Assistant Secretary General of UN.
National Archives (111-SC-298026)

la-wide elections and refused to give them access to the North. Soviet officials slammed the commission as a rubber stamp for the imperialist designs
of the United States. The Americans fired back, saying the Soviets just did
not want UNTCOK to see what was happening in the North. There was
probably some truth to both charges.

The news left the UNTCOK team in limbo. Their mandate was to oversee
elections for all of Korea, so now what would they do?

Hodge and the military government urged UNTCOK to proceed with the
elections in the South alone if the Soviets continued to refuse to participate.
A majority of the commission balked at the suggestion. It was not what
their mandate called for, and they feared that holding separate elections

would ruin any chance of reunifying the country. Moreover, they did not find the necessary conditions for free and fair elections in the South. In meetings with military government officials, Korean leaders, civil authorities, and election officials, they were told over and over again about the lack of free speech, press, and assembly, trials without juries, and the detention of thousands of political prisoners without due process. As a onetime prisoner of conscience, Syrian delegate Zeki Djabi demanded immediate amnesty for all political prisoners at the first meeting of the commission.

But what concerned UNTCOK most was the police state, which they observed firsthand when they tried to interview the heads of the Federation of Korean Trade Unions, the Farmer's Union, and the Women's Democratic Alliance. They discovered that these leftist and center-left leaders "were either in prison, under order of arrest, or under some form of police surveillance." And despite being given full immunity, none of them accepted requests for interviews, citing a "lack of confidence in the assurances given by the authorities."[3]

UNTCOK saw such conditions as favoring the major parties of the Right, "since they appear to have the advantage of some influence in the South Korean administration." The leftist parties, on the other hand, did not "enjoy the same favorable position and thus have not been able to maintain an effective and comprehensive framework of organization."[4] Yasin Mughir, the alternate Syrian delegate, put it more bluntly, calling right-wing activity "strong" and "blatant" in the South. The UN delegates later learned that the welcome at Tongdaemun Stadium had been sponsored entirely by the conservatives. Richard Johnston, the *New York Times* reporter in Seoul, dubbed it a "Rightist show."[5] It included the KDP, who now backed Rhee's demands for separate elections, after the US plans for south Korea became clear, although the rift between the two sides remained.

The military government trotted out legal advisers Charles Pergler and Ernst Fraenkel to defend its record on civil liberties. Pergler, a former Czech émigré, was dean of the National University College of Law in Washington, DC, and an expert on constitutional law. Fraenkel was a German-Jewish lawyer who opposed Nazi rule before fleeing to the United States in 1938. His book, *The Dual State: A Contribution to the Theory of Dictatorship*, which went on to become the classic study on the legal origins of totalitarianism in Nazi Germany, was published in 1941.

In presentations to the commission, the two legal scholars highlighted the AMG's efforts to promote civil liberties in south Korea. Pergler cited the

numerous Japanese laws that had been abolished under the military government, including those that discriminated on the basis of race, religion,
and nationality. "The spirit of the Military Government has been in favor of
civil liberties," he maintained. "That has a distinct bearing on the question
of free air for elections."

Fraenkel spent his time discussing the progress being made toward re-
forming the police. "The Japs had, so to speak, a dual judicial system. Criminal procedures could be carried out under the Japanese first by courts and
secondly by the police proper." This frequently led to convictions without
due process, he told the commission. Fraenkel touted how the military government ended the police power to administer summary justice. "This was
the first step taken by us in order to curb the power of the police in an extremely important field."[6]

In the questioning period, however, skeptical representatives kept coming back to the police. Australian representative S. H. Jackson said that "the
police we have here are, for the most part, Japanese-trained. They have been
operating under Japanese regulations, and their material is Japanese trained
material." Fraenkel acknowledged the colonial elements in the police force
but justified them on the practical grounds that "the Japanese did not permit the Koreans to study matters which had some practical significance . . .
we just did not have the people here, and in that managerial vacuum we had
to take the people we had."

Canadian delegate George Patterson followed up by asking whether it
would be possible to "go much further in removing these policemen?" Neither adviser directly answered his question, knowing full well that General
Hodge would never agree to it. Instead Pergler pointed to a recent order that
barred the police from joining political organizations. Signaling his dissatis-
faction, an exasperated Patterson wanted to know "if there is not something
more dramatic which can be done to promote a confidence in the people."[7]

Back in January, Hodge gave a full-throated defense of the Korean police
to the War Department. He praised them for their "excellent and patriotic
service." "Without them," Hodge told his superiors, "the October 1946
Communist Revolution would have succeeded." He acknowledged that the
Koreans hated the police, but it was because "Koreans do not like control in
any shape or form." But as "Oriental police go," Hodge wrote, "Korean police are doing a good job, [and] are comparatively democratic and reason-
ably effective." He talked about "certain basic handicaps," foremost among
them, "the stubborn character and psychology of the Korean people, their

resistance to sudden changes and their complete lack of political and social sensings beyond their own experiences under 4,000 years of feudalism and 40 years of Japanese oppression."[8]

The State Department's support for elections in the South put Fraenkel and Pergler in the uncomfortable position of defending policies they themselves had criticized. Both advisers privately agreed with UNTCOK's assessment of the police, having had their own fights with Police Chief Cho Pyŏngok over police procedure and personnel. They both viewed the South as a police state, and if anyone could recognize one, it would be Fraenkel, who narrowly had escaped the Gestapo in September 1938. Fraenkel thought "the terrorism under the South Korean police is such" that the UN might find that "free elections can't be held." He told Owen Jones that "the sins of two years are finding us out."[9] And, in fact, representatives Djabi and Jackson wanted to report back to the United Nations "that South Korea is a police state where no free atmosphere for elections exist," but the other UNTCOK members voted down the idea.[10]

The commission was divided over how to proceed. The Indian, Syrian, Australian, and Canadian representatives expressed grave concerns with supervising elections in the South alone. Delegates from China, El Salvador, and the Philippines, on the other hand, argued that the lack of Soviet cooperation left them no choice but to carry out their mandate in the South where they had access. Deadlocked, UNTCOK requested additional guidance from the UN Interim Committee (also known as the Little Assembly), which acted in place of the General Assembly when it was out of session.[11]

US occupation officials complained vociferously about commission members. Political adviser Joseph Jacobs called S. H. Jackson a "big problem," who was "definitely anti-American" and "clearly came to Korea with the preconceived idea of showing us up." "From the beginning," he wrote to the secretary of state, "he has taken the lead in the commission to find dirt on our administration here, under the guise of trying to discover whether a 'free atmosphere' exists in South Korea for the holding of fair elections."[12]

Hodge similarly blasted the trio of Jackson, Patterson, and Djabi as Soviet "apologists" and "appeasers" who "added greatly to the strength of the Communists' propaganda, as well as give the Communists new slogans for their attack against elections in south Korea."[13] He blamed them for the "snowballing loss of faith in the UN commission," telling the secretary that it was directly because of their "vacillation, fumbling, lack of unanimity, and uncertainty and inaction."[14]

The problem was that the Americans' own officials had raised many of the same concerns. Shortly after the UN vote in November 1947, General A. C. Wedemeyer undertook his fact-finding mission in Korea. Reporting on conditions, he condemned both rightist and leftist groups "for creating unrest and fomenting disorder" on the peninsula. But it was his evaluation of the Korean National Police that most alarmed American officials, since it cast serious doubt on the possibility for democratic elections in the South. "So long as there is no reform of the present police system and police brutality," Wedemeyer wrote, "there is little hope that a government can be established fully representative of the freely expressed will of the Korean people in South Korea." He noted that there were more political prisoners now than at the height of Japanese rule. Under existing conditions, he was certain that rightists, led by Syngman Rhee and Kim Koo, "would gain control of any government established in South Korea by such elections."[15]

Wedemeyer's assessment lined up closely with the judgment of Canadian representative Patterson, who told Hodge over dinner that the reason he opposed separate elections in south Korea was because "they will result in reactionary rightists getting in and they will maintain themselves in power for years to come."[16] Patterson thought his country had blundered badly by sending him to Korea without first reaching an understanding with the Soviet Union. The prime minister, Mackenzie King, had made it clear to him before his departure that he wanted nothing to do with the permanent division of Korea. King had seen this act the year before with Palestine, where the UN intervened in a similar manner. He had wanted to avoid Canadian involvement in the Palestine question, but under pressure from the United States, he reluctantly acquiesced to a UN proposal in 1947 to split Palestine into separate Jewish and Arab states. King vowed not to repeat the same mistake in Korea.[17]

But now Patterson was stuck in Korea, where he was entirely dependent on the US military government for housing, transportation, and communication. His government called him back to Tokyo, where he had been stationed prior to Korea, while UNTCOK waited for a response from the Interim Committee. While Patterson was in Japan, Canadian officials reiterated to him that they would not support separate elections in the South.[18]

Meanwhile, the US military government, in an attempt to present a separate election as a foregone conclusion, set a date without UN approval: May 9, 1948. (It was later changed to May 10, because of a solar eclipse on the previous day, considered a bad omen by the Korean people.) General Hodge also pressured UNTCOK members individually to immediately announce that the commission would oversee elections in the South. He did not want them to wait to hear back from the United Nations; he wanted the elections to be a done deal.[19]

Kim Kyusik complicated these efforts at a press conference, following his meeting with UNTCOK. To a reporter's question as to whether the UN commission should supervise elections in the South alone, he answered: "If the Commission cannot carry out its original mission, then it should refer Korea question back to interim committee for re-examination." Elaborating further, he said that "if the UN Commission observes elections and sets up government in south Korea only, it will merely perpetuate division of country into north and south." In a surprise move, he insisted that "there should be a conference of leaders of both north and south Korea under supervision of the UN Commission."[20]

He received support from an unlikely source. Appearing at the same meeting with UNTCOK, Kim Ku testified forcefully that "there must be a meeting of leaders of both north and south Korea after withdrawal of both US and Soviet Troops and there could be no national election without participation of north Korean people." Kim's plan sounded a lot like the Soviet proposal. According to Joseph Jacobs, Kim came out "rather strongly [that] he would work with Kimm Kiusic and other middle of the road leaders," so much so he didn't think it would be the worst backup plan if the Interim Committee ruled against separate elections in the South.[21]

What explains Kim Ku's sudden change of heart? The cynical answer would be that Kim realized he had no chance of being president. If he had been the frontrunner instead of Rhee, maybe he would have continued to advocate for separate elections. But it was also true that Kim genuinely feared that his country would be left permanently fractured if they went through with them. "Kim Koo finds it impossible to cooperate in the coming elections, because he does not wish to play a part in the permanent division of Korea," is what his closest adviser told Leonard Bertsch. "He believes that those who do play such a part will merit the eternal hatred of the people, who will someday classify them as national traitors." Perhaps it was a case of too little, too late, but this is where Kim stood now.[22]

What happened to Kim's partnership with Rhee? Kim thought Rhee's rule or bust mission would lead to Korea's ruin. But their differences went deeper than that. As Bertsch explained, "There is no political or personal

Syngman Rhee and Kim Ku shake hands in a show of solidarity after Chang Tŏksu's assassination. Kim was afraid the
military command would take punitive action against him
and asked Rhee to participate in the publicity stunt, who
reluctantly agreed.
Wikimedia Commons

affection between the two men, there is merely a temporary alliance for
limited purposes." Their public ceremonies of affection—including a famous
picture of the two men shaking hands after Chang Tŏksu's assassination—
concealed a simmering rivalry. Kim Kyusik confirmed the breach between
the two men in January 1948, saying that he "believed it to be permanent."[23]

"The hatred of the two men," according to Bertsch, "is rooted in part in
personal jealousy, in part in the over-weaning vanity of each and in part in

the radically different character of their training and of their present support." Kim's camp regarded Rhee's supporters as a bunch of pro-Japanese collaborators, while Rhee's followers viewed Kim's people as a ragtag group of revolutionary has-beens. The two rivals also had different political bases; not all rightists were the same, as ideology and class divided them.

Part of their rivalry stemmed from the fact that Rhee came back to Korea with no financial support, which forced him to rely heavily on wealthy Korean benefactors. Kim, on the other hand, had secured a large donation from the Kuomintang, the Chinese Nationalist Party, before leaving for Korea in November 1945. Of course this did not stop Kim from accepting assistance from rich Koreans with checkered pasts—he had accepted a villa from the gold-mining mogul Ch'oe Ch'anghak, after all. But it did mean that Kim was less beholden to wealthy conservatives for his support.

The consummate historian, Bertsch compared the relationship between Kim and Rhee to the triumvirate formed during the Roman Republic. Like Julius Caesar and Pompey, he explained, "Each man regards the other with fear and dislike, and each hopes to eliminate the other after having come to power through joint efforts."[24] With the separate elections, their rivalry had spilled into the open. There could only be one Caesar.

Back at the UN, the United States put forward a resolution recommending that UNTCOK carry out its mission in the South alone. In late February, the Interim Committee voted 31 to 2 in favor of the resolution. The Canadian and Australian delegates were the two lone holdouts. The committee relayed the vote and recommendation to UNTCOK. But even before UNTCOK had a chance to meet to discuss the recommendation, the acting chair of the commission, Liu Yuwan, publicly announced on March 1 that UNTCOK would observe elections in the South no later than May 10. General Hodge had been hounding Liu for days to set an election date. When the news reached Canada, government officials immediately telegraphed Patterson in Tokyo to instruct him to oppose the statement, publicly if necessary. If UNTCOK proceeded with the recommendation, Patterson was instructed to withdraw from the commission right away.

When UNTCOK met on March 9, Patterson, having returned from Tokyo, pressed the other members to issue a public statement saying that Liu's March 1 announcement was his own view, not the official position of the commission. But Patterson's proposal was defeated by a vote of 3 to 2, with

China, El Salvador, and the Philippines voting no; Canada and India voting yes; and Australia, Syria, and France abstaining.

Immediately after the vote, Patterson announced to the other members that he could no longer participate in commission activities and walked out of the meeting. The remaining members, stunned by his sudden withdrawal, quickly decided to vote again on Patterson's proposal. In the second round, the representatives who had formerly abstained joined India in voting in favor, while the former no votes flipped to abstentions. In hopes of luring Patterson back, the group released a statement saying that Liu's announcement was informal and the issue was still being decided by the commission.

Canada's withdrawal from the commission threatened to throw UNTCOK into a crisis of legitimacy. Americans viewed such a scenario as an existential threat to their exit strategy. So the United States, with assistance from its allies, dialed up the diplomatic pressure on Canada. In Washington, the State Department confronted the Canadian ambassador over Patterson's actions. In China, the minister of foreign affairs berated the Canadian ambassador to China for his country's opposition to separate elections in Korea.[25] And in Seoul, American officials met with Canada's UN representative, George McNaughton, and George Patterson to try to change their minds. Hodge invited Patterson over for dinner at his quarters to "talk informally."[26]

The pressure seemed to work. Patterson rejoined UNTCOK on March 12 during a session in which the divided commission agreed to "observe" the elections. But the meaning of "observe" was unclear. Were they approving the separate elections or not? The ambiguous language reflected the deep divisions within the commission. Jackson had introduced a resolution recommending that UNTCOK withdraw from Korea by April 15, which was ultimately voted down. In a compromise, the commission added a proviso to the agreement to observe the elections, requiring that "the elections will be held in a free atmosphere wherein democratic rights of freedom of speech, press, and assembly be recognized and respected."[27] Clearly, reforms would be necessary to get UNTCOK's approval.

Liberal advisers had made another push for their agenda after the UN adopted the resolution on Korea, starting with land reform. The Bunce-Yi land bill had languished in committee for months, and never received a vote on the floor of the Interim Assembly. Conservative lawmakers continued to block the bill by absconding before the vote. With reform looking all but dead, the price of land doubled, giving landowners an opportunity to sell their land at the highest price since liberation.[28]

However, with the elections on the horizon, occupation officials eyed a revival of the land reform bill. In fact, the day Leonard Bertsch met with KDP leaders for lunch—right before Chang Tŏksu's assassination—he was trying to convince them to drop their opposition to land reform. "The establishment of a sound and liberal system of land tenure, based on the wider ownership of the land by those who till the soil" Bertsch argued, "will go far toward a basis of solution of many of our economic problems."[29]

KDP leaders talked a good game about wanting land reform, but then they would find some excuse to drag their feet. Two months earlier, legislators had agreed to strip Korean-owned lands from the bill at their request. Despite the concession, lawmakers aligned with the KDP continued to refuse to allow the bill to come up for a vote. Shifting the goalposts yet again, they now talked about the need to wait for an independent government to be established before passing land reform legislation.[30]

"The real problem," a frustrated Hodge told the War Department, "is to get legislators who give lip service to the necessity of land reform to support and vote for program . . . *on the floor* of legislature."[31] His military governor had stressed the importance of this matter "with legislative leaders who are already aware of doing something to combat Leftist propaganda among the peasants in South Korea" and reminded them of the "urgent importance of removing this cause for criticism before the next elections."[32]

Hodge wanted the Koreans to carry out land reform by passing legislation in SKILA. But after the Interim Assembly adjourned without passing a bill in March 1948, the US military government decided it could not wait any longer, not with UNTCOK's approval of the upcoming elections on the line. Land reform was the quickest way to firm up support in the South. Several days after SKILA adjourned, Major General William F. Dean, who became military governor in October 1947, announced that the AMG would redistribute former Japanese lands to tenant farmers.

The AMG's land redistribution program allowed landless tenants to purchase between one and six acres of land. They would pay for the land on installment over a fifteen-year period at an annual rate of 20 percent of the harvest, with slight variations depending on the crop. Bunce and Yi added provisions to ensure that the lands stayed in the hands of the peasants. They banned the sale or mortgaging of land during the fifteen-year period; as an added incentive, new landowners earned equity on the land each year they held onto it. The redistributed land accounted for 20 percent of all farming lands in the South. "500,000 households will become free landowners in a free country," Military Governor Dean declared with great fanfare.[33]

The announcement did not exactly get the response Americans were hoping for. As expected, leftist groups like the NFPU harshly criticized the plan as a half-measure that failed to deliver on the promise of land reform. They renewed calls for land redistribution without payment and for large Korean estates to be included in the program. Their demands inspired pockets of resistance to the sale of former Japanese lands in the countryside, though they were quickly put down by the combined forces of the police and military.[34]

It wasn't only the Left that protested. The Kungsam-myŏn peasants in Naju also refused to participate in the redistribution program, despite the urging of American officials. They held firmly to the idea that they should not have to pay for lands that were rightfully theirs. In defiance, they continued to farm the land without paying rent. It would be another two decades before most Kungsam-myŏn peasants got their land back, and they would have to pay for it. None of the original petitioners, including Na Chaegi, lived to see it.[35]

Even the Federation of Korean Farmers, an anti-communist farmer's organization backed by Syngman Rhee, believed that redistributing Japanese lands alone was not enough. (The Federation was the farmers' equivalent of the conservative labor organization, Taehan Noch'ong.)[36] Rhee and Kim had joined their advisory board in August 1947 in an attempt to build a base of support among conservative peasants. The federation, along with every other farmer's group in the South, kept up the drumbeat for expanding land reform to include large Korean landholdings.[37]

Their persistence paid off. In 1950, on the eve of the Korean War, South Korea passed a land reform bill, which at long last broke up and redistributed large Korean estates. Under the bill, the government redistributed 26 percent of total farmland, including 40 percent of tenanted lands, to poor peasants. No one was allowed to own more than eight acres of land, which approximated the reform that took place in North Korea back in 1946. The reform bill destroyed feudalism once and for all in South Korea, including the traditional power of the *yangban*, the former landed gentry. By 1957, most farms in the South were operated by small, independent farmers, just as Yi Hun'gu and Arthur Bunce had envisioned.[38]

But the 1950 land reform proved to have a double edge. It compensated landowners and gave them first crack at buying former Japanese properties at a discount. This Faustian bargain enabled the largest and most powerful landlords to maintain—and in some cases, grow—their political and economic power. Ku Inhoe of LG and Ch'oe Chonghyŏn of SK Group were examples of big landlords who turned their landed wealth into future *chaebols*. Ch'oe started the SK Group—currently one of the five biggest conglomerates in South Korea—with the purchase of a former Japanese textile company.[39] These *chaebols* would help fuel South Korea's rapid development—the "Miracle on the Han"—but the concentration of economic power also entrenched political corruption and contributed to widening class inequality in South Korea. It is no coincidence that the country is the home of *Parasite* and *Squid Games*.[40]

The reforms kept coming. After land redistribution came an announcement on new criminal procedures, which among other things enshrined trial by jury and barred arrests without warrant. This was followed by an order from the military governor that pardoned thousands of political prisoners, many of whom had been held without due process—though thousands more, detained mainly for labor protests, continued to languish in prison. Finally, in a dramatic public appearance more typical of his commanding officer, General MacArthur, Hodge proclaimed the inviolable liberties of the Korean people with a new Bill of Rights. Incorporating elements from the newly adopted Japanese constitution and American Bill of Rights, Hodge's proclamation included guarantees of equality before the law, freedom of speech, assembly, and association, and the right to vote.[41]

The moment was not as inspirational as it seemed. "It was promulgated," Jacobs later told the secretary of state, "largely to meet the insistent queries of the United Nations Temporary Commission on Korea, in connection with that Commission's interest in the maintenance of a free atmosphere for elections to be observed by it, as to the substantive legal basis for civil liberties in South Korea."[42] Indeed, the need for UN approval had transformed General Hodge from a guardian of the status quo to a zealous reformer—save for one area. He adamantly refused to make changes to the police.[43] "The police have had wide power. They have to, in a war or in an occupation under conditions we face here," he lectured the commission. "As I explained to you, we have had continuously to wage what might be called a war against subversion, and the active forces need wide power or they could not function." Under these circumstances, Hodge argued, "we are underpoliced in South Korea."[44]

Yet to allay the commission's concerns, Hodge promised that "every effort is being made and will be made to exercise proper control over and direct the activities of the police toward free elections."[45] He saw to the task of securing police compliance personally. For the entire occupation, he had explicitly ordered his advisers not to interfere in the internal affairs of the Korean police. But at this point, a case of police misconduct or excess could sabotage America's exit strategy. In late March, the general addressed a combined meeting of provincial governors and police chiefs in Seoul. He impressed upon them the necessity for a free atmosphere for elections, explaining, "This one feature is of more concern to the United Nations General Assembly and to the United Nations Temporary Commission on Korea than any other." Hodge went on to say, "The primary duty of the U.N. Commission here is to observe the elections for the express purpose of determining if the representatives elected do in fact represent the will of the people."[46]

The focus on UN recognition was strategic. Hodge knew the rightists desperately wanted the creation of a separate government in the South. He reminded them that this could only happen if UNTCOK recognized the elections as democratic and free from police coercion. Finally, he warned them that international election observers would be paying close attention to their activities on Election Day.

Despite his worries about the police, Hodge did delegate one crucial task to them. As the final report on the American military government's involvement in the Korean elections acknowledged, "Registration was largely a police function."[47] Concerns with possible coercion were superseded by the need for high voter turnout. And by that standard, voter registration was a massive success: 80 percent of Koreans eligible to vote registered during the registration period between March 30 and April 9. But, as some had feared, police intimidation played a key role in this success.[48]

There was one area of reform the military government pushed without the prodding of UNTCOK—women's rights. The May elections would be the first for over four million Korean women, and the AMG needed as many of them to go to the polls as possible. As first-time voters, they would need a crash course on their democratic rights and responsibilities. "Women are eligible to vote and as soon as election proceedings have been worked out," US officials explained, "the Women's Bureau will have to inaugurate an all-out movement to teach Korean women how to vote."[49] They feared that the high illiteracy rate among Korean women—more than 80 percent according to their statistics—would result in their low turnout.

Pyongyang radio transmitted a steady diet of anti-election messages across the southern zone. One of them said, "The American election plan is a device to fool people and to confuse them. The people will be given a ballot with a large number of names, and there will be nothing on the ballot to tell them which name they are supposed to vote for."[50] (That last line might have been a slip of the tongue.) The AMG "solved" this problem, as well as the challenge of illiteracy, by printing photographs of the candidates next to their names on the ballot.

The military government had established the Women's Bureau back in August 1946, with the stated aim of improving the political, economic, and social situation of Korean women. Helen Begley Nixon, a graduate of Smith College and former director of the Red Cross in Holyoke, Massachusetts, was appointed American adviser of the Bureau. Evelyn Koh was named the Bureau's Chief. Koh had earned a PhD in sociology from the University of Michigan in 1937 and served as professor of economics and sociology at Ewha College from 1935 to 1944.

Evelyn Koh was part of a remarkable trio of Korean sisters. If China had the Soong sisters, which included Madame Chiang Kai-shek, Korea had the Koh sisters. Evelyn and her oldest sister, Gladys, started the "Sister's Garden" in 1937, a settlement village (a sort of rural version of Jane Addams's Hull House) that provided medical services to poor women villagers. They also ran a nursery and kindergarten, taught classes in home economics, and held regular Sunday school, before it was all shut down by the colonial authorities. The sisters were products of American missionary education.[51]

But for the first year, the Women's Bureau was largely moribund. The high command's aversion to reform had a lot to do with this, though to be fair, virtually every political party in the South, including the communists, subordinated women's rights to other interests and goals.[52] That changed with the arrival of the UN commission. According to Helen Nixon, "when the United Nations decided to send Commission to Korea to investigate the possibilities of a free election, our real task began."

Immediately following the UN vote, Nixon reached out to the president of the League of Women Voters and the editors of the popular national magazine *Ladies Home Journal*, requesting reading materials on everything from democratic procedure to personal hygiene. "I am convinced that the hope of Korea lies with Korean women," she wrote. "They will be a force for democracy if we supply the knowledge that they need and are seeking."[53]

Nixon teamed up with Evelyn Koh, who was selected as one of the twelve members of the National Election Committee, to organize millions of women into the Federation of Korean Women. Members had to sign a pledge to devote themselves to the independence of the country and to "the best interests of all women regardless of individual beliefs and opinions." Nixon made it clear that their agenda was not a radical one. "This is definitely not a feminist movement," she wrote. "We Americans have no right to try to superimpose our Western structure on them in violation of Oriental tradition. All we want to do is to correct existing abuses."[54]

The Women's Bureau worked closely with rightist women's organizations, which supported the goal of establishing an independent government in south Korea. After splitting from the Founding Women's Association (FWA) in September 1945, rightist women pursued a pared-down agenda that included the right to vote, literacy education, and the abolition of prostitution and sex trafficking. Any economic rights they had agreed to while part of the FWA were dropped from the program.[55]

Leftist women activists maintained that women's liberation "could not be realized merely by the fact that they wore the same clothes as men, socialized with men, ate like men, or had equal political rights as men."[56] They argued women also needed equal pay for equal work, the right to inherit and own property (especially land), and guaranteed childcare. They touted the gender equality laws passed in the North, which contained many of the provisions they sought.

But women's rights in the North looked better on paper than in reality. The laws, especially on marriage and divorce, sparked a furious backlash from men (and some women), especially in the countryside, so much so that a number of communist leaders wanted to roll them back, thinking they were doing too much too soon, given the country's deeply rooted patriarchy. Some North Korean men, for example, boycotted the elections in August 1948, when the North held their own separate elections, to protest women voting. Moreover, while North Korean leader Kim Il Sung spoke about women being "a powerful driving force that pushes one side of the wheels of the cart of the revolution" (reminiscent of Mao Zedong's "women hold up half the sky"), his ruling party was sorely lacking in women leaders.[57]

Both Helen Nixon and Evelyn Koh acknowledged that more reforms were necessary if they were to advance women's rights in south Korea. They thought laws on marriage, divorce, and inheritance, and the working of the family registry, which only allowed men to be heads of households, all needed thorough revisions. But, in their mind, there was no time for such reforms now—there was an election to be held. They pinned their hopes on the newly established South Korean government enacting these changes.[58]

If March was the month of reform, April was the month of resistance. It opened with the people of Jeju, the island province off the southern coast of Korea, rebelling against the scheduled elections. "Today, on this day of April 3," the People's Liberation Army declared, "your sons, daughters, and little brothers and sisters rose up in arms for the reunification and independence of our homeland, and for the complete liberation of the people." The rebels saw themselves as defenders of Korean sovereignty, a "save-the-nation-movement." They urged the people of Jeju to "rise up along with us" to answer "the call of the country and its people."[59]

What had happened to Jeju? For most of the occupation, Korea's largest island was the smoothest running province, having avoided the unrest that had plagued most of the southern zone. Thanks largely to the leadership of the People's Committee, Jeju had escaped the upheavals of the Autumn Uprising, and conducted peaceful elections in November 1946, sending two leftist candidates to represent them in the Interim Assembly in Seoul.[60] In fact, as late as October 1947, General Hodge was telling a group of visiting American congressmen that Jeju was "a truly communal area that is peacefully controlled by the People's Committee without much Communist influence."[61] Up till then, Jeju provided a counter-history, a glimpse into what south Korea could have been if the AMG had decided to work with the people's committees.

The relationship, however, soured with the appointment of law and order governor Yu Haejin, who brought polarization from the mainland to the island in April 1947. He arrived with members of the rightist youth group, Northwest Youth Association. In his first acts as governor, he ended the power-sharing arrangement with the People's Committee and reconstituted the police into an arm of the Right. "Many terrorist acts have been caused by the police under Governor Yoo's [Yu's] regime," wrote Lieutenant Colonel Lawrence A. Nelson, a special investigator of the military government. "All top police positions are filled with non-natives of Jeju and he has filled many positions of appointment with mainland people which has not been placidly accepted by the natives of Jeju-do." The island's jails were soon packed, presenting "the worst case of crowding found in any penal institution in Korea. Thirty-five prisoners in a cell, ten by twelve," according to American investigators from the Counter Intelligence Corps (CIC).[62]

In March 1948, the CIC recommended Yu be replaced. "Governor Yoo Hae-jin has repeatedly demonstrated his inability to properly administer a Province as a governor," their report explained. "He has made futile attempts to control political thought by ruthless and dictatorial methods." Most worrisome, they thought his actions were backfiring. "He has driven the Leftist factions underground, where their activities have grown more dangerous. Leftist members and sympathizers have increased."[63] But the high command in Seoul refused to replace Yu, not with elections right around the corner.

Sure enough, at the crack of dawn on April 3, armed guerrillas rushed down from Halla Mountain, the highest point on the island, and attacked police boxes, raided elections offices, and intimidated election workers. They had set up their headquarters on the mountain, today the most popular tourist attraction in Jeju, using the caves and fortifications established by the Japanese during the war. As one US official reported, "Difficulty developed in holding the election on Jeju because of the reluctance of election officials to open polls or to handle any election material because of fear of communist reprisals." Indeed, voter registration in Jeju was by far the lowest among all the provinces in the South.

Fearing the guerrillas would upend the elections, the military government sent 1,700 police and three constabulary battalions from the mainland to put down the rebellion. But any hope of settling the situation with a show of force, as one US commander naively predicted, was quickly dashed. Instead, American-backed forces became mired in a protracted campaign against the rebels that left in doubt the ability to hold elections on the island.[64]

The second challenge to the elections came from a North-South Unity Conference that was to be held April 19 to April 23 in Pyongyang. The North, with the Soviet Union's blessing, planned to convene a gathering of southern and northern political leaders to discuss how to reunify Korea. They invited over two hundred delegates from the South, but the two stars on the list were unquestionably Kim Ku and Kim Kyusik. The attendance of the two longtime nationalists would have lent instant credibility to the event.

The State Department saw "cause for grave concern over the possible effects" the Pyongyang conference would have on the forthcoming elections. "Should Kim Koo and Kimm Kiu Sic join forces with north Korean group," the acting secretary of state wrote to Jacobs on April 5, "it would appear not unlikely that increasing number of their followers and sympathizers would boycott elections in the South." He urged the US military government to go on the offensive in order that "the aggressive propaganda campaign on behalf of the Pyongyang conference be matched by equally forceful campaign on our part."[65]

Heeding the secretary's advice, General Hodge took to the airwaves the next day to forcefully discredit the conference:

> We have been hearing much recently concerning the so-called North-South Korea Leaders Conference for reuniting Korea. . . . The Korean people must not be fooled by tricks. The one surest way in which there can be an effective and lasting uniting of North and South Korea by the Koreans themselves is through the action of electing representatives of the people. Hence it is absolutely essential that every man and woman over 21 full years of age go to their place of registry immediately and register. They must go to the polling places on election day and vote for their own selection of representatives who can in a truly representative capacity take steps to bring about the unification of Korea and make it a truly sovereign state.[66]

Hodge and his advisers also met with the two Kims to dissuade them from participating. They found that there was no changing Kim Ku's mind; he was adamant about going. He saw himself as the savior of the nation—the only person who could prevent the country from being divided: "I would risk my life at the 38th parallel in trying to form a unified government rather than participate in forming a separate government in the South."[67]

The less messianic-minded Kim Kyusik, however, started to get cold feet, afraid he would be lending his prestige to a communist propaganda event. American officials thought they had convinced him not to attend the conference. But at the last minute, he changed his mind and departed for Pyongyang on the morning of April 19. Apparently, the night before, UNTCOK delegates S. H. Jackson and George Patterson had urged him to attend the

Kim Ku, center, with his son, Kim Sin, right, about to
cross into north Korea in April 1948. The border was
marked with a simple post.
Wikimedia Commons

conference, saying that "if Kimm's or other reasonable terms were accepted,
UNTCOK might postpone elections scheduled for May 10th." The chance
to hold off the elections appeared to be the deciding factor for Kim Kyusik,
who had been "leaning toward not going to Pyongyang and was even attempting to find excuses why he should not go." He, along with the entire
contingent of center-left assemblymen, had recently resigned from the Interim Assembly in protest of the separate elections.[68]

Around the same time, Pak Hŏnyŏng also left for the North, but this time
for good. He had been going back and forth since the warrant for his arrest
was issued. He went on to become Kim Il Sung's right-hand man as the
chairman of the Great People's Congress, and he would serve as foreign
minister during the Korean War. In relocating to the North, Pak was also
able to be reunited with his daughter, Vivian. She traveled to Pyongyang
from Moscow in 1949 to meet the father she had only recently learned ex-

isted. Her mother, Chu Sejuk, who was released at the end of World War II after having served her sentence in Kazakhstan, had reluctantly revealed to her daughter, who was eighteen years old at the time, that Pak Hŏnyŏng was her father. (By then, Pak was married to his third wife and had other children. Soviet officials had kept Chu's existence a secret from Pak, perhaps because then they would have had to explain why she was imprisoned in a labor camp.) Vivian had been raised in an orphanage run by communist cadres in Moscow since her parents' arrest.[69]

But there would be no communist paradise for either Chu or Pak. After her release, Chu petitioned Stalin to be allowed to return to Korea. Her request was denied. She fell sick while visiting Vivian in Moscow in 1953 and died shortly thereafter. Pak was tried for being an American spy in 1954 and sentenced to death by a firing squad. His execution was part of a mass political purging ordered by Kim Il Sung, as he sought to eliminate "internal enemies" after the North's failure to win the Korean War.[70] It was not lost on Vivian that the tragedies that befell her parents came at the hands of "comrades." It seems she never joined the Communist Party. In 2007, the South Korean government posthumously awarded Chu Sejuk the National Medal of Merit for her patriotic acts as an independence fighter. Vivian, who was seventy-nine at the time, received the award on her mother's behalf.

The conference in Pyongyang attracted over five hundred delegates from forty-six political parties in north and south Korea. It was held at the Moranbong Theatre, which recently had been built on the site of a former Japanese Shinto shrine. According to one report, the Soviet Union "spared no expense or effort to provide an ideal atmosphere for the conference." Kim Ku was the undisputed star of the show. "Separate elections," he declared resolutely in his speech to the delegates "must be opposed and defeated at any cost." Kim Sin, the son of Kim Ku, who accompanied his father to the North in April 1948, recalled the reaction to his father's speech at the packed theater: "The audience clapped passionately when father said he was against a separate government in the South." But he also remembered: "It became completely silent when he said he didn't want a separate government in the North, either."[71] A month earlier, North Korean authorities arrested thousands of dissidents calling for a unified Korean government and demanding that UNTCOK be allowed access to the North to oversee peninsula-wide elections.[72]

The conference ended with a resolution calling for a boycott of the southern elections and the immediate withdrawal of all foreign troops. The resolution also denounced Americans for holding "a unilateral election in South

Korea for the purpose of delaying the unification and independence of our fatherland." It declared, "The Korean people have the ability to establish a united, democratic government with their own hands."[73] But the resolution did little to stop the slide toward separate governments—not that it was supposed to. A few days following the conference, the North promulgated the country's first constitution and scheduled elections that would create a separate government based in Pyongyang, all with the explicit approval of the Soviet Union. Soviet officials appeared as keen on legitimizing a client state through democratic processes and institutions as their American counterparts.[74]

General Hodge dismissed the conference as little more than a political stunt designed to undermine the scheduled elections and make the United States look bad. He pointed out how all the speeches made at the conference had been attacks on the United States, the UN Commission, and the May 10 elections. "The bombastic propaganda is to try to prevent any Koreans from expressing themselves in democratic elections," he said in a public statement on May 3. "They have even gone into the propaganda song and dance that the United States wants Korea as a colony and a place for American military bases, which are the most fantastic lies of all."[75] (Hodge might have wanted to take that last one back: the United States built a network of military bases during the Korean War and currently has fifteen military bases in South Korea.)[76] Furious with Kim Ku and Kim Kyusik for providing legitimacy to what he called an "all Korean Communist conference," Hodge deemed the two men personae non gratae upon their return to the South, and their public life largely came to an end. Kim Kyusik announced his retirement from politics, while Kim Ku did what he could to not become completely irrelevant.

In 1949, Kim Ku was assassinated by a South Korean military officer, possibly at the order of Syngman Rhee. A year later, Kim Kyusik was abducted and taken to the North, where he was reportedly killed in December 1950. Cho Mansik, the "Gandhi of Korea," who had been under house arrest in the North since 1946 for opposing trusteeship, was executed by northern forces in 1950. The three longtime nationalists had spent most of their lives fighting, organizing, and conspiring for Korean independence—not to mention enduring years in prison and exile—but in the end, all they would know of liberation was occupation and war.

Despite the challenges, Hodge went full steam ahead with the elections. They were key to a face-saving American withdrawal strategy from Korea; there was no plan B. When a reporter, in an off-the-record press conference on May 7, raised the possibility of the Commission rejecting the election results, Hodge answered: "If the UN should reject it, I don't know the answer. It would be pretty hard after all the promises, all the hulabaloo [sic] on the election, to tell the Koreans, well, you have two hundred elected people, now they are no good to you." As a result, he did not think "anything like that will happen."[77]

Still, Hodge was not leaving anything to chance. The US military government took full charge of election preparations, everything from locks on the ballot boxes to the registration of candidates. No detail was too small. The Justice Department drew up and publicized election laws and regulations; advisers from the Department of Communication aired radio programs and organized film screenings through a fleet of sound trucks; and members of the Department of Education established a speaker's series on the historical importance of voting.

Adding to the sense of urgency, in April 1948 President Truman set a timeline for the withdrawal of American forces from south Korea. "Every effort," he wrote in NSC-8, "should be made to create conditions for the withdrawal of occupation forces by December 31, 1948."[78] General Hodge had every intention of making the deadline. Probably no one wanted out of Korea more than he did. Ironically enough, hours before the election, Pyongyang radio broadcasted a message telling the general "to pack his bags and get out of Korea." This might have been the first and only time Hodge and the North agreed on anything.[79]

10 Strongman Rising

On May 10, 1948, millions of Koreans headed to the polls for the first time. They would cast their ballots for members of the National Assembly, who would later elect the president, much as in a parliamentary system. The atmosphere was tense—hundreds of people had been killed in political violence leading up to election day. The week before, North Korean radio aired a broadcast calling "for countermeasures for fighting against the South Korean separate elections." South Koreans might have recognized the voice. It was Hŏ Hŏn, the onetime member of the Left-Right Coalition, who had left for the North to be reunited with his daughter, Hŏ Chŏngsuk. "Make the people refuse to vote in the elections," he declared over the airwaves.[1]

The elections took place under a state of alert, with the deployment of nearly 35,000 police across the South. The United States also sent two battleships to Busan in a show of force. Meanwhile, the United Nations Temporary Commission on Korea (UNTCOK) team dispersed—as much as thirty persons could—to different corners of the South to do what they could to observe the elections. Given their minuscule numbers, the Commission could only monitor a fraction of the 13,800 voting sites. Throughout the day, they received a steady stream of complaints of police and rightist youth groups intimidating and harassing voters.[2]

Yet almost immediately after the polls closed, Secretary of State George Marshall sent a note congratulating south Koreans "on the success of Korea's first democratic election, held under the observation of the United Nations Temporary Commission on Korea." He wrote, "The fact that some 90 percent of the registered voters cast their ballots, despite the lawless efforts of a Communist-dominated minority to prevent or sabotage the election, is

One of the nearly four million Korean women who voted on May 10, 1948.
National Archives

a clear revelation that the Korean people are determined to form their own government by democratic means."[3]

The Chinese delegate, Liu Yuwan, provided the first comment from a UNTCOK member. "I was greatly surprised and absolutely satisfied with the orderly manner in which elections were conducted. In many other countries I have seen the people voting for candidates; here today the Korean people were voting for independence." Liu said he found no irregularities in the polling areas he observed, and, in his opinion, the election took place in an "orderly, quiet and dignified manner." He added that "there was no question in [my] mind that the atmosphere of the election there was completely free."[4] That could only be true if the elections were graded on a curve. The press reported nearly forty people killed in election-day violence (the numbers were surely higher), and hundreds detained for protest or what the authorities called "rioting."

The North called the election a "device of American imperialists implemented by their stooges in the United Nations Commission," which was expected. But some of the "stooges" had serious misgivings about the elections. At least four members of UNTCOK did not believe the conditions on May 10 met the standards for democratic elections. The Syrian delegate, Yasin Mughir, thought the elections were outright stolen by the rightists.[5] The strongest case for not recognizing the elections came from the island province of Jeju.

In Jeju, a boycott of the elections, as well as the threat of violence, resulted in far lower turnout, 62.8 compared to 95.95 percent nationwide. In the days leading up to the elections, rebels called on—and, in some cases, forced—residents to escape to one of the mountains on the island or hide out in one of its forests. Despite heavy police presence on election day, rebels also successfully conducted hit-and-run raids on polling places to suppress the vote. They stole or destroyed voting rolls in more than half the 133 polling stations on the island.[6]

Hodge dismissed the election results in Jeju as an outlier and blamed "outside" communist agitators for the low turnout. Other officials, however, held different views on the underlying factors that had led to the outcome. Major General Orlando Ward believed "the uprising was caused by people's hatred of the police" and thought "the riots will continue until provocative causes are removed." The public prosecutor from the Kwangju District, Kim Hŭiju, who was assigned to investigate conditions on the island in early May, came to the same conclusion, attributing the unrest to the excess of the police and the rightist youth groups aligned with them.[7]

Two weeks before the election, the insurgents had reached a ceasefire deal with Lieutenant Colonel Kim Ingnyŏl, commanding officer of the ninth regiment of the Korean constabulary. The two sides negotiated a tentative agreement in which the rebels would gradually disarm in exchange for amnesty. As part of the deal, they also received assurances that police who had committed atrocities would be held to account, which caused tensions between the constabulary and the police. In his memoirs, Kim said he desperately wanted to find a peaceful solution to the conflict.

But the truce accord collapsed on May 1, when Ora-ri village along the north coast of Jeju was set ablaze by arsonists. Kim rushed to Ora-ri to find out what had happened. His investigation revealed that rightists from the Northwest Youth Association, with police support, had started the fire. "The police did not intend to quell the riot but to aggravate and expand it in order to conceal their fault and guilt," Kim reported to American officials. "They disguised themselves as rioters and set fire to private houses, spreading a rumor that the rioters committed arsons."[8]

Armed police on the lookout for rebels at a police station in Jeju.
National Archives

When Kim tried to present evidence for his case at a meeting with his superiors, the national police chief, Cho Pyŏngok, shouted him down, accusing him of being a communist. The two men nearly came to blows. But US officials had already made up their mind that the fire was started by the rebels. General Hodge had always been circumspect about the ceasefire agreement. The military government cemented the narrative about the rebels in a short propaganda film, *May Day on Cheju-do*, using footage from a US aircraft that caught the arson on camera.[9]

On May 3, Military Governor William Dean nullified the ceasefire and ordered an all-out attack on the rebels. He replaced Kim Ingnyŏl with a hardliner, Lieutenant Colonel Pak Chin'gyŏng, as commanding officer. Pak was selected for his knowledge of the island's terrain, which he had acquired in his time as a soldier in Jeju in the Japanese army during the war. His reputation preceded him—not in a good way—with his subordinates. Dozens of members of the ninth regiment deserted to join the rebels soon after he was promoted. Pak was shot in his sleep by his own men a month later.

In the days leading up to the elections, thirty-five police were killed—some of them brutally, including by decapitation—and hundreds of villagers

Police force being trained on school grounds by a Japanese-trained officer, Jeju,
May 1948.
Carl Mydans / The LIFE Picture Collection / Shutterstock

were interrogated, tortured, and murdered. Yet even among the police there
were dissenters, though they were in the distinct minority. One police chief
in Jeju, Mun Hyŏngsun, rejected orders to execute rebels in his custody. In
doing so, he probably saved close to two hundred lives. (He would later be
referred to as the Korean Schindler.) Nevertheless, any chance of a peaceful
settlement went up in flames with the thatched roofs of Ora-ri village.[10]

The American military government annulled the May 10 results of the
two voting districts on Jeju Island and rescheduled new elections for June
23. Having a little over a month to pacify the island, Korean troops, joined
by the police, went mountain to mountain to try to ferret out the armed
rebels. Using what amounted to an early version of the strategic hamlet program later used in Vietnam, security forces relocated civilians to the coasts
in hopes of isolating the insurgents. Colonel Rothwell R. Brown, who led
the campaign, thought it would take two weeks to bring the rebellion to
heel. His prediction was off by more than a little. New elections would not
be held for another year, and even then under heavy security. The insurgency would not be completely pacified until 1954. Brown learned that guerrillas with local support could fight a superior armed force to a stalemate for

a long time. But the human costs were staggering: close to 30,000 islanders perished, about 10 percent of Jeju's total population, many of them killed indiscriminately by American and South Korean security forces.

In 2000, the South Korean government established a National Truth Commission to investigate the Jeju events. Six years later, President Roh Moo-hyun officially apologized to the people of Jeju and acknowledged state responsibility for the atrocities, which had been denied by the government for decades.

To no one's surprise, the election results showed the political parties allied with Syngman Rhee winning a majority in the new Assembly. The newly elected body convened its first session on May 31, 1948, to overwhelmingly select Rhee as chairman of the Assembly. On June 11, Rhee contacted UNTCOK to formally notify its members of the establishment of the National Assembly in south Korea. His first official communiqué as chairman was met with a long silence. In Shanghai, UNTCOK members were divided over validating the recent elections. Representatives from Australia, Canada, India, and Syria argued that the elections "were not held in a sufficiently free atmosphere to earn the approval of the Commission."[11]

George McCune, former head of the Korea desk at the US State Department, also questioned the validity of the elections: "The American command and the South Korean Interim Government described the elections as a great victory for democracy and a repudiation of communism. Some unofficial reports were less favorable, many observers holding the view that the elections had been fraudulently conducted in an atmosphere of terrorism. A more moderate view, widely held, was that elections should not be accepted as a free expression of the Korean will."[12]

The Commission was torn. "Some of them [UNTCOK] doubt whether the very outcome of these elections will contribute to the solution of the Korean problem, and even if they do not entertain such doubts, they do not want to regard the elections in the south as nation-wide," Joseph Jacobs explained to the secretary of state. "They want to call them 'decidedly rightists' elections.'" But he also noted that there were other members who were "inclined to think that these elections may be one step towards the unification and sovereignty of Korea."[13]

UNTCOK seemed intractably divided. Yet, on June 25, the Commission issued a statement acknowledging the establishment of the Korean National Assembly. The United States had exerted enormous pressure on the commission's national leaders in the intervening weeks. On June 30, UNTCOK released another statement saying that the elections were "a valid expression of the free will of the electorate in those parts of Korea which were accessible to the Commission."

With the announcement, a sense of relief washed over the US military government. The long radio silence had cast doubt on whether UNTCOK would in fact recognize the election results, making for a tense few weeks in south Korea.[14] But UNTCOK's announcement at the end of June broke the tension. For the moment, Hodge and his conservative advisers could take comfort in executing an exit strategy that would allow the US to draw down its forces while maintaining a foothold in Korea. Rhee and his rightist associates may not have been their first (or second or third) choice, but at least he was a trusted anti-communist.

Liberal advisers also took solace in the recognition of the elections, viewing it as an important milestone in Korean democracy, despite their ambivalence with the final results. They told themselves the election of Syngman Rhee was the painful but unavoidable birth pangs of democracy in Korea. But whatever good feelings the elections generated would not last. Several weeks later, American legal experts and senior advisers found translated copies of the Korean constitution on their desks. They were stunned with what they read: core principles they had tacitly agreed to with members of the Korean drafting committee and Rhee himself were either absent or substantially changed. This was not the document they had been expecting.

Liberal reformers felt particularly blindsided. Arthur Bunce, the senior economic adviser with socialist sensibilities, explained that "the original document, which pays homage at least to liberalism, was altered beyond recognition in committee, and the resulting compromise draft which made its way to the Assembly floor provided for a presidential dictatorship rooted in economic oligarchy."[15] How did this happen?

Shortly after the elections, US legal advisers met with drafters of the constitution and leaders of the two parties who won the most seats, Kim Sŏngsu and Sin Ikhŭi of the KDP (Sin had taken the place of Chang Tŏksu as the party's number two after Chang's assassination), and Syngman Rhee, who led the NSRRKI. In their conversations, American advisers pushed for a parliamentary system with powers vested mostly in the legislative body.

Under their proposal, the president would largely be a figurehead. Apart from the system of government, they were willing to grant Korean drafters wide latitude.

The Koreans involved in these discussions, including an unusually quiet Syngman Rhee, agreed to a parliamentary government with a British-style cabinet system. KDP leaders were quite pleased with the outcome, believing a parliamentary model would provide a check on a Rhee presidency. They also viewed a parliamentary system as a better vehicle for patronage and favor-peddling.[16] Rhee and the KDP may have found themselves back on the same side on the elections, but the resentment and suspicion between the two parties did not go away.

The drafting process began on June 3, when the constitutional committee, consisting of thirty newly elected assemblymen and ten legal experts, convened its first session. It was led by the dean of Korea University's College of Law, Yu Chino, Minister of Justice Kim Pyŏngno, and Prosecutor General Yi In. These principal drafters of the constitution all had legal training from Japanese universities. Yu Chino received his law degree from Keijo University in Seoul; Kim Pyŏngno and Yi In graduated from Meiji University. Other than Yu, the members of the committee had little expertise in constitutional law. The military government assigned Charles Pergler and Ernst Fraenkel to advise the committee, but a compressed schedule as well as other legal work limited their involvement.

American advisers had dismissed an earlier Korean effort to write a national charter. In March 1947, a committee in the Interim Assembly, led by Sin Ikhŭi, drafted a constitution. Sin submitted it to the military governor for approval, requesting it take effect following the transfer of power from the occupation to the new Korean government. The military government's Justice Department saw little value in writing a constitution at the time and questioned its legality. "The drafting of a national constitution, temporary in name but permanent in character, by an improvised body provisionally representing only a part of the country and its population would seem to be unpractical under any circumstances." Joseph Jacobs ridiculed the "many amateurish features, contradictions, and defects," including the language that qualified civil rights guarantees. The bill was vetoed by the military government.[17]

This trial run with the constitution confirmed the high command's worst suspicions about the Koreans (though it was entirely a rightist affair). "Politically immature Koreans," Hodge warned the State Department in June

1947, "will be strongly influenced along oriental lines and despite their experience with a tyrannical dynasty and domination by Japanese will in the end gravitate toward a highly centralized government while giving lip service to 'democracy' which they understand in practical effect only vaguely."[18]

And yet, less than a year later, Korean drafters found themselves largely alone to write the actual document. Part of this had to do with Pergler and Fraenkel being stretched too thin. But the hands-off approach was also a function of their legal philosophies. Fraenkel was a liberal pluralist who specialized in European parliamentary law. Based on his legal expertise and linguistic skills, an assignment in US-occupied Germany would have seemed more appropriate. But the head of the US Justice Department, a lawyer with a PhD in international law from Yale, believed that European continental law was a better fit for Korea, so Fraenkel found himself there.

As a liberal pluralist, Fraenkel eschewed a one-size-fits-all approach to law and democracy, which gave him pause about imposing democracy from above: "We enact statutes and even a constitution, establish institutions which are wholly based on occidental thinking and apply ideas to the government of this country which are meaningful only in the framework of our tradition and civilization."[19] This criticism was fine in theory but perhaps not the best approach when the person overwhelmingly favored to come into power had authoritarian impulses.

Between June 3 and June 23, the committee met sixteen times to draft a constitution to submit to the National Assembly for ratification. Yu Chino drafted a constitution beforehand to serve as the basis for debate. While the political affiliation of the committee ranged narrowly from moderate to Far Right, the group split over a number of issues. Despite the earlier agreement with American advisers, members clashed over the form of government, relitigating the merits of a presidential versus parliamentary system. Those favoring a strong presidential system came from Rhee's party. They argued that a strong executive was necessary to ensure order in the South and to deal with a hostile, communist regime in the North.

Anticipating some of these concerns, Yu incorporated elements of both presidential and parliamentary systems. His draft included extraordinary executive powers in case of national emergencies, known as the "crisis clause." But Yu also designed the government so that lawmaking powers were vested in the National Assembly, and the prime minister and the cabinet—*not* the president—were responsible to the Assembly. Yu's constitution made the parliament the chief organ of state power. Throughout the debate, members of the KDP held fast to the core principles in Yu's constitution.

A series of liberal reforms in Yu's initial draft, recommended by Pergler and Fraenkel, did not survive. The committee killed a constitutional ban on torture and nullified a provision prohibiting arrest without a warrant on national security grounds. To the disappointment of US advisers, the committee also removed a provision applying the Bill of Rights to non-Koreans.[20] The committee also agreed broadly on constitutional principles for a planned economy. Leading up to the elections, the different rightist parties campaigned on the promise to nationalize the economy, implement land and labor reforms, and increase educational and medical access. Why would rightists support a "socialist platform," as Joseph Jacobs called it? Because it was what a large portion of ordinary Koreans wanted, and rightist candidates could only ignore their aspirations at their electoral peril. On the campaign trail, they could be heard shouting the slogan "Give land to farmers, factories to workers."[21]

The military government's own internal polling showed that a large majority of Koreans favored government ownership of farmlands and large industries. The polling also indicated that the public wanted large Korean landholdings to be redistributed to landless peasants. The revolution could not be denied—at least not completely, anyway. Despite the disappointment of the last two and half years, Koreans still expected economic justice and a dignified life as an essential part of their independence.

The newly drafted constitution spoke to these popular aspirations. Article 84, the opening section on the economy, read: "The principle of the economic order of the Korean Republic shall be to realize social justice, to meet the basic demands of all citizens and to encourage the development of a balanced economy." Rightist lawmakers, however, did what they could to kill or weaken the provisions aimed at these purposes. For example, a law guaranteeing private sector workers an equal share in the profits made it into the first full draft of the constitution but lawmakers later watered it down by removing the adverb "equally" from the language and adding the qualifier "in accordance with the provisions of the law."[22]

The committee was making good progress on the draft constitution when Syngman Rhee, without warning, showed up to their June 15 meeting and called for a presidential system of government. Just a week earlier, he had said that he would accept the will of the National Assembly. But now Rhee was saying that a strong presidency was absolutely necessary. He talked about how the president would need powers to respond quickly and decisively to northern aggression. His words failed to sway the committee, which held firm to a parliamentary system.

Rebuffed by the committee, Rhee took his demands to the National Assembly a few days later, where he put forth a resolution calling for a special session. He planned to use the special session to force through a constitution with strong presidential powers. But his resolution was soundly defeated by a vote of 130 to 2. On June 21, Rhee reappeared before the committee but this time told them that he would not be taking up any official post under the current constitution. He spoke ominously of forming an outside group. It was a thinly veiled threat to undermine the legitimacy of any government without him.[23]

Rhee had considerable leverage—and, as always, was not afraid to use it. It was still unclear at this point whether UNTCOK would approve the elections; they were still deliberating and would not make their announcement until June 30. Rhee's withdrawal would have thrown Korean politics into turmoil and sowed further doubt in the minds of UN observers about recognizing a new South Korean government. Rhee's power play, however, was not without risk: if he followed through with this threat, it would put his lifelong dream of ruling an independent Korea in jeopardy. Rhee's rightist rivals knew of his ambitions, and thus it became a matter of who would blink first. The answer came quickly. On the same night, top KDP officials decided to capitulate to Rhee's demands for strong executive powers. The next day, June 22, following a lengthy discussion between KDP bosses and the drafting committee, members revised the constitution to accommodate Rhee's wishes. As Joseph Jacobs reported several weeks later, "Almost all members seemed to accept these provisions as drafted on which Syngman Rhee had reportedly insisted as the price of his participation."[24]

For unknown reasons, Yu Chino, the leading drafter, was not at the meeting that day. So that evening, KDP party heads, with drafts of the revised constitution in hand, visited Yu at his home to inform him of the changes. They also needed to ask the constitutional expert how the revisions would affect other parts of the constitution. In his memoir, Yu recalled responding indignantly: "Why worry about minor logistical inconsistencies and conflicts when the major change is a fundamental shift in the structure of power?"[25] He then resigned his position on the committee, refusing to be a party to Rhee's power grab, according to his telling.

His recollection of a principled stand did not square with what followed. Contrary to his account, Yu returned to the committee to work on revisions to make the different parts of the constitution fit with a presidential system. More tellingly, he was appointed chief of the Office of Legislation, a cabinet-level position, in the new South Korean government.[26] Rhee was not a man known for generosity to those who opposed him.

The KDP thought they had wrangled some concessions from Rhee to limit presidential authority. Rhee had agreed to their proposal to create a State Affairs Council, an executive body that would work with the president to decide national policies. Any order originating from the presidency would require the majority vote of the State Affairs Council. Since the Assembly would select more than half of the council members, the KDP believed the Council would act as an effective check on Rhee's expected presidency.[27]

Working furiously, the committee incorporated the "Rhee revisions" into the final draft of the constitution and submitted it to the National Assembly on June 23. Ernst Fraenkel looked over the draft a few days later. Why didn't he catch the changes? Probably because they were not what he was looking for. His task at that moment was to identify potential *international* violations in the laws that might draw the scrutiny of UNTCOK. The commission's mandate spoke only about observing elections in Korea, so it was highly unlikely they would have anything to say about the constitution, but American officials were not taking any chances. So, when Fraenkel reviewed the draft, he was checking to see that the laws related, for example, to foreigners' rights and that the president's power to ratify treaties did not run afoul of international standards. It was all about getting UNTCOK's approval.[28]

The Assembly began debate on the constitution in early July. Despite the agreement between the KDP and Rhee, assemblymen spent most of the time arguing over the specific powers of the presidency. The outcome would determine the balance of power in the new government, which, as a result of Rhee's prior maneuvering, had tilted toward the executive. The most contentious issue involved the president's authority to veto laws passed in the Assembly. Opponents feared that the provision would reduce the Assembly to a mere advisory organ to the president. Once again, Rhee exerted influence to get his desired policies. As chairman of the proceedings, he cut off debate and made it nearly impossible for legislators to reject presidential veto power. He exercised his authority as chairman to fast-track passage of most of the 102 articles comprising the constitution. The Assembly passed articles 18 to 42 on the afternoon of July 5, and articles 43 to 102 on July 6. By calling for a vote on each provision in quick succession, Rhee prevented the opposition from organizing against his favored proposals.[29]

Rhee's previous concessions to the KDP were gutted in the final version of the constitution. In the final draft, the president appointed and removed members of the State Affairs Council at his discretion. As Charles Pergler noted, "The State Affairs Council created by Sec. II of Chap. IV confers power of decision in words, but in view of the powers of the President to remove, the power of Council in such a situation are little more than advisory."[30] The Assembly ratified the constitution on July 12 and officially promulgated it on July 17.

Helen Begley Nixon and Evelyn Koh were likely let down by the final constitution. Among the more than one hundred articles was virtually nothing on women's rights. It likely didn't help that not a single woman was elected to the National Assembly, though nineteen women candidates had run for office. One writer for the Women's Bureau tried to put a happy face on the results: "Although none of the women candidates was elected, we did not feel too upset, because the women had served their purpose."[31] Unless that purpose was to provide democratic cover for a questionable election, they had little to show for their efforts. The changes to the laws on marriage, divorce, and inheritance that Nixon and Koh had been hoping for never materialized. It would be decades before Korean women secured the same rights as men in these areas. The family registry system (*hoju*), which only permitted males to be heads of households, was only abolished in 2005. Without economic rights, women would receive less than half the wages of their male counterparts until 1987. South Korea continues to have one of the worst gender pay gaps in the world. Suffrage alone, just as leftist women activists predicted, would not be enough to achieve gender equality in Korea.[32]

The military government was behind the frantic pace of the constitution-making process. The entire process, from drafting to ratification, took less than forty days, a fraction of the time it took in occupied Japan and Germany. The tight timetable was necessary to meet the year-end deadline for withdrawing American troops from Korea, scheduled to commence on August 15.

The military command also rushed to have the constitution in place in order to present the new South Korean government as a fait accompli to UNTCOK. Members of UNTCOK saw through the strategy but thought there was little they could do to stop it. "Syngman Rhee temporary chairman of Korean Assembly favours the earliest formation of national government," S. H. Jackson reported to the Australian foreign ministry. "His view is likely to prevail, Korean constitution has been approved."[33]

On July 20, the United States reported to the UN that all requirements for recognition had been fulfilled.[34] Earlier that day, the members of the National Assembly voted for the first president of South Korea. Any uncertainty over the outcome—if there really was any—had been put to rest two weeks earlier when Philip Jaisohn announced, "Even if the position is offered, I will not accept it. I am a citizen of the United States and intend to remain so."[35]

Jaisohn as president was always a long shot. He was eighty-three when he returned to Korea in 1947 and looked every bit his age. In fact, he nearly didn't make it back to Korea; his doctors initially refused to clear him for the flight, owing to his poor health.[36] Rhee, at seventy-two, seemed young in comparison. Just as important, most Koreans had no idea who Jaisohn was. He devoted a good portion of his life to the cause of Korean independence but most of his activities took place more than four decades earlier. Since then, he had married a white American woman, the niece of President James Buchanan, become a United States citizen, and enjoyed a long career as a physician in the Philadelphia area.

Shortly after his announcement, Jaisohn returned to Philadelphia, where he died from cancer three years later. In 1994, his ashes were repatriated and buried in Seoul National Cemetery, a recognition reserved for patriots who had given their lives during the Korean independence movement. The cemetery was established by Syngman Rhee in 1956; it is where his body, too, lies.

Charles Pergler reviewed the ratified constitution a few days before Rhee was elected president. He found critical defects in the document, starting with the phrase "as specified by the law," that made the guarantees of free speech, press, assembly, and association all but "meaningless." This was exactly the kind of hedging language that had prompted US occupation authorities to take over the constitution writing process in Japan.[37]

He also expressed deep reservation with Article 57, the so-called "crisis clause," which conferred extraordinary powers upon the president in "time

Philip Jaisohn speaks at the ceremony welcoming him back to Korea in 1947.
The Picture Art Collection / Alamy Stock Photo

of civil war or in dangerous situation arising from foreign relations or in case of a natural calamity or in event of a grave economic or financial crisis." This language, he noted, "is rather reminiscent of the unfortunate Art. 48 of the German Weimar Constitution. It also is a repetition of Art. 8 of the defunct Japanese Constitution which provided that the Emperor in cases of urgent necessity to maintain public safety or avert public calamities issue . . . imperial ordinances in place of laws."

The provision did provide that "such orders shall be reported without delay to the National Assembly for confirmation." Failure to obtain confirmation would result in the emergency order being annulled. Pergler was, however, skeptical that it could safeguard against presidential abuse of power, noting that "the fact is that prior to the meeting of the Assembly the President can so establish himself in power that his acts could not be undone." The provision, he analogized, "might be something in the nature of locking the door of the barn after the horse has been stolen or escaped."[38] The nation's founding document, as Bruce Cumings has so memorably put it, had enough "loopholes through which Syngman Rhee could drive a truck."[39] It would take another forty years and four constitutions for South Korea to get its national charter right. The country is now on its fifth constitution, passed in 1988. Meanwhile, the Japanese constitution has not been amended once since it was promulgated under American auspices in 1946.[40]

Conservative and liberal advisers alike skewered the constitution for its undemocratic features. Joseph Jacobs condemned the concentration of power in the executive, as he listed the broad powers of the presidency for the secretary of state in August 1948.

> In addition to being the supreme executive authority, commander of the armed forces, controller of all appointments and dismissals and possessor of veto power over all Assembly bills; the president also has virtual control of items and lists of national expenditures; can issue orders to all government department agencies, and local governmental bodies and revoke orders which they may have issued; classify, assign, and control the civil service; and exercise extraordinary legislative and appropriation powers in times of self-proclaimed national emergencies.[41]

The conservative adviser also slammed the "socialistic" provisions that gave the government control over natural resources, public utilities, and transportation and banking systems. "In view of traditional Korean ideas of patronage and graft, in which the new government will almost certainly also be addicted," Jacobs wrote, "it is highly probable that utilities and industries will be operated under direct control or license for private rather than public gain."[42]

Arthur Bunce read the constitution in much the same way. As a Christian socialist, he was not opposed to state intervention in the economy. In fact, for more than two years, Bunce had lobbied the military government and the Interim Assembly to redistribute former Japanese-owned lands and factories to Korean farmers and workers. He had also favored a planned economy guaranteeing a minimum standard of living for Koreans. But under the existing constitution, he feared a command economy would only aggrandize the power of an imperial presidency. Bunce thought Article 87, which brought "any enterprises having public character" under the authority of the government, "the most dangerous politico-economic provision of the constitution." By the terms of the article, he worried that "the railway system, the post-office, every bank and insurance company and public utility in South Korea could become subject to allocation as a reward for political service, with disastrous results to the public interest."[43]

This outcome was the result of a rightist civil war in which Rhee and his allies emerged triumphant. "From the foregoing, it is not too much to say that Rhee has deliberately fostered this spirit," Jacobs wrote to the secretary of state, "and is now seeking to reduce the Hankook [Han'guk] Democratic Party [KDP] to a negligible force and the remainder of Rightists to dutiful lackeys." "With vast powers of industrial and financial control in his hands, together with the prerogatives of patronage," he predicted Rhee would eventually "wean away wealthy Hankook supporters and wreck the one substantial opposition to his rule."[44]

Nothing could be done at this point. On July 10, two days before the National Assembly ratified the constitution, Secretary of State George Marshall gave American officials strict orders to avoid "any acts" that "could be construed as a disavowal of the new government." He warned, "Any weakening of prestige and authority of the new government in the south would inevitably redound to the advantage of the Soviet puppet regime in the north." Occupation reformers therefore had no choice but to accept a flawed constitution, one that "could evolve into a government by a strongman," according to one legal expert.[45]

The hand-wringing over Rhee's power grab obscured the role US officials played in paving the way for authoritarianism in South Korea. This is not to diminish Rhee's part in all of this. The fact was, he outmaneuvered the Americans to seize power. Both these things could be true at once. Even the CIA gave Rhee his due, noting that he "has proved himself to be a remarkably astute politician." As his speechwriter Robert Oliver once said, Rhee could be dealt deuce seven—the worst starting hand in poker—and come away winning the pot.[46]

The Republic of Korea (South Korea) was inaugurated on August 15, 1948, on the third anniversary of Korea's liberation from Japan. Ten days later, the North held its own elections for what was called the Supreme People's As-

Syngman Rhee, Douglas MacArthur, and John Hodge at the opening ceremony of
the founding of South Korea, August 15, 1948.
National Archives (SC-306878)

sembly. Perhaps in an attempt to one-up the Americans, North Korean authorities claimed that 99.97 percent of registered voters cast a ballot. North
Korea was on its way to becoming an authoritarian state. Two weeks later,
the People's Assembly ratified a constitution, and the Democratic People's
Republic (North Korea), led by Kim Il Sung, was formally established. Korea was officially divided.[47]

The United States made a big show of the establishment of South Korea.
General MacArthur left Tokyo for just the second time since his installation
as Supreme Commander of Japan to be in attendance. (The only other time
he had left was to Manila in 1946 when the Philippines became independent.) In the fete for South Korea, MacArthur addressed the elephant in the
room: "In this hour, as the forces of righteousness advance, the triumph is
dulled by one of the greatest tragedies of contemporary history—an artificial barrier has divided your land." But he assured his Korean audience that
"unity was not a long ways away."[48] That was over seventy-five years ago.

During his short address, Hodge made it known that effective midnight, the military government of the last three years would cease to exist. It would be replaced by a civilian administration led by the new US ambassador, John R. Muccio from Rhode Island. Hodge was eager for the ceremony to be over. He asked MacArthur to be relieved of duty as soon as possible. Hodge did not want to be around when Rhee's entourage of sycophants from the United States, Hawai'i, and China came into town. The contempt was mutual. Rhee and his wife continued to tell anyone who would listen that Hodge was a closet communist.[49]

By now, everyone knew that the two old hands hated one another bitterly. Going back to before the elections, American officials had worried about "the acute personal animosity existing between General Hodge and Dr. Rhee." They thought that because Rhee was "expected to emerge as the dominant figure of the new government in South Korea, it would make it highly desirable that General Hodge be replaced before that relationship could be allowed to jeopardize the success of the negotiations incidental to the transfer of authority to that government."[50] But the State Department recommended that "his replacement as such by new Chief of Mission take place only after Aug 15 ceremonies, which would seem to provide fitting juncture for Gen Hodge to consider his mission accomplished."[51]

Hodge got what he wanted not long after the inauguration. He was reassigned to Fort Monroe in Virginia, where he was later given the title of Chief of Army Field Forces. During the Korean War, he ran war-game exercises for American troops in North Carolina, simulating North Korean and Chinese military tactics. But as for the actual war, Hodge said virtually nothing. He also stayed silent on his three-year stint in Korea. Did he have any regrets, feel any responsibility? Or did he feel vindicated? Or maybe as the consummate soldier, he just thought he did his job and that was that. We will never know. He left no personal papers, no diary. It seemed he was content to just fade away. Hodge died shortly after North Korea and UN forces agreed to an armistice ending the conflict. (Without a formal treaty, however, the war is technically not over.)[52]

Rhee ruled South Korea with an iron fist until he was forced out of office by pro-democratic forces in 1960. The opposition finally caught up with him. Rhee went into exile in Hawai'i, where he lived out the rest of his days in a small cottage owned by a Korean-American businessman. The *New York Times* reported, "The 86-year-old former President has refused to see almost all of his old friends." This was a man who would spend hours talking about anything pertaining to Korea. His discussion of Korean poetry and calligraphy was known to have put more than one official to sleep. Knowing he would never realize his lifelong ambition of ruling over a unified Korea had crushed his once indomitable spirit.[53]

Whatever one may think of Syngman Rhee, he was a true believer. He and his wife left Korea nearly penniless, not having profited off his presidency one bit. The same could not be said of his circle of flatterers and hangers-on. When Rhee was admitted to the hospital in O'ahu for a stroke, his friends had to take up a collection from the Korean community in Hawai'i to pay his medical bills. After he recovered, Rhee was hoping to return to South Korea in 1962 to retire there but was denied entry by the new government. The government dropped its objections the following year, but Rhee's doctor prohibited him from traveling, owing to his poor health. Rhee died in O'ahu in 1965 at the age of ninety. Following his death, his body was returned to South Korea for burial.[54]

Conclusion   Paths Not Taken

Under Syngman Rhee, South Korea descended into authoritarianism. His government tortured, imprisoned, and executed tens of thousands of political opponents. "The jails in Seoul are overcrowded with political prisoners," Ernst Fraenkel, who stayed on in South Korea to advise the Rhee government, wrote in 1950. "Six weeks ago, I inspected a police jail in Inchŏn. The prisoners there were living under conditions which I hesitate to describe in this letter. It reminds you of a scene of Dante's Divina Comedia." The police, he added, "exercise unlimited and uncontrolled power of arrest, torture, extortion, and detainment."

Rhee's repressive policies made reunification with the North even more improbable. As Fraenkel explained, "Although the Rhee Government pays lip service to the idea of peaceful unification, it brands all those who sponsor the slightest effort to come to terms with the North as Communists and national traitors."[1] As an imperial president, Rhee radically redefined who and what a "collaborator" was. They were no longer individuals who abetted and profited from Japanese colonial rule. They were now pro-communist sympathizers. Ch'oe Nŭngjin, who previously led the Detective Bureau, was among those Rhee had thrown in prison—Ch'oe had become an outspoken critic of Rhee's presidency—and was sentenced to death for being a communist conspirator in 1951. (In 2016, Ch'oe was acquitted of the charges, and his family was awarded monetary compensation for his wrongful conviction and death.) This revision shielded some of Rhee's most important allies from prosecution. In fact, only sixteen Koreans were ever tried for collaborating with the Japanese, and only four were convicted for treason.[2]

It would be another six decades before South Korea attempted to come to terms with its colonial past.

In 2009, the Presidential Committee for the Inspection of Collaboration for Japanese Imperialism identified over a thousand Koreans who had collaborated with the Japanese during the colonial period. But given they were all deceased, there was no one to prosecute. In a belated attempt at justice, the South Korean government confiscated almost 100 million US dollars' worth of property from the descendants of collaborators. It seems South Koreans will never get closure on an issue they expected to be resolved long ago.[3]

The actions of Rhee's government shattered Fraenkel's faith in what America had done, and perhaps more importantly, not done, in Korea. "Did we pave the way for democracy? Did we insist on local self-government, trade unions, rural cooperatives, and a minimum of the rule of law?" he asked rhetorically. Fraenkel didn't think the Soviets acted much better, accusing them of establishing a puppet government in the North (Kim Il Sung was no more of a puppet than was Syngman Rhee), but he expected more of the United States. Writing from Kyoto, after being evacuated from Seoul at the start of the Korean War, Fraenkel confided to his sister, Marta, that "our policy in Korea is bankrupt." Betraying a sense of regret, he conceded, "It is to a large extent our fault."[4]

The war started in June 1950 when North Korean forces invaded the South following a yearlong series of skirmishes along the border. During the war, each side took turns trying to conquer the peninsula—the North during the summer of 1950 and the South during the winter of 1950. But after three years of fighting that lay the peninsula to waste and cost some five million lives—General Curtis LeMay, the architect of America's bombing campaign during the war, liked to brag that "we burned down every town in North Korea and South Korea"—the two sides were right back where they started: separated along the 38th parallel.[5]

Both regimes managed to survive the war and grew more repressive in the years after. Rhee's authoritarian government lasted until 1960. His twelve-year rule was followed by almost thirty years of military dictatorship. One of the many people who paid the price for democracy in South Korea included Yi Hun'gu, who had joined the opposition party to challenge Rhee in the late 1950s. After the military coup in 1961, Yi was arrested and detained. Several days later, he died in Taejon prison, the former colonial penitentiary that once held Yŏ Unhyŏng.[6] In all, South Korea spent four decades under a dictatorship of one form or another. Only after decades of protests and bloodshed did South Korea finally break the string of autocratic governments, holding its first truly democratic election in December 1987.[7]

A similar process occurred in postwar North Korea but without the belated democratization. After the Korean War, Kim Il Sung systematically eliminated rivals, including his foreign minister, Pak Hŏnyŏng, in 1954, and consolidated one-man, one-family rule in North Korea, which continues to this day. His grandson, Kim Jong Un, represents the third generation of supreme leaders in North Korea.[8]

Of the Cold War partitioned countries, Korea is the only one that is still divided. North and South remain locked in an endless standoff—the two sides agreed to a ceasefire, not a peace treaty, in 1953. The prospects for reunification are as remote today as they have ever been. Korea seems hopelessly, permanently divided.

It is hard to look at the Korean peninsula today without thinking about the paths not taken during the occupation era. What if General Hodge had chosen to work with the people's committees instead of disbanding and outlawing them? Counterfactual speculations are typically not that useful. We know what happened. We can never know what might have happened if the course of events had been different. But in this case, there is the *factual* example of the Jeju's People's Committee, a leftist-leaning group, which pursued a peaceful path to independence, with the support of the local US military government.

As in Jeju, most local people's committees in Korea had formed organically from the bottom up. Their politics ran the gamut from doctrinaire communist to moderately conservative. Yet, despite their differences, the various people's committees held broadly shared goals for liberation. As Richard Robinson wrote, "They demanded long overdue land and labor reforms and protection from the terroristic Japanese-trained police and dishonest politicians."[9] Moreover, liberal and socialist advisers in the military government proposed an agenda that would have fulfilled most of their hopes and expectations, which is what happened in Japan, where "the first few years even the Communists found it easy to speak of the occupation forces as an army of liberation," according to historian John Dower.[10] Considering that a hated wartime enemy received democratization and reform—while Korea didn't— brings home just how badly the American occupation let Koreans down.

Roger Baldwin, who advised the US military government in Japan and Korea on civil liberties, admitted as much when he said, "It's too bad Korea isn't a defeated country, we'd do better by them."[11]

Another alternative scenario involves Hodge removing Cho Pyŏngok and Chang T'aeksang as chiefs of police. The drafted statement in political adviser Leonard Bertsch's personal papers, dated April 21, 1947, shows it was a real possibility. "Ever since liberation, Koreans have been hoping and expecting that the police forces would be cleansed of those who betrayed their people to the Japanese invaders," the statement said. "With the passing months it has become sadly apparent that it was the intention of those in control of the police force not to remove, but rather to strengthen, the influence of those who had betrayed their own people." And for this reason, it declared, "I am hereby removing Chough, Pyung Ok from his office as Director of the Department of Police, effective immediately; and I am removing, Chang, Taik Sang from his office as Chief of Division "A" of the National Police, effective immediately."[12]

What might have happened if Hodge had signed and made good on this statement? Might the centrist coalition have succeeded? At the very least, it would have boosted the Right-Left coalition's chances and it is why the two co-chairs, Yŏ Unhyŏng and Kim Kyusik, made the removal of Cho and Chang their top priority and even threatened at one point to resign from the committee unless Hodge ousted them. In Bertsch's opinion, it was "the absolute minimum of concession which would enable them to carry forward their program and winning public support."[13] This minimum concession might have saved Yŏ from assassination and given the Right-Left Coalition a genuine opportunity to show a third way was possible in Korea. One could also imagine the Soviets being more amenable to compromise at the Second Joint Commission (1947) if Americans had Yŏ and Kim and their social democratic agenda to offer as alternatives to Rhee and Kim Ku. In other words, things could have played out differently if Cho and Chang were purged and the police was reformed. Alas, the drafted statement was never signed; the police state, under Cho and Chang, continued unabated; and Yŏ was assassinated. The dream of "a mass-supported, middle of the road political movement, which would weaken the extremes and establish a democratic-minded leadership," died along with him.[14]

At every critical juncture when a different policy decision could have changed the course of the occupation, General Hodge chose maintaining the status quo over fulfilling Korean aspirations. Some of this could be attributed to Hodge's deep-seated fear of communism, which led him to dismantle the people's committees, reinstate the colonial police, and oppose meaningful reforms. It's also what led him to empower the police and its reactionary allies to brutally suppress the Autumn Uprising, despite intelligence indicating they were uncoordinated and spontaneous, arising out of daily grievances over unjust rice collection and police brutality. Hodge's "fear of communism," as one of his advisers put it, "became a fear of democracy."[15]

And yet, Hodge's anti-communism did not blind him to seeing Rhee as a fascist threat, nor did it stop him from supporting the Right-Left Coalition. And even after the demise of the coalition, he sought desperately to find an alternative to Rhee. "We cannot and must not overlook his potential to do irreparable damage," Hodge wrote empathically to the US secretary of state in 1947. But if Hodge recognized Rhee's authoritarian impulses, he could not bring himself to arrest or exile him, as he did with the communist leaders in the South. On several occasions, he sent MPs to arrest Rhee only to take back the order at the last minute.[16] The same went for police chiefs Cho and Chang. Hodge's political adviser, Leonard Bertsch, had prepared a fully drafted statement removing them as heads of the police but Hodge could not get himself to sign it (perhaps he pulls the trigger if the Autumn Uprising doesn't occur). He had serious doubts about Rhee, Cho, and Chang, but he trusted the Soviets and communists even less, though it got close near the end.[17]

Immediately after World War II, the Soviet Union had accommodated the United States on Korea, agreeing to the American proposal to partition and separately occupy the peninsula, as well as their idea for trusteeship. And as an occupying power, Soviet officials supported moderate Christian nationalist Cho Mansik over the Korean Communist Party, which created an opening for a broad coalition in the North. Stalin's policies in Korea, at least at the start, "were especially moderate and cautious," according to historian Norman Naimark.[18]

The opening, however, closed fairly quickly. In January 1946, Soviet officials arrested Cho Mansik for his opposition to trusteeship and, during the First Joint Commission, demanded the exclusion of rightist parties from participating in the Korean Provisional Government, which was a non-starter for the United States. And the Soviets stuck to this stance, more or less, the rest of the occupation. The two sides could not get their timing right: when the Soviets backed Cho, a center-right nationalist, Hodge supported the KDP and brought back rightists Rhee and Kim Ku. And when the US backed a centrist coalition led by Yŏ Unhyŏng and Kim Kyusik in the summer of 1946, Kim Il Sung, with Soviet support, had clearly established himself as the front-runner in the North. American and Soviet officials just could not get their openings to align for reunification, with tragic consequences for the Korean people.

Kim Ku, Syngman Rhee, and Kim Il Sung and their allies played a part in the closing of political possibilities in Korea, as they tried to outmaneuver occupation officials and each other to seize and consolidate power. Ultimately, however, foreign powers bear the lion's share of the responsibility. As Ernst Fraenkel reminded everyone in 1950, "The Koreans are not responsible for the artificial division of their country into two states, we are." He added, "The 38th parallel, the idea of trusteeship, the establishment of the Joint Commission, and all basic decisions on Korea were not thought through."[19] North and South were not inevitable. The two Koreas were the result of policies and decisions not of the Koreans making, and they have lived with division and conflict ever since, more than seventy-five years and counting.

Notes

Prologue

1. As Bruce Cumings explains, reporters cite the 70 percent figure each time a crisis flares up on the Korean peninsula, while ignoring the American military presence in the South, including their arsenal of nuclear weapons. Bruce Cumings, "Time to End the Korean War," *Atlantic Monthly* 279, no. 2 (February 1997): 71–79.

2. Viet Thanh Nguyen, *Nothing Ever Dies: Vietnam and the Memory of War* (Cambridge, MA: Harvard University Press, 2016), 4.

Introduction

1. John Dower, *Embracing Defeat: Japan in the Wake of World War II* (New York: Norton, 1999), 34. KBS kwangbok 60-chunyŏn t'ŭkpyŏl p'ŭrojekt'ŭ t'im [KBS Special Project Team for 60th Anniversary of Liberation], ed. *8.15 ŭi kiŏk: Haebang konggan ŭi p'ungkyŏng, 40-in ŭi yŏksa ch'ehŏm* [Memories of August 15: Landscape of Liberation Space, Historical Experiences of Forty People] (P'aju: Tosŏ Ch'ulp'an Han'gilsa, 2005), 105.

2. Japanese colonial policies to "assimilate" Koreans were not terribly successful. For instance, less than 20 percent of Koreans were fluent in Japanese by 1945. To understand how Koreans navigated and resisted Japanese assimilation efforts, see Mark Caprio, *Japanese Assimilation Policies in Colonial Korea, 1910–1945* (Seattle: University of Washington Press, 2009); Todd A. Henry, *Assimilating Seoul: Japanese Rule and the Politics of Public Space in Colonial Korea, 1910–1945* (Berkeley: University of California Press, 2016).

3. Quoted in Joel Stevenson, "Korean Short Fiction from the Liberation Period, 1945–1948" (MA thesis, University of British Columbia, 1999), 112. To see how Korean writers narrated under colonial repression, see Janet Poole, *When the Future Disappears: The Modernist Imagination in Late Colonial Korea* (New York: Columbia University Press, 2014).

4. Glenn T. Trewartha and Wilbur Zelinsky, "Population Distribution and Change in Korea, 1925–1949," *Geographical Review* 45, no. 1 (1955): 1–26; Yun Kim, "Some Demo-

graphic Measurements for Korea Based on the Quasi-Stable Population Theory," *Demography* 2, no. 1 (1965): 567–578.

5. KBS kwangbok 60-chunyŏn t'ŭkpyŏl p'ŭrojekt'ŭ t'im, 105 and 185.

6. Yŏng-ho Ch'oe, Peter Lee, and Wm. Theodore de Bary, ed., *Sources of Korean Tradition*, vol. 2, *The Modern Period* (New York: Columbia University Press, 2000), 356.

7. Carter Eckert, *Offspring of Empire: The Colonial Origins of Korean Capitalism 1876–1945* (Seattle: University of Washington Press, 1991).

8. KBS kwangbok 60-chunyŏn t'ŭkpyŏl p'ŭrojekt'ŭ t'im, 105.

9. Dower, *Embracing Defeat*, 26.

10. Bruce Cumings, *The Origins of the Korean War*, vol. 1, *Liberation and the Emergence of Separate Regimes, 1945–1947* (Princeton, NJ: Princeton University Press, 1981), 117. Challenging conventional wisdom, which identified the war's beginnings with the June 1950 Soviet-sponsored invasion, Cumings argued that the Korean War was a civil war fought between Koreans to come to terms with the legacies of Japanese colonialism. In his analysis, the partition of the country in August 1945 and US policies enacted immediately following it ensured the emergence of separate regimes on the peninsula, which, in turn, made the outbreak of war inevitable.

11. Scholars have largely adopted Cumings's occupation as a prelude to war framework while identifying different "origins" moments and assigning responsibility for the war differently. Yet for all their differences, which are far from minor, the reason to study the occupation remains the same: to investigate the origins of the Korean War and Cold War divisions. See William Stueck, *The Korean War: An International History* (Princeton, NJ: Princeton University Press, 1995); Allan Millett, *The War for Korea, 1945–1950: A House Burning* (Lawrence: University of Kansas Press, 2005); Wada Haruki, *The Korean War: An International History* (Lanham, MD: Rowman & Littlefield, 2014); James Irving Matray, *The Reluctant Crusade: American Foreign Policy in Korea, 1941–1950* (Honolulu: University of Hawai'i Press, 1985). For Korean-language scholarship on the period, see Pak Myŏngnim, *Han'guk chŏnjaeng ŭi palbal kwa kiwŏn* [The Korean War: The Outbreak and Its Origins], 2 vols. (Seoul: Nanam Ch'ulp'an, 1996); and Tae Gyun Park, *An Ally and Empire: Two Myths of South Korea-United States Relations, 1945–1980*, trans. Ilsoo David Cho (Sŏngnam: The Academy of Korean Studies Press, 2012).

12. For interventions calling for histories outside of the bipolar Cold War frame, see Matthew Connelly, "Taking Off the Cold War Lens: Visions of North-South Conflict during the Algerian War for Independence," *American Historical Review* 105, no. 3 (June 2000): 739–769; Kuan-Hsing Chen, *Asia as Method: Toward Deimperialization* (Durham, NC: Duke University Press, 2010); Heonik Kwon, *The Other Cold War* (New York: Columbia University Press, 2010); and Odd Arne Westad, *The Global Cold War: Third World Interventions and the Making of Our Times* (Cambridge: Cambridge University Press, 2005).

13. Quoted in An T'aejŏng, *Chosŏn Nodong Chohap Chŏn'guk P'yŏngŭihoe* [The National Council of Labor Unions] (Seoul: Hyŏnjang esŏ Mirae rŭl, 2002), 429.

14. Cumings, *Origins of the Korean War,* 1:135.

15. As Fredrick Logevall reminds us, "To the decision makers of the past, the future was merely a set of possibilities." Fredrick Logevall, *Embers of War: The Fall of an Empire and the Making of America's Vietnam* (New York: Random House, 2014), 17.

16. Quoted from Roger N. Baldwin, "Why Democracy Fails in Korea," *New Leader,* January 24, 1948.

17. "The Economic Objectives of the Occupation," Report on Occupation South Korea, Part 2: Economics, 1947, p. 10, Record Group (hereafter RG) 554, box 41, National Archives and Records Administration (hereafter NARA), College Park, MD.

18. Gregg A. Brazinsky, *Nation Building in South Korea: Koreans, Americans, and the Making of Democracy* (Chapel Hill: University of North Carolina Press, 2009).

1. Pursuing Liberation

1. KBS kwangbok 60-chunyŏn t'ŭkpyŏl p'ŭrojekt'ŭ t'im [KBS Special Project Team for 60th Anniversary of Liberation], ed. *8.15 ŭi kiŏk: haebang konggan ŭi p'ungkyŏng, 40-in ŭi yŏksa ch'ehŏm* [Memories of August 15: Landscape of Liberation Space, Historical Experiences of Forty People] (P'aju: Tosŏ Ch'ulp'an Han'gilsa, 2005), 105.

2. KBS kwangbok 60-chunyŏn t'ŭkpyŏl p'ŭrojekt'ŭ t'im, 87–88.

3. Bruce Cumings calculates that almost 12 percent of the Korean population had been sent abroad as part of Japan's wartime mobilization. Bruce Cumings, *The Origins of the Korean War,* vol. 1, *Liberation and the Emergence of Separate Regimes, 1945–1947* (Princeton, NJ: Princeton University Press, 1981), 54. Other scholars believe the numbers were higher. See Andre Schmid, "Historicizing North Korea: State Socialism, Population Mobility, and Cold War Historiography," *American Historical Review* 123, no. 2 (Apr. 2018): 439–462, at 442. On Japanese conscription of Korean soldiers during war, see Takashi Fujitani, *Race for Empire: Koreans as Japanese and Japanese as Americans during World War II* (Berkeley: University of California Press, 2011).

4. KBS kwangbok 60-chunyŏn t'ŭkpyŏl p'ŭrojekt'ŭ t'im, 164.

5. Ji Young Kim, "Representations of Colonial Collaboration and Literature of Decolonization in Korea, 1945–1950" (PhD diss., University of Chicago, 2016), 1. Yi T'aejun was one of Korea's most influential writers during the colonial period. He left Seoul for north Korea in 1946. After he moved north, Yi rewrote the scene on the bus, showing Koreans jubilantly celebrating liberation upon hearing the news. His writings were banned in South Korea until 1988. "Before and After Liberation" chronicles key events and developments in Yi's life in the years right before and after liberation. See Chŏng Hyŏn'gi, "Chakkajŏk chŭngosim ŭi hyŏngsanghwa" [The Formation of a Writerly Hatred], in *Wŏlbuk munin yŏn'gu* [Study of North Korean Literary Writers], ed. Kwŏn Yŏngmin (Seoul: Munhak Sasangsa, 1989).

6. The dialogue is from Joel Stevenson, "Korean Short Fiction from the Liberation Period, 1945–1948" (MA thesis, University of British Columbia, 1999), 128–129.

7. KBS kwangbok 60-chunyŏn t'ŭkpyŏl p'ŭrojekt'ŭ t'im, 23.

8. Ch'oe Yisan, *Mutchi mara Ŭrhaesaeng: Haebang chŏnhu Kwangju iyagi* [Do Not Ask Those Born in 1935, the Year of Ŭrhae: Kwangju Before and After Liberation] (Seoul: P'urŭn Yŏksa, 2018), 172–173.

9. KBS kwangbok 60-chunyŏn t'ŭkpyŏl p'ŭrojekt'ŭ t'im, 185.

10. An Hoenam, "Pul" [Fire], *Munhak* [Literature], no.1 (July 1946): 35–47. Like his fictional character, An Hoenam was conscripted to work for the Japanese empire, in the coal mines of North Kyushu during the war. Influenced by the Japanese i-novel, Korean writers fictionalized their daily lives and experiences, making the authors, themselves, the main protagonist of the story. See Kim, "Representations of Colonial Collaboration," 44–45.

11. Pak Kŏlsun, "3·1 Undong kwa kungnae tongnip undong" [3·1 Movement and National Independence Movement], *Tongyanghak* 47 (2010): 259–280; and Pak Myŏngsu, "Kŏn'guk tongmaeng kwa chwaik minjok t'ongil chŏnsŏn" [National Foundation League and Left-Wing National United Front], *Sŏngsil sahak* 37 (2016): 239–284.

12. Pyŏn Ŭnjin, "1932–1945-nyŏn Yŏ Unhyŏng ŭi kungnae hwaltong kwa kŏn'guk chunbi" [Yŏ Unhyŏng's Domestic Activities and Preparation for National Foundation in 1932–1945], *Han'guk inmulsa yŏn'gu* 21 (2014): 473–504, at 499.

13. Yi Chŏngsik, *Yŏ Unhyŏng: Sidae wa sasang ŭl ch'owŏl han yunghwa chuŭija* [Yŏ Unhyŏng: An Advocate for Harmony Who Transcends Time and Thought] (Seoul: Seoul Taehakkyo Ch'ulp'anbu, 2008), 492–493.

14. Quoted from Yi, *Yŏ Unhyŏng*, 502.

15. Cumings, *Origins of the Korean War,* 1:87–88.

16. Hwasook Nam, *Women in the Sky: Gender and Labor in the Making of Modern Korea* (Ithaca, NY: Cornell University Press, 2021), 39–60.

17. Quoted in Mun Kyŏngnan, "Mi kunjŏnggi Han'guk yŏsŏng undong e kwanhan yŏn'gu" [Study on Korean Woman's Liberation Movement under US Military Government (1945–1948)] (MA thesis, Ewha Womans University, 1988), 35–36. Also see Mun Chihyŏn, "Haebang hu chwaikkye yŏsŏng undong ŭi panghyang kwa han'gye: Chapchi *Yŏsŏng kongnon* ŭl chungsim ŭro" [Post-Liberation Leftist Women's Movement and Their Limitations with a Focus on *Yŏsŏng kongnon*], *Ihwa sahak yŏn'gu* 54 (June 2017): 243–278.

18. Inyoung Kang, "Overlooked No More: Yu Gwansun, a Korean Independence Activist Who Defied Japanese Rule," *New York Times,* March 28, 2018.

19. Kang, "Overlooked No More."

20. Quoted in Mun, "Mi kunjŏnggi Han'guk yŏsŏng undong e kwanhan yŏn'gu," 35–36.

21. This bottom-up organizing varied from province to province. See Pak Myŏngnim, *Han'guk chŏnjaeng ŭi palbal kwa kiwŏn* [The Korean War: The Outbreak and Its Origins], 2 vols. (Seoul: Nanam Ch'ulp'an, 1996).

22. A. C. Bunce to A. W. Hanson Esq., October 28, 1933, Records of YMCA International Work in Korea, Collection Y.USA.9-2-21, box 6, folder 3, Kautz Family YMCA

Archives, University of Minnesota, Minneapolis, https://archives.lib.umn.edu/repositories /7/resources/948/inventory, see "PDF Collection Inventory."

23. Chŏnghŭi Ch'oe, *The Cry of the Harp and Other Korean Short Stories,* trans. Genell Y. Poitras (Arch Cape, OR: Pace International Research, 1983), 157.

24. Yong-Sŏp Kim, "The Landlord System and the Agricultural Economy during the Japanese Occupation Period," in *Landlords, Peasants, and Intellectuals in Modern Korea,* ed. Kie-Chung Pang and Michael Shin (Ithaca, NY: Cornell University Press, 2005).

25. Yi Hyesuk, "Mi kunjŏnggi nongmin undong ŭi sŏnggyŏk kwa chŏn'gae kwajŏng" [Characteristics and Development Process of the Peasant Movement during US Occupation], in *Haebang chikhu ŭi minjok munje wa sahoe undong* [National Issues and Social Movements Immediately after Liberation], ed. Han'guk sahoesa yŏn'guhoe (Seoul: Munhak kwa Chisŏngsa, 1988).

26. Chang Sanghwan, "Haebang kwa chŏnjaeng, kŭrigo chŏnjaeng ihu ŭi nongmin undong" [Emancipation and War, Peasant Movement after Korean War], *Nongch'on sahoe* 20, no. 1 (2010): 7–16.

27. Ch'ae Mansik, "Non iyagi" [Once upon a Rice Paddy], reprinted in *T'aep'yong Ch'onha,* ed. Kim Yunsik and Pak Wansŏ, *Han'guk sosŏl,* vol. 15 (Seoul: Tusan Tonga, 1996), 402–425. Quoted from Stevenson, "Korean Short Fiction from the Liberation Period," 23.

28. James C. Scott, *Seeing Like a State: How Certain Schemes to Improve the Human Condition Have Failed* (New Haven, CT: Yale University Press, 1999). On the great land surveys and how they were used to dispossess poor peasants of their land in colonial Korea, see Peter Duus, *The Abacus and the Sword: The Japanese Penetration of Korea, 1895–1910* (Berkeley: University of California Press, 1998).

29. Edwin Gragert, *Landownership under Colonial Rule: Korea's Japanese Experience, 1900–1935* (Honolulu: University of Hawai'i Press, 1994). Kim, "Landlord System."

30. Lori Watt, "Embracing Defeat in Seoul: Rethinking Decolonization in Korea, 1945," *Journal of Asian Studies* 74, no. 1 (2015): 153–174, at 158.

31. KBS kwangbok 60-chunyŏn t'ŭkpyŏl p'ŭrojekt'ŭ t'im, 87–88.

32. Quoted in John W. Treat, "Choosing to Collaborate: Yi Kwang-su and the Moral Subject in Colonial Korea," *Journal of Asian Studies* 71, no. 1 (2012): 81–102, at 94–95.

33. As historian Hong Sŏngch'an explains, "The Japanese knew that security measures alone would not suffice to establish a colonial system. They needed a permanent ruling structure to appease anti-Japanese sentiments." Quoted in Gi-Wook Shin, *Peasant Protest and Social Change in Colonial Korea* (Seattle: University of Washington Press, 1996), 51.

34. Ch'oe Chŏnghŭi, "P'ungnyu chaphinŭn maŭl" [Village Where Music Is Sung], *Paekmin,* September 1947, 67.

35. Charles K. Armstrong, *The North Korean Revolution, 1945–1950* (Ithaca, NY: Cornell University Press, 2003), 82.

36. Kim Soryun. "Han'guk hyŏndae sosŏl e nat'anan Ilbon'gun "Wianbu" sŏsa yŏn'gu" [Study of Narrations of Japanese Military "Comfort Women" Represented in Modern Korean Novels], *Kukche ŏmun* 77 (June 2018): 303–326.

37. KBS kwangbok 60-chunyŏn t'ŭkpyŏl p'ŭrojekt'ŭ t'im, 87–88.

38. "Summary of Statement of Choy Nueng (Daniel) Chin [Ch'oe Nŭngjin] (Head of the Detective Bureau)," Police Corruption, RG 554, box 64, NARA, College Park, MD.

39. "History of the Department of Police," Police Corruption, RG 554, box 64, NARA, College Park, MD.

40. "Police and Public Safety," p.1, Police Hist: Drafts, RG 554, box 26, NARA, College Park, MD.

41. Armstrong, *North Korean Revolution*, 76; and Suzy Kim, *Everyday Life in the North Korean Revolution, 1945–1950* (Ithaca, NY: Cornell University Press, 2013), 37.

42. Quoted in Sayaka Chatani, *Nation-Empire: Ideology and Rural Mobilization in Japan and Its Colonies* (Ithaca, NY: Cornell University Press, 2018), 242.

43. Yi Imha, *Haebang konggan, ilsang ŭl pakkun yŏsŏngdŭl ŭi yŏksa: Chedo wa kyujŏng, ŏgap e kyunyŏl ŭl naen yŏsŏngdŭl ŭi pallan* [The History of Women Who Changed Everyday Life and Liberation Space: The Mutiny of Women Who Clove through Institutions, Rules, and Oppression] (Seoul: Ch'ŏlsu wa Yŏnghŭi, 2015), 33–38.

44. KBS kwangbok 60-chunyŏn t'ŭkpyŏl p'ŭrojekt'ŭ t'im, 166.

45. Quoted in An T'aejŏng, *Chosŏn Nodong Chohap Chŏn'guk P'yŏngŭihoe* [The National Council of Labor Unions] (Seoul: Hyŏnjang esŏ Mirae rŭl, 2002), 65.

46. Kim Muyong, "Haebang chikhu nodongja kongjang kwalli wiwŏnhoe ŭi chojik kwa sŏnggyŏk" [Organization and characteristics of the Workers' Factory Self-Management Committee immediately after liberation], *Yŏksa yŏn'gu* 3 (1994): 81–145; Cho Sun'gyŏng and Yi Sukjin, *Naengjŏn ch'eje wa saengsan ŭi chŏngch'i: Mi kunjŏnggi ŭi nodong chŏngch'aek kwa nodong undong* [The Cold War System and the Politics of Production: Labor Policy and Labor Management during the US Military Government in South Korea] (Seoul: Ihwa Yŏja Taehakkyo Ch'ulp'anbu, 1995), 101.

47. The Korean communist movement was started by exiles in Moscow, Shanghai, and Tokyo in the late 1910s and early 1920s. Some of these overseas activists returned to Korea to establish an underground Communist Party in April 1925. At its peak, there were several thousand communists in Korea, who tried to organize workers, students, and peasants, but they had limited success owing to colonial repression and internal divisions. For a recent study on the Korean communist movement during the colonial period, see Vladimir Tikhonov, *The Red Decades: Communism as Movement and Culture in Korea, 1919–1945* (Honolulu: University of Hawai'i Press, 2023).

48. KBS kwangbok 60-chunyŏn t'ŭkpyŏl p'ŭrojekt'ŭ t'im, 246–247.

49. Janice Kim, *To Live to Work: Factory Women in Korea, 1910–1945* (Palo Alto, CA: Stanford University Press, 2009).

50. My description of Kang Churyong's life and activism draws from Nam, *Women in the Sky*, 12–38. .

51. Quoted in Hyaeweol Choi, Barbara Molony, and Janet Theiss, *Gender in Modern East Asia: An Integrated History* (New York: Routledge, 2016), 289.

52. Nam, *Women in the Sky,* 170–180; and Seol Kap, "The Welder Who Helped Bring Democracy to South Korea," *Jacobin,* December 16, 2020. In 2019, Kim Yong-hee, a former Samsung worker, staged a similar protest against his unjust firing when he spent almost a year atop an 82-foot traffic camera in Seoul. See Choe Sang-Hun, "'My Last Stand': In South Korea, a Protester's Lone Fight against Samsung," *New York Times,* April 20, 2020, A17; and Choe Sang-Hun, "South Korean Ends Yearlong Tower Protest after Samsung Apologizes," *New York Times,* May 30, 2020, A13.

53. Nam, *Women in the Sky,* 18.

54. An, *Chosŏn Nodong Chohap Chŏn'guk P'yŏngŭihoe,* 56–75.

55. Kim Ch'angsu, "Haebanggi chaju kwalli undong kwa Yi Kyuwŏn ŭi '"Haebang Kongjang'" [Autonomous Management Movement during the Liberation Period and Yi Kyuwŏn's "Liberation Factory"], *Chakkadŭl* 67 (2018): 179–195. A number of novels were written on the workers' self-management movement; see Sin Tŏkryong, ed. *P'okp'ung: Haebang konggan ŭi nodong undong sosŏl sŏnjip* [Selected Novels on Labor Movements in Liberation Space] (Seoul: Siinsa, 1990).

56. Yi Kyuwŏn, "Haebang kongjang" [Liberation Factory], *Uri munhak* [Our Literature] 10 (September 1948).

57. These loans, as Carter Eckert writes, "had become the very lifeblood of the company." Carter Eckert, *Offspring of Empire: The Colonial Origins of Korean Capitalism 1876–1945* (Seattle: University of Washington Press, 1991), 87.

58. Eckert, *Offspring of Empire,* 220.

59. An, *Chosŏn Nodong Chohap Chŏn'guk P'yŏngŭihoe,* 67–68.

2. Fractures Appear

1. An Hoenam, "Pul" [Fire], *Munhak* [Literature] 1 (July 1946).

2. "There were not that many Japanese people out and about," recalled Kang Ch'angdŏk, which he thought "unusual because many orchards were managed by Japanese." The few Japanese faces he did see walking around were deadly pale (*sasaek*). See KBS kwangbok 60-chunyŏn t'ŭkpyŏl p'ŭrojekt'ŭ t'im [KBS Special Project Team for 60th Anniversary of Liberation], 185.

3. Ch'oe Chŏnghŭi, *The Cry of the Harp and Other Korean Short Stories,* trans. Genell Y. Poitras (Arch Cape, OR: Pace International Research, 1983), 157. On peasant passivity after liberation, see Chŏn Sangin, "Mi kunjŏnggi ŭi nongŏp munje wa t'oji chŏngch'aek" [Agrarian Problem and Land Policy under the US Military Government], in *Nongji kaehyŏk yŏn'gu* [Farmland Reform Research], ed. Hong Sŏngch'an (Seoul: Yŏnse Taehakkyo Ch'ulp'anbu, 2001), 58–59.

4. Scholars have debated what inspired peasants to rebel in 1894, but there's no denying that they were driven—at least in part—by perceived injustice and inequality. See Young Ick Lew, "The Conservative Character of the 1894 Tonghak Peasant Uprising: A

Reappraisal with Emphasis on Chŏn Pong-jun's Background and Motivation," *Journal of Korean Studies* 7 (1990): 149–180.

5. Bruce Cumings, *The Origins of the Korean War*, vol. 1, *Liberation and the Emergence of Separate Regimes, 1945–1947* (Princeton, NJ: Princeton University Press, 1981), 282–286; and Gi-Wook Shin, *Peasant Protest and Social Change in Colonial Korea* (Seattle: University of Washington Press, 1996), 144–173.

6. Chang Sanghwan, "Haebang kwa chŏnjaeng, kŭrigo chŏnjaeng ihu ŭi nongmin undong" [Emancipation and War, Peasant Movement after Korean War], *Nongch'on sahoe* 20, no. 1 (2010); Yi Hyesuk, "Mi kunjŏnggi nongmin undong ŭi sŏnggyŏk kwa chŏn'gae kwajŏng" [Characteristics and Development Process of the Peasant Movement during US Occupation], in *Haebang chikhu ŭi minjok munje wa sahoe undong* [National Issues and Social Movements Immediately after Liberation], ed. Han'guk sahoesa yŏn'guhoe (Seoul: Munhak kwa Chisŏngsa, 1988).

7. Kim Sŭnghwan and Sin Pŏmsun, eds., *Haebang konggan ŭi munhak* [Literature of the Liberation Space] (Seoul: Tol Paegae, 1988), 290–291, cited in Chŏn Hŭngnam. "An Hoenam ŭi "Nongmin ŭi Piae"-ron" [Discussion of An Hoenam's "The Sorrows of Peasants"], *Han'guk ŏnŏ munhak* 29 (May 1991), 180.

8. Korean scholars have argued these land sales should be seen as the beginning of land reform in South Korea, which was not formally enacted until 1948. See Lee Yong-ki, "Taking Another Look at Land Reform in South Korea: A Focus on Kinship Networks," *Seoul Journal of Korean Studies* 26, no. 1 (June 2013): 103–128; Chang Sanghwan, "Nongji kaehyŏk kwajŏng e kwanhan siljŭngjŏk yŏn'gu," [An Empirical Study on the Process of Land Reform in the Area of South Korea (I)] *Kyŏngje sahak* 8 (1984): 195–272; Hong Song-chan, "Trends of the Landlord Pre- and Post-Land Reform," in Kim Seongho et al., *Nongji gaehyeoksa yongu* [Studies on the History of Korean Land Reform] (Seoul: Hanguk nongchon gyeongje yeonguwon, 1989); Cho Sŏkgon, "Nongji kaehyŏk jinhaeng kwajŏng kwa chŏngbu, chiju, nongmin ŭi ipchang: Kwangju-kun Namjong-myŏn sarye rŭl chungsim ŭro" [Study of the Response of Peasants, Landlords, and the Korean Government to Land Reform in South Korea: The Case of Namjong-myŏn in Kwangju-kun], *Taedong munhwa yŏn'gu* 75 (2011): 343–411; Pak Chindo, "Nongji kaehyŏk ŭi yŏksajŏk han'gye [The Historical Limitations of Land Reform]," *Kŭnhyŏndaesa kangjwa* 3 (1993): 122–134.

9. Owner-cultivators farmed their own small plots of land, semi-tenants both owned and leased land (because they didn't own enough), landless tenants strictly leased land, and farmhands and servants worked for others, and thus were the poorest of the poor. See Shin, *Peasant Protest*.

10. Ch'oe, *Cry of the Harp*, 157–165.

11. On the Naju farmers' six decade long struggle for restitution, see Ham Hanhŭi, "Mi kunjŏng ŭi nongji kaehyŏk kwa Han'guk nongmin ŭi taeŭng" [The US-Led Land Reform and the Korean Peasants' Response: Cultural Conflicts and Confrontations], *Han'guk munhwa illyuhak* 31, no. 2 (1998): 407–437; and Pak Ijun, "Mi kunjŏnggi Naju

Kungsam-myŏn nongji t'arhwan undong ŭi chŏn'gae kwajŏng" [The Land-Retaking Movement in Kungsam-myŏn, Naju under the US Military Administration], *Chibangsa wa chibang munhwa* 6, no. 1 (May 2003): 197–223. Disputes between small landowners and local elites were widespread during this period. See Yumi Moon, *Populist Collaborators: The Ilchinhoe and the Japanese Colonization of Korea, 1896–1910* (Ithaca, NY: Cornell University Press, 2013).

12. The 2018 South Korean miniseries *Hymn of Death,* based on a true story, illustrates how class hierarchy among Koreans was as much the cause of injustice as Japanese colonialism.

13. Yi Kyusu, "Chŏnnam Naju-kun Kungsam-myŏn ŭi t'oji soyu kwan'gye ŭi pyŏndong kwa Tongyang Chŏksik Chusik Hoesa ŭi t'oji chipchŏk" [Changes in Land Ownership Relations in "Kungsam-township" of Naju County, South Chŏlla Province, and Oriental Development Company's Land Accumulation], *Hanguk tongnip undongsa yŏn'gu* 14 (October 2000): 193–194.

14. Ham Hanhŭi, "Haebang ihu ŭi nongji kaehyŏk kwa Kungsam-myŏn nongmin ŭi sahoe kyŏngjejŏk chiwi mit kŭ pyŏnhwa" [Agrarian Reform after Liberation and Socioeconomic Standing of Kungsam-myŏn Peasants and Its Changes], *Hanguk munhwa illyuhak* 23 (1991): 26–27.

15. Kim, "Haebang chikhu nodongja kongjang kwalli wiwŏnhoe ŭi chojik kwa sŏnggyŏk," 109–110; An T'aejŏng, *Chosŏn Nodong Chohap Chŏn'guk P'yŏngŭihoe* [The National Council of Labor Unions] (Seoul: Hyŏnjang esŏ Mirae rŭl, 2002).

16. "History of the Department of Labor," p.3, RG 554, box 39, NARA, College Park, MD.

17. Kim, "Haebang chikhu nodongja kongjang kwalli wiwŏnhoe ŭi chojik kwa sŏnggyŏk"; An, *Chosŏn Nodong Chohap Chŏn'guk P'yŏngŭihoe.*

18. Yi Tonggyu, *Yi Tonggyu sŏnjip* [Collected Writings of Yi Tonggyu], ed. Song Yŏngsun (Seoul: Hyŏndae Munhak, 2010), 160–164.

19. An, *Chosŏn Nodong Chohap Chŏn'guk P'yŏngŭihoe,* 57.

20. Ijŏng Pak Hŏn-yŏng Chŏnjip P'yŏnjip Wiwŏnhoe, *Ijŏng Pak Hŏn-yŏng Chŏnjip* [Editorial Committee of I Chŏng- Pak Hŏn-yŏng's Complete Works], vol. 2 (Seoul: Yŏksa Pip'yŏngsa, 2004), 47–55.

21. Chang Sejin, "Ch'ian kwa chŏngch'i sai esŏ: haebanggi pin'gon taejung ŭi chonjaeron" [Between the Police and the Politics: How the Poor Masses Were Called by the Rulers during Korea's Liberation Period], *Hyŏndae munhak ŭi yŏn'gu* 56 (2015): 267.

22. Hwang Sunwŏn. "Sul iyagi" [The Story of Liquor], *Sinch'ŏnji* 2, no. 2 (February 1947); and *Sinch'ŏnji* 2, no. 3 (March/April 1947).

23. Sin Tŏkryong. "'Sul iyagi' e natanan nodong undong yangsang yŏn'gu: Haebang chikhu nodongja kongjang kwalli rŭl chungsim ŭro" [Study of Labor Movement Represented in "The Story of Liquor" with a Focus on Factory Management by Workers after Liberation], *Han'guk munye ch'angjak* 14, no. 1 (April 2015): 35–52.

24. Hwasook Nam, *Building Ships, Building a Nation: Korea's Democratic Unionism under Park Chung Hee* (Seattle: University of Washington Press, 2011), 31.

25. Kim Kyŏngil, *Ilche ha nodong undongsa* [The History of the Labor Movement under Japanese Colonial Rule] (Seoul: Ch'angjak kwa Pip'yŏngsa, 1992).

26. As Chŏn Sangin argues, "There are problems with categorizing the post-liberation landlord class as simply reactionary or anti-reformist. . . . Not all of the landlord class was progressive and reformist but their tendency to lead leftist movements was not insignificant." See Chŏn, "Mi kunjŏnggi ŭi nongŏp munje wa t'oji chŏngch'aek," 78.

27. Ruth Barraclough, "Red Love in Korea," in *Red Love across the Pacific: Political and Sexual Revolutions in the Twentieth Century,* ed. Heather Bowen-Struyk, Paula Rabinowitz, and Ruth Barraclough (New York: Palgrave Macmillan, 2015).

28. Hwasook Nam, *Women in the Sky: Gender and Labor in the Making of Modern Korea* (Ithaca, NY: Cornell University Press, 2021), 48.

29. The Japanese developed an elaborate system of surveillance, including a network of Korean informants and spies (Lee Jung-jae plays one in the 2015 South Korean blockbuster movie *Assassination*), to infiltrate Korean communist cells and track down their leaders. See Chong-Sik Lee and Robert A. Scalapino, *Communism in Korea,* vol. 1, *The Movement* (Berkeley: University of California Press, 1973).

30. Im Kyŏngsŏk. "Tongji ŭi son e kkŏkkin 'isanghyang ŭl hyang han kkum'" ["The Dream for a Utopia," Destroyed at the Hands of a Comrade], *P'ŭresian,* August 8, 2005.

31. Barraclough, "Red Love in Korea," 28.

32. These industrial cooperatives showed mixed results. See Nam, *Women in the Sky,* 80–81.

33. On independent worker activism during the colonial period, see Kim, *Ilche ha nodong undongsa;* Kim, *To Live to Work;* Nam, *Women in the Sky;* Ken Kawashima, *The Proletarian Gamble: Korean Workers in Interwar Japan* (Durham, NC: Duke University Press, 2009).

34. On anarchism in Korea, see Yi Horyong, *Han'guk ŭi anak'ijŭm: Sasang p'yŏn* [Anarchism in Korea: On Thoughts] (P'aju: Chisik Sanŏpsa, 2001); and Yi Horyong, *Han'guk ŭi anak'ijŭm: Undong p'yŏn* [Anarchism in Korea: The Movement] (P'aju: Chisik Sanŏpsa, 2015); Dongyoun Hwang, *Anarchism in Korea: Transnationalism and the Question of National Development, 1919–1984* (Albany: SUNY Press, 2016).

35. Nam, *Building Ships,* 31–32.

36. Quoted in Yi, *Yŏ Unhyŏng,* 501–502.

37. Erez Manela, *The Wilsonian Moment: Self-Determination and the International Origins of Anticolonial Nationalism* (New York: Oxford University Press, 2009).

38. In a last-ditch effort to find a political home, Yŏ went to Taiwan to join Chiang Kai-shek's Whampoa Clique, which would become the Blue Shirts Society. But in a familiar pattern, he left the group after being disappointed by Chiang Kai-shek's partisan anti-communism. Kyu-hyu Jo, "The Rise of the South Korean Left, The Death of Unitary Socialism, and the Origins of the Korean War, 1945–1947" (PhD diss., University of Chicago, 2019), 199–207.

39. Kim Samung, *Mongyang Yŏ Unhyŏng P'yŏngjŏn: Chinbojok Minju chuŭija* [Yŏ Unhyŏng: A Biography of a Progressive Democratic Thinker] (Seoul: Ch'aeryun, 2015), 47.

40. Quoted in Yi, *Yŏ Unhyŏng*, 521.

41. Yi, *Yŏ Unhyŏng*, 533–534.

42. Yi, *Yŏ Unhyŏng*, 532–549.

43. Jo, "Rise of the South Korean Left," 54.

44. On the fluctuating land prices in the South and how they related to political developments, see Chang, "Nongji kaehyŏk kwajŏng e kwanhan siljŭngjŏk yŏn'gu."

45. Mun Kyŏngnan, "Mi kunjŏnggi Han'guk yŏsŏng undong e kwanhan yŏn'gu" [Study on Korean Woman's Liberation Movement under US Military Government (1945–1948)] (MA thesis, Ewha Womans University, 1988); Mun Chihyŏn, "Haebang hu chwaikkye yŏsŏng undong ŭi panghyang kwa han'gye: Chapchi *Yŏsŏng kongnon* ŭl chungsim ŭro" [Post-Liberation Leftist Women's Movement and Their Limitations with a Focus on *Yŏsŏng kongnon*], *Ihwa sahak yŏn'gu* 54 (June 2017): 243–278.

3. The Race to Korea

1. Dean Rusk, *As I Saw It* (New York: W. W. Norton, 1990), 124.

2. Rusk, *As I Saw It*, 124.

3. Rusk said later: "I remember at the time that I was somewhat surprised that the Soviets accepted the 38th parallel since I thought they might insist upon a line further south in view of our respective military positions in the areas." Draft Memorandum to the Joint Chief of Staff, [undated], *Foreign Relations of the United States, 1945, vol. 6, The British Commonwealth, the Far East,* ed. John P. Glennon et al. (Washington, DC: Government Printing Office, 1969), doc. 771 (hereafter *FRUS,* 1945, vol. 6).

4. "Translation of Message from Harry S. Truman to Joseph Stalin," trans. Sergey Radchenko, August 19, 1945, History and Public Policy Program Digital Archive, Wilson Center, original in Russian State Archive of Socio-Political History (RGASPI), fond 558, opis 11, delo 372, listy 112–113, https://digitalarchive.wilsoncenter.org/document/122333.

5. Stalin accommodated the United States almost everywhere in Asia, even when the favor wasn't returned. See Norman M. Naimark, *Stalin and the Fate of Europe: The Struggle for Sovereignty* (Cambridge, MA: Harvard University Press, 2019), 12.

6. Jongsoo James Lee, *The Partition of Korea after World War II: A Global History* (New York: Palgrave Macmillan, 2006), 6.

7. Quoted in Bruce Cumings, *The Origins of the Korean War,* vol. 1, *Liberation and the Emergence of Separate Regimes, 1945–1947* (Princeton, NJ: Princeton University Press, 1981), 106.

8. Quoted in Cumings, *Origins of the Korean War,* 1:109.

9. Dipesh Chakrabarty, *Provincializing Europe: Postcolonial Thought and Historical Difference* (Princeton, NJ: Princeton University Press), 8.

10. Walter LaFeber, *The Clash: US-Japanese Relations throughout History* (New York: W. W. Norton, 1998), 85–86.

11. Roosevelt-Stalin Meeting, February 8, 1945, 3:30 p.m., Livadia Palace, Bohlen Minutes, *Foreign Relations of the United States, Diplomatic Papers, Conferences at Malta and Yalta, 1945*, ed. Bryton Barron, Pt. 3, *The Yalta Conference*, February 4–11, 1945, doc. 393 (Washington, DC: US Government Printing Office, 1955), https://history.state.gov /historicaldocuments/frus1945Malta/comp3.

12. Quoted from Lee, *Partition of Korea*, 9.

13. The Political Adviser in Korea (Benninghoff) to the Secretary of State, September 15, 1945, *FRUS*, 1945, vol. 6, doc. 781.

14. Cumings, *Origins of the Korean War*, 1:123; James I. Matray, "Hodge Podge: American Occupation Policy in Korea, 1945–1948," *Korean Studies* 19 (1995): 17–38.

15. "Gen. John R. Hodge Dies at 70," *New York Times*, November 13, 1963, 41.

16. David Halberstam, *The Fifties* (New York: Random House, 1994), 81.

17. John Dower, *Embracing Defeat: Japan in the Wake of World War II* (New York: Norton, 1999), 223.

18. Cumings, *Origins of the Korean War*, 1:127.

19. Cumings, *Origins of the Korean War*, 1:448.

20. MacArthur was simultaneously head of the Japanese occupation, the US Far East Command, and the US Army in the Far East, which put him in control over close to 80 million people. See Daniel Immerwahr, *How to Hide an Empire: A History of the Greater United States* (New York: Farrar, Straus, and Giroux, 2019), 224.

21. Quoted in Pak Myŏngnim, *Han'guk chŏnjaeng ŭi palbal kwa kiwŏn*, vol. 2 [The Korean War: The Outbreak and Its Origins], 55–56.

22. E. Grant Meade, *American Military Government in Korea* (New York: King's Crown Press, 1951), 49.

23. Beginning in 1942, the US government, in collaboration with Harvard, Stanford, Columbia, Northwestern, and the University of Chicago, designed a study program to train civilians in civil affairs and military governance in preparation for the war's end. For the Far Eastern theater, 1,600 civilian officers were trained for the postwar occupation of Japan. Henry H. Em, "Civil Affairs Training and the US Military Government in Korea," in *Chicago Occasional Papers in Korea*, ed. Bruce Cumings (Chicago: Center for East Asian Studies, University of Chicago, 1991), 94–135.

24. Cumings, *Origins of the Korean War*, 1:128.

25. Philip H. Taylor, "Administration and Operation of Military Government in Korea," in *American Experiences in Military Government in World War II*, ed. Carl J. Friedrich (New York: Rinehart, 1948), 355.

26. Meade, *American Military Government*, 49, 51.

27. See National Committee for the Investigation of the Truth about the Jeju April 3 Incident, Jeju 4·3 Peace Foundation, *The Jeju 4·3 Incident Investigation Report* (Jeju: Jeju 4·3 Foundation, 2014), 76; Kyengho Son, "The 4:3 Incident: Background, Development

and Pacification, 1945–1949" (PhD diss., Ohio State University, 2008), 52–55.

28. Numerous people's committees formed at the township and village levels on the island after liberation. The leaders of these local PCs comprised the executive leadership of the main Jeju's People's Committee, which made coordination between the different PCs possible. See *The Jeju 4·3 Incident Investigation Report*, 87–89; and Son, "The 4:3 Incident," 69–74.

29. John Merrill, "The Cheju-do Rebellion," *Journal of Korean Studies* 2 (1980): 151–152; *The Jeju 4·3 Incident Investigation Report*, 87–90.

30. A number of the leaders of the People's Committee had served multiyear prison sentences during the colonial period for organizing Jeju's famous women divers against Japanese exploitation. Meade, *American Military Government*, 185–186; Son, "The 4:3 Incident," 68, 96–97; Bruce Cumings, *The Origins of the Korean War*, vol. 2, *The Roaring of the Cataract, 1947–1950* (Princeton, NJ: Princeton University Press, 1990), 252.

31. Report of trip to the Province of Jeju during the period 4–6 December 1946, December 9, 1948, Bertsch Papers, box 4, folder K-74, Harvard-Yenching Library, Harvard University, Cambridge, MA.

4. Reversing the Tide

1. Richard J. H. Johnston, "U.S. Keeps Japanese Rulers in Korea to Enforce Orders," *New York Times,* September 10, 1945.

2. Gordon Walker, "Blunder May Provoke Civil War in Korea," *The Observer,* November 18, 1945, 5; The Acting Political Adviser in Korea (Langdon) to the Secretary of State, November 26, 1945, *Foreign Relations of the United States,* 1945, vol. 6, *The British Commonwealth, the Far East,* ed. John P. Glennon et al. (Washington, DC: Government Printing Office, 1969), doc. 846 (hereafter *FRUS,* 1945, vol. 6).

3. Johnston, "U.S. Keeps Japanese Rulers in Korea to Enforce Orders."

4. Quoted in Bruce Cumings, *The Origins of the Korean War,* vol. 1: *Liberation and the Emergence of Separate Regimes, 1945–1947* (Princeton, NJ: Princeton University Press, 1981), 138.

5. "Truman Defends Policy in Korea; Korea: Rising Sun Flag Lowered and Old Glory Raised," *New York Times,* September 13, 1945.

6. If Stalin wasn't interested in fomenting socialist revolutions in Eastern Europe at this time, he was certainly not interested in doing so in southern Korea. See Norman M. Naimark, *Stalin and the Fate of Europe: The Struggle for Sovereignty* (Cambridge, MA: Harvard University Press, 2019), 11.

7. The Political Adviser in Korea (Benninghoff) to the Secretary of State, September 15, 1945, *FRUS,* 1945, vol. 6, doc. 781.

8. "Korea Gets Pledge by U. S. to Oust Japanese Rapidly: The Japanese Surrender and Bring to an End to Their Rule on Korea," *New York Times,* September 12, 1945.

9. Stewart Meacham, Labor Adviser to the Commanding General of the United

States Armed Forces in Korea, "Korean Labor Report," Prepared for the Secretary of Labor, November 1947, p. 14, box 1, folder 2, American Friends Service Committee Archives on Korea, Philadelphia, PA (hereafter AFSC Archives on Korea).

10. E. Grant Meade, *American Military Government in Korea* (New York: King's Crown Press, 1951), 72.

11. The Acting Political Adviser in Korea (Langdon) to the Secretary of State, November 26, 1945, *FRUS*, 1945, vol. 6, doc. 834.

12. The Political Adviser in Korea (Benninghoff) to the Secretary of State, September 29, 1945, *FRUS*, 1945, vol. 6, doc. 788.

13. Mun Kyŏngnan, "Mi kunjŏnggi Han'guk yŏsŏng undong e kwanhan yŏn'gu" [Study on Korean Woman's Liberation Movement under US Military Government (1945–1948)] (MA thesis, Ewha Womans University, 1988), 37–38.

14. Cumings, *Origins of the Korean War,* 1:97.

15. "Yi Myo-muk," *Han'guk minjok munhwa taebaekkwa sajŏn* [Encyclopedia of Korean Culture], https://encykorea.aks.ac.kr/Article/E0044264 (accessed January 4, 2023).

16. Richard J. H. Johnston, "Korea Awakening," *New York Times,* September 12, 1945.

17. Cumings, *Origins of the Korean War,* 1:142.

18. "Report of Investigation to Commanding General XXIV Corps," January 11, 1947, Bertsch Papers, box 1, folder G, Harvard-Yenching Library, Harvard University, Cambridge, MA (hereafter Bertsch Papers).

19. The Political Adviser in Korea (Benninghoff) to the Acting Political Adviser in Japan (Atcheson), October 9, 1945, *FRUS*, 1945, vol. 6, doc. 793.

20. Kyu Ho Youm, *Press Law in South Korea* (Ames: Iowa University Press, 1996), 38–40.

21. Quoted from Cumings, *Origins of the Korean War,* 1:498.

22. Richard J. H. Johnston, "Radicals in Korea Hit Gen. A. V. Arnold: Claim to Represent Country—Great Number of Parties Adds Confusion to Politics," *New York Times,* October 30, 1945.

23. Johnston, "Radicals in Korea."

24. The Political Adviser in Korea (Benninghoff) to the Acting Political Adviser in Japan (Atcheson), October 10, 1945, *FRUS*, 1945, vol. 6, doc. 794.

25. Cumings, *Origins of the Korean War,* 1:135.

26. Chengpang Lee and Myungsahm Suh, "State Building and Religion: Explaining the Diverged Path of Religious Change in Taiwan and South Korea, 1950–1980," *American Journal of Sociology* 123, no. 2 (2017): 465–509, 479.

27. Sungik Yang, "Myo Mook Lee," Korean Alumni Biographies Project, Harvard University, June 3, 2023, https://projects.iq.harvard.edu/koreanalumnibiographiesproject/people/myo-mook-lee. "Yi Myo-muk," *Han'guk minjok munhwa taebaekkwa sajŏn* [Encyclopedia of Korean Culture], https://encykorea.aks.ac.kr/Article/E0044264 (accessed January 4, 2023); *Han'gyŏre,* July 20, 2019. https://www.hani.co.kr/arti/culture/religion/902607.html (accessed January 4, 2023).

28. Pak So-yŏng, "Migunjŏnggi t'ongyŏk chŏngch'i: Yi Myo-muk ŭl chungsim ŭro"

[Interpreter Politics during the U.S. Army Military Government: Focusing on Myo Mook Lee], *T'ongbŏnyŏkhak yŏn'gu*, 23, no. 2 (2019): 93–116, at 109.

29. For a short biography of Cho, see "Cho Pyŏngok," *Han'guk minjok munhwa tae-baekkwa sajŏn* [Encyclopedia of Korean Culture], https://encykorea.aks.ac.kr/Article /E0051799 (accessed January 6, 2024); and Bruce Cumings, *Korea's Place in the Sun: A Modern History* (New York: W.W. Norton, 2005), 452. There were others in the KDP, besides Cho, with anticolonial credentials. See Allan Millett, *The War for Korea, 1945– 1950: A House Burning* (Lawrence: University of Kansas Press, 2005), 47.

30. Cumings, *Origins of the Korean War*, 1:166.

31. Summary of Statement of Choy Nueng (Daniel) Chin (Head of Detective Bureau), NARA, RG 554, box 64, 1, College Park, MD.

32. "Report on Chough Pyung Ok [Cho Pyŏngok]," Bertsch Papers, box 4, folder G-5.

33. Roger N. Baldwin, "Why Democracy Fails in Korea," *New Leader*, January 24, 1948, Roger Nash Baldwin Papers, series 3: Writings and Papers, box 22, folder 14, Public Policy Papers, Department of Special Collections, Princeton University Library.

34. Herbert Bix, *Hirohito and the Making of Modern Japan* (New York: HarperCollins, 2000).

35. MacArthur ordered his officials to sanitize Hirohito's war record, which had enormous ramifications for how Japanese society would remember the war. "If the man in whose name imperial Japan had conducted foreign and military policy for twenty years was not held accountable for the initiation or conduct of the war," John Dower writes, "why should anyone expect ordinary people to dwell on such matters, or think seriously about their own personal responsibility." John Dower, *Embracing Defeat: Japan in the Wake of World War II* (New York: Norton, 1999), 28.

36. In addition to police officers, village and town secretaries, and other government officials were exempt from military and labor conscription. See Sayaka Chatani, *Nation-Empire: Ideology and Rural Mobilization in Japan and Its Colonies* (Ithaca, NY: Cornell University Press, 2018), 224.

37. Kyu-hyu Jo, "The Rise of the South Korean Left, the Death of Unitary Socialism, and the Origins of the Korean War, 1945–1947" (PhD diss., University of Chicago, 2019), 178.

38. "History of the Department of Labor," p. 4, RG 554, box 39, NARA, College Park, MD.

39. "History of the Department of Labor," p. 7, RG 554, box 39, NARA, College Park, MD.

40. "History of the Department of Labor," p. 6, RG 554, box 39, NARA, College Park, MD.

41. "Remembering Stewart Meacham: For Peace, Justice, and Life," *Christianity and Crisis*, October 14, 1985, Stewart Meacham Obituary and Articles, AFSC Archives on Korea.

42. Meacham, "Korean Labor Report," 7.

43. Meacham, "Korean Labor Report," 7.

44. Quoted in "Report" issued by the American Committee to Aid Korean Trade Unions, WDSCA 014 Korea (1 July 47 to 3 Aug 47), RG 165, entry 463, box 250, NARA, College Park, MD.

45. Meacham, "Korean Labor Report," 15.

46. Yi Sŏngkyun, "Mi kunjŏnggi nodong undong ŭi chŏn'gae kwajŏng e kwanhan il yŏn'gu" [A Study on the Development Process of the Labor Movement during the US Military Government], in *Han'guk kŭnhyŏndae ŭi minjok munje wa nodong undong* [Ethnic Problems and Labor Movement of Modern and Contemporary Korea], ed. Han'guk sahoesa yŏn'guhoe (Seoul: Munhakkwa Chisŏngsa, 1989), 170–174.

47. An T'aejŏng, *Chosŏn Nodong Chohap Chŏn'guk P'yŏngŭihoe* [The National Council of Labor Unions] (Seoul: Hyŏnjang esŏ Mirae rŭl, 2002), 67.

48. Thomas H. Lee, "The Origins of the Taegu Insurrection of 1946" (BA thesis, Harvard University, 1990), 70.

49. Socialist activists encouraged workers to collaborate with "conscientious" capitalists to raise productivity and rehabilitate the country's industrial base. In fact, they organized associations in the factories "to get workers to arrive on time, avoid absences, clean the factory, follow work rules, restrain strikes, and compete with other unions in productivity-doubling campaign." See Yi, "Mi kunjŏnggi nodong undong ŭi chŏn'gae kwajŏng e kwanhan il yŏn'gu," 173; and Hwasook Nam, *Building Ships, Building a Nation: Korea's Democratic Unionism under Park Chung Hee* (Seattle: University of Washington Press, 2011), 33.

50. Dower, *Embracing Defeat*, 82.

51. Owen Jones, diary entry for June 15, 1946, folder Diary 6/15/1946–3/16/1947, box 4, Owen T. Jones Papers, Harry S. Truman Presidential Library, Independence, MO (hereafter Jones Papers).

52. "The Rice Problem," p.4, Rice 1946–47, RG 554, box 17, NARA, College Park, MD.

53. "Press Conference—23 October 1945," Control and Disposition of Former Japanese Property, RG 554, box 37, NARA, College Park, MD.

54. Richard D. Robinson, "Betrayal of a Nation," unpublished manuscript, 1950, p. 78, Harvard-Yenching Library, DS917.52 .R63 1950x, Harvard University, Cambridge, MA.

55. "General Notice No. 1," National Issues: Inflation, Currency, Rice, Housing Problems, RG 554, box 65, NARA, College Park, MD.

56. Baldwin, "Why Democracy Fails in Korea."

57. Arthur C. Bunce to Edwin Martin, July 22, 1947, RG 59, File 895.00/2-2447, NARA, College Park, MD.

58. Kie-chung Pang, "Yi Hun-gu's Agricultural Reform Theory and Nationalist Economic Thought," *Seoul Journal of Korean Studies* 19, no. 1 (2006): 61–89.

59. Yi Hyesuk, "Mi kunjŏnggi nongmin undong ŭi sŏnggyŏk kwa chŏn'gae kwajŏng"

[Characteristics and Development Process of the Peasant Movement during US Occupation], in *Haebang chikhu ŭi minjok munje wa sahoe undong* [National Issues and Social Movements Immediately after Liberation], ed. Han'guk sahoesa yŏn'guhoe (Seoul: Munhak kwa Chisŏngsa, 1988), 244.

60. Yi Yonggi, "Ŏnŭ pinnong ŭi chŏnjaeng kwa "Ppalgaengi" ranŭn chŏnhyŏng" [A Poor Peasant's Experience of the War and Retribution Called "Commie"], *Kusulsa yŏn'gu* 2, no.1 (2011): 51–74.

61. Ch'ae Mansik, "Non iyagi" ["Once Upon a Rice Paddy"], reprinted in *T'aep'yong Ch'onha*, ed. Kim Yunsik and Pak Wansŏ, *Han'guk sosŏl*, vol. 15 (Seoul: Tusan Tonga, 1996), 402–425. Quoted in Stevenson, "Korean Short Fiction from the Liberation Period," 23–24.

62. Cited in Chŏn Hŭngnam, "An Hoenam ŭi "Nongmin ŭi Piae"-ron" [Discussion of An Hoenam's "The Sorrows of Peasants"], *Han'guk ŏnŏ munhak* 29 (May 1991): 165–186, at 180.

63. "Press Conference—23 October 1945," Control and Disposition of Former Japanese Property, RG 554, box 37, NARA, College Park, MD.

64. See Ladejinsky memorandum on "Agrarian Reform in Korea," July 4, 1946, Supreme Commander of Allied Powers (hereafter SCAP), RG 331, box 8968, NARA, College Park, MD. Ladejinsky also later advised on land reform in Taiwan and South Vietnam.

65. Quoted from Yi Hyesuk, "Mi kunjŏnggi nongmin undong ŭi sŏnggyŏk kwa chŏn'gae kwajŏng" [Characteristics and Development Process of the Peasant Movement during US Occupation], 245.

66. The phenomenal growth of the NFPU was part of an associational explosion in liberated Korea in which the popular classes sought organizations to represent their interests. See Sunhyuk Kim, *The Politics of Democratization in Korea: The Role of Civil Society* (Pittsburgh, PA: University of Pittsburgh Press, 2000), 26.

67. Chang Sanghwan, "Haebang kwa chŏnjaeng, kŭrigo chŏnjaeng ihu ŭi nongmin undong" [Emancipation and War, Peasant Movement after Korean War], *Nongch'on sahoe* 20, no. 1 (2010), 10–11.

68. Quoted in Pak, "Mi kunjŏnggi Naju Kungsam-myŏn nongji t'arhwan undong ŭi chŏn'gae kwajŏng," 206.

69. Pak, "Mi kunjŏnggi Naju Kungsam-myŏn nongji t'arhwan undong ŭi chŏn'gae kwajŏng"; and Ham Hanhŭi, "Mi kunjŏng ŭi nongji kaehyŏk kwa Han'guk nongmin ŭi taeŭng" [The US-Led Land Reform and the Korean Peasants' Response: Cultural Conflicts and Confrontations], *Han'guk munhwa illyuhak* 31:2 (1998).

70. Quoted in Pak, "Mi kunjŏnggi Naju Kungsam-myŏn nongji t'arhwan undong ŭi chŏn'gae kwajŏng," 208. To understand why blue and green were seen as the same in Korean culture, see Andrew I. Kim, "Korean Color Terms: An Aspect of Semantic Fields and Related Phenomena," *Anthropological Linguistics* 27, no. 4 (1985): 425–436.

5. False Starts and Missed Opportunities

1. United States Army Forces in Korea (USAFIK) to Supreme Commander Allied Powers (SCAP), Secret Cable on Conditions in Korea, December 1945, National Issues: Inflation, Currency, Rice, Housing Problems, RG 554, box 65, NARA, College Park, MD.

2. Stewart Meacham, Labor Adviser to the Commanding General of the United States Armed Forces in Korea, "Korean Labor Report," http://library.haverford.edu/eastasian/Files/Survey_of_AFSC_Archives_on_Korea_(1938-2000).pdf. Prepared for the Secretary of Labor, November 1947, p. 14, box 1, folder 2, American Friends Service Committee Archives on Korea, Philadelphia, PA.

3. Jongsoo James Lee, *The Partition of Korea after World War II: A Global History* (New York: Palgrave Macmillan, 2006), 82. Soviet negotiators also wanted written into the final communiqué the goals of "developing the country on democratic principles and the earliest possible liquidation of the disastrous results of the protracted Japanese domination in Korea."

4. The Chargé in the Soviet Union (Kennan) to the Secretary of State, January 25, 1946, *Foreign Relations of the United States,* 1946, vol. 8, *The Far East,* ed. John G. Reid and Herbert A. Fine (Washington, DC: Government Printing Office, 1971), doc. 466 (hereafter *FRUS,* 1946, vol. 8).

5. "Big Three Re-Establish Unity in Wide Accord," *New York Times,* December 28, 1945.

6. Quoted in John Lewis Gaddis, *The United States and the Origins of the Cold War, 1941–1947* (New York: Columbia University Press, 1973), 289.

7. "Koreans Riot, Stone Yanks in Protest of Big 3 Plan," *Washington Post,* December 31, 1945, 1.

8. H. Merrill Benninghoff and Richard Robinson wanted the "Provisional" changed to "Interim" to avoid confusion and because they feared Kim would use the similarity in the names for political purposes. The Political Adviser in Korea (Benninghoff) to the Secretary of State, January 7, 1946, *FRUS,* 1946, vol. 8, doc. 455.

9. Kyengho Son, "The 4:3 Incident: Background, Development and Pacification, 1945–1949" (PhD diss., Ohio State University, 2008), 33. Quote from the *Donga Ilbo,* December 30, 1945.

10. Chŏn Pong-gwan, *Hwanggŭmgwang sidae: Singminji sidae Hanbando rŭl twihŭndŭn t'ugi wa yongmang ŭi in'gansa* [The Age of Gold: The History of Speculation and Desire That Shook the Korean Peninsula during the Colonial Era] (Seoul: Sallim, 2005); Grace Cho, "Last Office for Korea's Provisional Gov't in 1940s to Regain Former Glory," *Younhap News,* February 28, 2013, http://en.yna.co.kr/view/AEN20130228008700315.

11. Robert S. Kim, *Project Eagle: The American Christians of North Korea in World War II* (Lincoln: Potomac Books of the University of Nebraska Press, 2017), 41–46.

12. Alastair Middleton, "Kim Gu [Kim Ku]—'Baek Beom' [Paekbŏm]—Independence Fighter, Writer, Politician, and Punter," February 29, 2012, https://korearacing.live/tag/sinsel-dong.

13. Hyung Kyung Lee, "Recreating Dongdaemun [Tongdaemun] Stadium in South Korea: Beyond Japanese Colonial Memories and Towards a Global City," *Seoul Journal of Korean Studies* 31, no. 1 (2018): 99–128, at 109.

14. There are still questions surrounding the assassination of Song Chinu. Bruce Cumings assembled evidence that pointed to Kim as the killer. Tae Gyun Park [Pak T'aegyun], on the other hand, thinks there was "little chance" Kim ordered the hit based on his reading of the available evidence. See Bruce Cumings, *The Origins of the Korean War*, vol. 1, *Liberation and the Emergence of Separate Regimes, 1945–1947* (Princeton, NJ: Princeton University Press, 1981), 219; and Tae Gyun Park, *An Ally and Empire: Two Myths of South Korea-United States Relations, 1945–1980,* trans. Ilsoo David Cho (Sŏngnam: Academy of Korean Studies Press, 2012), 52.

15. Kyengho Son, "The 4:3 Incident: Background, Development and Pacification, 1945–1949" (PhD diss., Ohio State University, 2008), 34.

16. Before Kim Ku and Syngman Rhee were allowed to return to Korea, the high command made both men sign a pledge stating, "We shall be allowed to enter as strictly as private individuals and not in any official capacity. I further have the honor to state that on entering Korea we do not expect to function, either collectively or individually, as a government or such body exercising civil and/or political power. Our aim shall be to cooperate with the United States Military Government in establishing order as will benefit the Korean people." Kim Ku to Lt. Gen A. C. Wedemeyer, CG US Forces in China, November 19, 1945, AG files, *History of the United States Army Forces in Korea*, part 2, https://db.history.go.kr/contemp/level.do?levelId-husa_002_0010_0060#notehusa_002 _0010_0060_0018.

17. Cumings, *Origins of the Korean War*, 1:221.

18. Cumings, *Origins of the Korean War*, 1:221.

19. Cho Mansik's nationalist record was not perfect. He had been stained by his public efforts to recruit Korean students for Japan's war efforts, which left him vulnerable to charges of collaborating after the war. See Charles K. Armstrong, *The North Korean Revolution, 1945–1950* (Ithaca, NY: Cornell University Press, 2003), 55.

20. "Soviet Report on Communists in Korea, 1945," n.d., trans. from Russian by Gary Goldberg, Wilson Center Digital Archive, AGShVS RF. F. 172. OP 614631. D. 23, pp. 21–26, https://digitalarchive.wilsoncenter.org/document/soviet-report-communists-korea-1945.

21. Pak Myŏngnim, *Han'guk chŏnjaeng ŭi palbal kwa kiwŏn*, vol. 2 *Wŏnin kwa kiwŏn*, [The Korean War: The Outbreak and Its Origins, vol. 2: The Origins and the Causes of the Conflict], 45–46; Andrei Lankov, *From Stalin to Kim Il Sung: The Formation of North Korea, 1945–1960* (New Brunswick, NJ: Rutgers University Press, 2002), 10–12.

22. Owing to the weakness of the Communist Party in the North, Soviet officials initially sought to establish a united front, including conscientious capitalists and landowners, which they envisioned Cho leading. See Lee, *Partition of Korea*, 133–134. Also see Erik Van Zee, *Socialism in One Zone: Stalin's Policy in Korea, 1945–1947* (Oxford: Berg, 1989), 115, in which Van Zee contends that the Soviets wanted Kim Il Sung to

work with Cho Mansik as his communist partner in the KDP in the North. In November 1945, Kim and Cho had met to discuss forming a new party together.

23. Oliver wrote Rhee's speeches in the United States when he was in exile and served as a political adviser when Rhee became president of South Korea. For the Rhee-Oliver relationship, see David A. Frank and WooSoo Park, "Syngman Rhee, Robert T. Oliver, and the Symbolic Construction of the Republic of Korea during the Global Cold War," *Rhetoric Review* 37, no. 1 (2018): 105–117.

24. For Rhee's life in exile, see David P. Fields, *Foreign Friends: Syngman Rhee, American Exceptionalism, and the Division of Korea* (Lexington: University of Kentucky Press, 2019).

25. Mark Gayn, *Japan Diary* (New York: William Sloan Associates, 1948), 358.

26. The Ambassador to the Soviet Union (Harriman) to the Secretary of State, January 25, 1946, *FRUS*, 1946, vol. 8, doc. 468.

27. General of the Army Douglas MacArthur to the Joint Chiefs of Staff, February 2, 1946, *FRUS*, 1946, vol. 8, doc. 473.

28. Secret Cable on Conditions in Korea from USAFIK to SCAP, December 1945, National Issues: Inflation, Currency, Rice, Housing Problems, RG 554, box 65, NARA, College Park, MD.

29. Cumings, *Origins of the Korean War*, 1:227.

30. The Chargé in the Soviet Union (Kennan) to the Secretary of State, January 25, 1946, *FRUS*, 1946, vol. 8, doc. 465.

31. General of the Army Douglas MacArthur to the Joint Chiefs of Staff, January 23, 1946, *FRUS*, 1946, vol. 8, doc. 463.

32. A. C. Bunce to Charles Herschleb Esq., April 14, 1929, Records of YMCA International Work in Korea, Collection Y.USA.9-2-21, box 3, folder 7, Kautz Family YMCA Archives, University of Minnesota, Minneapolis (hereafter YMCA International Work in Korea Collection), https://archives.lib.umn.edu/7/repositories/948/inventory, see "PDF Collection Inventory." Danish cooperatives drew the interest of Christians and Christian missionaries looking for an alternative to communism. See Albert L. Park, "Reclaiming the Rural: Modern Danish Cooperative Living in Colonial Korea, 1925–37," *Journal of Korean Studies* 19, no. 1 (Spring 2014): 115–151.

33. Bunce was born in Manchester, England, before emigrating to Canada with his family as a young boy. He became a naturalized American citizen in 1941. A. C. Bunce, November 28, 1931, box 6, folder 2, YMCA International Work in Korea Collection.

34. Arthur C. Bunce, "The Future of Korea: Part II," *Far Eastern Survey* 13, no. 10 (1944): 85–88, at 85.

35. A. C. Bunce to Charles Herschleb Esq., April 14, 1929, box 3, folder 7, YMCA International Work in Korea Collection.

36. A. C. Bunce to Frank V. Slack Esq., September 14, 1934, box 1, folder 13, YMCA International Work in Korea Collection.

37. A. C. Bunce to Charles Herschleb Esq., March 6, 1934, box 6, folder 4, YMCA International Work in Korea Collection.

38. A. C. Bunce to Frank V. Slack Esq., November 14, 1933, box 6, folder 3, YMCA International Work in Korea Collection.

39. Gayn, *Japan Diary,* 351.

40. Gayn, *Japan Diary,* 433.

41. Gayn, *Japan Diary,* 432.

42. Letter from GHQ SCAP to CG USAFIK, April 12, 1946, 014-1 #1 Korea, SCAP, RG 331, box 785-2, NARA, College Park, MD.

43. Yun Taeyŏp, "Kŏn'guk ŭi chŏngch'i wa Mi kunjŏng: Kŏn'guk hŏnbŏp nongji kaehyŏk chohang ŭi kyubŏmjŏk kiwŏn kwa chŏngch'ijŏk hyŏnsil" [Politics of State Building and the US Military Government: Norm and Political Reality of the Farmland Reform Article of the 1948 Constitution], *Sahoe kwahak nonjip* 41, no. 1 (2010): 117–138, at 126.

44. Quoted in Suzy Kim, *Everyday Life in the North Korean Revolution, 1945–1950* (Ithaca, NY: Cornell University Press, 2013), 78.

45. Kim Sŏngbo, *Nam-Pukhan kyŏngje kujo ŭi kiwŏn kwa chŏn'gye: Pukhan nongŏp ch'eje ŭi hyŏngsŏng ŭl chungsim ŭro* [Origins and Development of the North and South Korean Economic Structure: On the Formation of the North Korean Agricultural System] (Seoul: Yŏksa Pip'yŏngsa, 2000); and Armstrong, *North Korean Revolution,* 76.

46. Armstrong, *North Korean Revolution,* 77.

47. As Charles Armstrong notes, many of the artists who went to the North "sympathized with the Left-leaning political orientation of the new regime in Pyongyang, but there was [also] a considerable degree of artistic freedom in North Korea until the spring of 1947." Armstrong, *North Korean Revolution,* 167. On the politics and aesthetics of writers who fled to the North, see Theodore Hughes, *Literature and Film in Cold War South Korea: Freedom's Frontier* (New York: Columbia University Press, 2014); for their often brilliant writings during the colonial period, see Janet Poole, *When the Future Disappears: The Modernist Imagination in Late Colonial Korea* (New York: Columbia University Press, 2014).

48. Mun Woong Lee, "Rural North Korea under Communism: A Study of Sociocultural Change" (PhD diss., Rice University, 1975), 24.

49. United States Department of State, *North Korea: A Case Study in the Techniques of Takeover* (1951; Washington, DC: US Government Printing Office, 1961), 56.

50. Sung-Chan Hong, "Land Reform and Large Landlords in South Korea's Modernization Project," *Seoul Journal of Korean Studies* 26, no. 1 (June 2013): 23–45, at 32.

51. Kim, *Everyday Life,* 224; and Ruth Barraclough, "Red Love and Betrayal in the Making of North Korea: Comrade Hŏ Chŏngsuk," *History Workshop Journal* 77 (2014): 86–102, at 98.

52. Leonard M. Bertsch to General Brown, June 13, 1947, Bertsch Papers, box 4, folder H-40, Harvard-Yenching Library, Harvard University, Cambridge, MA.

53. Ham Hanhŭi, "Mi kunjŏng ŭi nongji kaehyŏk kwa Han'guk nongmin ŭi taeŭng" [The US-led Land Reform and the Korean Peasants' Response: Cultural Conflicts and Confrontations], *Han'guk munhwa illyuhak* 31, no. 2 (1998).

54. Gayn, *Japan Diary*, 433.

55. "Agrarian Reform in Korea," July 4, 1946, SCAP, RG 331, box 8968, NARA, College Park, MD.

56. "Agrarian Reform in Korea," July 4, 1946, SCAP, RG 331, box 8968, NARA, College Park, MD.

57. "Agrarian Reform in Korea," July 4, 1946, SCAP, RG 331, box 8968, NARA, College Park, MD.

58. Gayn, *Japan Diary*, 433.

59. General MacArthur "reversed course" in 1947 to remake Japan into a communist bulwark, ending reform and putting the former conservative elite back into power. See Michael Schaller, *The American Occupation of Japan: The Origins of the Cold War in Asia* (New York: Oxford University Press, 1987).

60. Owen Jones, diary entry for June 19, 1946, folder Diary 6/15/1946–3/16/1947, box 4, Owen T. Jones Papers, Harry S. Truman Presidential Library, Independence, MO.

61. "History of the Department of Labor," p.8, RG 554, box 39, College Park, MD.

62. Meacham, "Korean Labor Report," 33.

63. "History of the Department of Labor," p.9, NARA, RG 554, box 39, College Park, MD.

64. "History of the Department of Labor," p.9, NARA, RG 554, box 39, College Park, MD.

65. See Guy Podoler, "The Effect of Japanese Colonial Brutality on Shaping Korean Identity: An Analysis of a Prison Turned Memorial Site in Seoul," in *War and Militarism in Modern Japan*, ed. Guy Podoler (Leiden: Brill, 2009).

66. "Robert-Robinson Investigation, July 1946," History of the Police Department, RG 554, box 25, NARA, College Park, MD.

67. Richard D. Robinson, "Betrayal of a Nation," 155, unpublished manuscript, 1950, Harvard-Yenching Library, DS917.52.R63 1950x, Harvard University, Cambridge, MA.

68. Interview Mr. B. Stockton, G-2 History Section XXIV Corps, with Mr. Richard D. Gilliam, USAMGIK Dept. of Justice Assistant Adviser, Oct. 6, 1948, Notes, Documents, Early Drafts on Justice w/ some interviews, RG 554, box 21, NARA, College Park, MD.

69. "Troop Information Hour," April 24, 1947, Police Corruption South Korea, RG 554, box 64, NARA, College Park, MD.

70. Summary of Statement of Choy Nueng (Daniel) Chin (Head of Detective Bureau), p.1, Police Corruption South Korea, RG 554, box 64, NARA, College Park, MD.

71. Lee, *Partition of Korea*, 105–106; and Benjamin R. Young, "Meet the Man Who Saved Kim Il Sung's Life," *NK News*, December 12, 2013, https://www.nknews.org/2013/12/meet-the-man-who-saved-kim-il-sungs-life/.

72. Mark Caprio, "The Contradictory Achievement of the 1946–47 US-USSR Joint Commission: Strengthening North-South Korean Divisions," *Proceedings of the XXX International Congress on Historiography and Source Studies of Asia and Africa,* vol. 1 (conference held June 2019), Faculty of Asian and African Studies, University of St. Petersburg, 2021, 334, https://orienthist.spbu.ru/arhiv/2019/Proceedings-HSSAA-2019 -2020.pdf.

73. Lieutenant General John R. Hodge to the Secretary of State, undated [received March 22, 1946], *FRUS,* 1946, vol. 8, doc. 489.

74. Quoted in Caprio, "The Contradictory Achievement of the 1946–47 US-USSR Joint Commission," 179.

75. Lieutenant General John R. Hodge to the Secretary of State, undated, [received March 22, 1946], *FRUS,* 1946, vol. 8, doc. 489.

76. Robinson, "Betrayal of a Nation," 98.

77. Robinson, "Betrayal of a Nation," 79.

78. Robinson, "Betrayal of a Nation," 77.

79. Cumings, *Origins of the Korean War,* 1:204.

80. Meade, *American Military Government in Korea,* 66.

81. On the collection and rationing of rice, see report attached from Representatives from Korean Command to the War Department, Dec. 17, 1947, NARA, RG 165, entry 463, box 249, NARA, College Park, MD and "History of the National Price Administration," USAMGIK: History of National Price Administration, RG 554, box 14, NARA, College Park, MD.

82. John C. Caldwell, *The Korea Story* (Chicago: Henry Regnery Company, 1952), 22–23.

83. Quoted in Yi Sŏngkyun, "Mi kunjŏnggi nodong undong ŭi chŏn'gae kwajŏng e kwanhan il yŏn'gu," [A Study on the Development Process of the Labor Movement during the US Military Government], in *Han'guk kŭnhyŏndae ŭi minjok munje wa nodong undong* [Ethnic Problems and Labor Movement of Modern and Contemporary Korea], ed. Han'guk sahoesa yŏn'guhoe (Seoul: Munhakkwa Chisŏngsa, 1989), 181.

84. "Goodfellow Ends His Work in Korea," *New York Times,* May 24, 1946, 12.

85. Meacham, "Korean Labor Report," ii.

6. Rising Up

1. Chang Sanghwan, "Haebang kwa chŏnjaeng, kŭrigo chŏnjaeng ihu ŭi nongmin undong" [Emancipation and War, Peasant Movement after Korean War], *Nongch'on sahoe* 20, no. 1 (2010): 7–16, at 14.

2. "History of the Police Department," Police History: Notes, RG 554, box 27, NARA, College Park, MD.

3. Quoted in Joel Stevenson, "Korean Short Fiction from the Liberation Period, 1945–1948" (MA thesis, University of British Columbia, 1999), 26.

4. Chang, "Haebang kwa chŏnjaeng, kŭrigo chŏnjaeng ihu ŭi nongmin undong," 14.

5. "Robert-Robinson Investigation, July 1946," History of the Police Department, RG 554, box 25, NARA, College Park, MD.

6. "Robert-Robinson Investigation, July 1946." As Thomas H. Lee put it, "USAMGIK's rice policy served to alienate everyone and to gain favor with no one." Lee, "The Origins of the Taegu Insurrection of 1946" (BA thesis, Harvard University, 1990), 60.

7. Quoted from A. Wigfall Green, *The Epic of Korea* (Washington, DC: Public Affairs Press, 1950), 95. Green served as judge advocate in Korea during the military occupation.

8. Chang, "Haebang kwa chŏnjaeng, kŭrigo chŏnjaeng ihu ŭi nongmin undong," 14.

9. Albert L. Park, "Reclaiming the Rural: Modern Danish Cooperative Living in Colonial Korea, 1925–37," *Journal of Korean Studies* 19, no. 1 (Spring 2014): 115–151.

10. Gi-wook Shin, "The Historical Making of Collective Action: The Korean Peasant Uprisings of 1946," *American Journal of Sociology* 99, no. 6 (May 1994): 1596–1624, at 1605.

11. Quoted in Bruce Cumings, *The Origins of the Korean War,* vol. 1: *Liberation and the Emergence of Separate Regimes, 1945–1947* (Princeton, NJ: Princeton University Press, 1981), 199.

12. "Robert-Robinson Investigation, July 1946," History of the Police Department, RG 554, box 25, NARA, College Park, MD.

13. Pak Yijun, "Naju Kungsam-myŏn t'oji t'alhwan undong yŏn'gu," [Land Ownership Recovery Movement by Naju Kungsam-myŏn Peasants: A History] (PhD diss., Chŏnnam Taehakkyo, 2003), 126–132.

14. Quoted in Ham Hanhŭi, "Mi kunjŏng ŭi nongji kaehyŏk kwa Han'guk nongmin ŭi taeŭng" [The US-Led Land Reform and the Korean Peasants' Response: Cultural Conflicts and Confrontations], *Han'guk munhwa illyuhak* 31, no. 2 (1998): 407–437, at 428.

15. "Robert-Robinson Investigation, July 1946," History of the Police Department, RG 554, box 25, NARA, College Park, MD.

16. Hwang Sunwŏn, *Tok chinnŭn nŭlgŭni: Hwang Sunwŏn tanp'yŏnsŏn* [Old Man Making a Jar: Selected Short Stories of Hwang Sunwŏn] and Pak Hyegyŏng, ed., *Han'guk munhak chŏnjip* [Collected Works of Korean Literature], vol. 8 (Seoul: Munhak kwa Chisŏngsa, 2005). The translated quotes that follow are from Hwang Sunwŏn, *Lost Souls: Stories,* trans. Bruce Fulton and Ju-Chan Fulton (New York: Columbia University Press, 2009), 208–226.

17. Stewart Meacham, Labor Adviser to the Commanding General of the United States Armed Forces in Korea, "Korean Labor Report," http://library.haverford.edu/eastasian/Files/Survey_of_AFSC_Archives_on_Korea_(1938-2000).pdf. Prepared for the Secretary of Labor, November 1947, p. 14, box 1, folder 2, American Friends Service Committee Archives on Korea, Philadelphia, PA.

18. "History of Department of Labor," p.8, RG 554, box 39, NARA, College Park, MD.

19. Yi Hyesuk, "Mi kunjŏnggi nodong undong ŭi sŏnggyŏk kwa chŏn'gae kwajŏng" [The Character and Development Process of Labor Movements during the US Military Occupation Period], *Hyŏnsang kwa insik* 10, no. 4 (1986): 72–103, at 86.

20. KBS kwangbok 60-chunyŏn t'ŭkpyŏl p'ŭrojekt'ŭ t'im, 166.

21. Sŏng Hanp'yo, "9-wŏl ch'ongp'aŏp kwa nodong undong ŭi chŏnhwan," [September General Strike and the Turn of the Labor Movement], in *Haebang chŏnhusa ŭi insik 2: Chŏngch'i, kyŏngje, sahoe, munhwajŏk kujo ŭi siljŭngjŏk yŏn'gu* [Understanding of Pre- and Post-Liberation History, vol. 2: Empirical Studies on Political, Economic, Social, Cultural Structures], ed. Kang Man'gil, Kim Yunsik, Pak Hyŏnch'ae et al. (Seoul: Han'gilsa, 1993), 359–404; An T'aejŏng, *Chosŏn Nodong Chohap Chŏn'guk P'yŏngŭihoe* [The National Council of Labor Unions] (Seoul: Hyŏnjang esŏ Mirae rŭl, 2002).

22. Meacham, "Korean Labor Report," 32.

23. An, *Chosŏn Nodong Chohap Chŏn'guk P'yŏngŭihoe*, 90.

24. Song, "9-wŏl ch'ongp'aŏp kwa nodong undong ŭi chŏnhwan." Early on, the Chŏnp'yŏng had adopted many of the priorities of the military government. Its activists, for example, organized associations to maintain workplace discipline in the factories "to get workers to arrive on time, avoid absences, clean the factory, follow work rules, restrain strikes, and compete with other unions in productivity-doubling campaign." See Hwasook Nam, *Building Ships, Building a Nation: Korea's Democratic Unionism under Park Chung Hee* (Seattle: University of Washington Press, 2011), 33.

25. Leonard Bertsch to General Hodge, October 17, 1947, Subject: Extortion by Police, Bertsch Papers, box 1, folder M, Harvard-Yenching Library, Harvard University, Cambridge, MA (hereafter Bertsch Papers).

26. Quoted from Song, "9-wŏl ch'ongp'aŏp kwa nodong undong ŭi chŏnhwan."

27. Meacham, "Korean Labor Report," 33.

28. Writer Kim Yŏngsŏk captured the conflict between labor and management in the textile mill in his story, "Storm," published in 1946. See Cho Yuri, "Haebang konggan ŭi 'P'okp'ung,' Chosŏn Nodong Chohap Chŏn'guk P'yŏngŭihoe: Sosŏl kwa hamkke ponŭn Han'guk nodongja undong yŏksa" ["Storm" of the Liberation Space, the National Labor Union Council: Reading History of Korea's Labor Movement through Fiction], *Sahoe chinbo yŏndae*, vol. 168 (2019); and Meacham, "Korean Labor Report," 34.

29. "Remembering Stewart Meacham," *Christianity and Crisis*, October 14, 1985.

30. Meacham, "Korean Labor Report," 32; and Cumings, *Origins of the Korean War*, 1:252.

31. Kyu-hyu Jo, "The Rise of the South Korean Left, The Death of Unitary Socialism, and the Origins of the Korean War, 1945-1947" (PhD diss., University of Chicago, 2019), 364.

32. KBS kwangbok 60-chunyŏn t'ŭkpyŏl p'ŭrojekt'ŭ t'im, 249–252.

33. On the general strike, see Cumings, *Origins of the Korean War*, 1:352–356; Lee, "Origins of the Taegu Insurrection," 75–77; and *Seoul Times*, September 24, 1946.

34. Quoted in Lee, "Origins of the Taegu Insurrection," 76.

35. General of the Army Douglas MacArthur to the Joint Chiefs of Staff (Eisenhower), October 28, 1946, *Foreign Relations of the United States, 1946*, vol. 8, *The Far East*, ed. John G. Reid and Herbert A. Fine (Washington, DC: Government Printing Office, 1971), doc. 556 (hereafter *FRUS, 1946*, vol. 8).

36. Memorandum by the Director of the Office of Far Eastern Affairs (Vincent) to the Secretary of State, October 29, 1946, *FRUS,* 1946, vol. 8, doc. 557.

37. Erik Mobrand, "Street Leaders of Seoul and the Foundations of the South Korean Political Order," *Modern Asian Studies* 50, no. 2 (2016): 636–674, at 652.

38. Meacham, "Korean Labor Report," 34.

39. KBS kwangbok 60-chunyŏn t'ŭkpyŏl p'ŭrojekt'ŭ t'im, 254.

40. Meacham, "Korean Labor Report," 34. The military government opened negotiations with the Taehan Noch'ong that yielded a number of concessions, which enhanced its standing with workers who had lost faith in the Chŏnp'yŏng because of the outcome of the strikes.

41. A missionary friend eventually intervened with the Labor Department to get Kim his job back but other people in a similar situation were probably not as lucky. Meacham, "Korean Labor Report," 35.

42. Cumings, *Origins of the Korean War,* 1:321; and Meacham, "Korean Labor Report," 36, 41–42.

43. "Petition on Behalf of Mr. Oh Pyung-Mo [O Pyŏngmo]," April 28, 1947, Roger Nash Baldwin Papers, series 2: Subject Files, box 18, folder 8, Public Policy Papers, Department of Special Collections, Princeton University Library (hereafter Baldwin Papers).

44. Baldwin's fellow ACLU board members were skeptical about MacArthur's commitment to democracy in Japan; some thought Baldwin's judgment had been clouded by the general's stature and charm. See Robert Cottrell, *Roger Nash Baldwin and the American Civil Liberties Union* (New York: Columbia University Press, 2001), 319.

45. Roger Baldwin, "Chaos in Korea," June 1947, Baldwin Papers, series 3: Writings and Speeches, box 22, folder 14.

46. Roger Baldwin, "More Civil War," May 17, 1946, Baldwin Papers, series 2, box 18, folder 8.

47. "Statement by Lieutenant General John Hodge," Oct. 14, 1946, Civil Disturbance: Department of Labor and Commerce: Strikes and Riots, 9/45-4/47, RG 554, box 62, NARA, College Park, MD.

48. "Summation of United States Army Military Government Activities in Korea, No. 12 (September 1946), p.13. SCAP, RG 331, box 8303, NARA, College Park, MD.

49. "A Korean Worker Writes to His American Friend," as part of the report of the American Committee to Aid Korean Trade Union's Report, Records of the War Department General and Special Staffs, RG 165, entry 463, box 250, College Park, MD.

50. Meacham, "Korean Labor Report," 34.

51. John R. Hodge to Chief, Civil Affairs Division, War Department Special Staff, Jan. 9, 1948, RG 165, entry 463, box 410, NARA, College Park, MD.

52. Roger Baldwin, "Why We Fail in Korea," December 1947, Baldwin Papers, series 3, box 22, folder 12.

53. Yang Soo Kim, "Cholera Outbreaks in Korea after Liberation in 1945: Clinical and Epidemiological Characteristics," *Infection and Chemotherapy* 51, no. 4 (2019): 427–434; and KBS kwangbok 60-chunyŏn t'ŭkpyŏl p'ŭrojekt'ŭ t'im, 157–158.

54. Pak graduated from Taegu Medical School in 1944 and was employed as deputy doctor military officer of Taegu University's Medical School Hospital in 1946. See KBS kwangbok 60-chunyŏn t'ŭkpyŏl p'ŭrojekt'ŭ t'im, 171–172.

55. Report of Investigation of Disorder in Taegu Conducted by Major General Albert E. Brown, October 4, 1946, Bertsch Papers, box 4, folder G.

56. Cumings, *Origins of the Korean War,* 1:356.

57. KBS kwangbok 60-chunyŏn t'ŭkpyŏl p'ŭrojekt'ŭ t'im, 193.

58. Cumings, *Origins of the Korean War,* 1:363; and KBS kwangbok 60-chunyŏn t'ŭkpyŏl p'ŭrojekt'ŭ t'im, 193.

59. Scholars have provided different interpretations of the Autumn Uprising. For Cumings, they represented a last-ditch stand of revolutionary forces in the South, which resulted in dismal failure because the spontaneity that gave the movement its initial burst of energy also made the resistance inchoate and fragile, leaving it vulnerable to a sophisticated campaign of suppression. Others have argued that the uprisings were spontaneous, arising from locally specific grievances having to do with bread and butter issues, as opposed to being driven by dreams of transformative change (i.e., revolution). For different perspectives, see Cumings, *Origins of the Korean War,* 1:351–381; Chŏng Haegu, *10-wŏl inmin hangjaeng yŏn'gu* [A Study of the October's People's Uprisings] (Seoul: Yŏrŭmsa, 1988); Gi-Wook Shin, *Peasant Protest and Social Change in Colonial Korea* (Seattle: University of Washington Press, 1996), 110–127; Lee, "Origins of the Taegu Insurrection"; and Jin-Yeon Kang, "Colonial Legacies and the Struggle for Social Membership in a National Community: The 1946 People's Uprisings in Korea," *Journal of Historical Sociology* 24, no. 2 (2011): 321–354.

60. Pak, "Naju Kungsam-myŏn t'oji t'alhwan undong yŏn'gu," [Land Ownership Recovery Movement by Naju Kungsam-myŏn Peasants: A History], 133–140.

61. This story came from one of dozens of eyewitness testimonies published by the Truth and Reconciliation Commission in South Korea, formed in 2005 to investigate and uncover past incidents of human rights abuses and state violence, from the colonial period through the end of authoritarian rule in the late 1980s. One of the primary researchers for the Commission, Kim Sangsuk, published her findings in *10-wŏl hangjaeng: 1946-nyŏn 10-wŏl Taegu, pongin toen sigan sok ŭro* [The October Uprising: October 1946 in Taegu, in Sealed Time] (P'aju: Tol Pegae, 2016).

62. For full transcript of the letter, see Bertrand M. Roehner, *Relations between US Forces and the Population of South Korea,* 15–18. The author cites NARA, State Department Records, Central Decimal Files, Time Segment 1945-1949, RG 59, box 7389, 895.00/4-247, as the original source.

63. Leonard M. Bertsch, the political adviser to Hodge, received numerous reports of police brutality during the Autumn Uprising. Leonard M. Bertsch to General Brown, October 31, 1946, Bertsch Papers, box 4, folder G-5.

64. Cumings, *Origins of the Korean War,* 1:379.

65. Memorandum of Conversation with Major General A. V. Arnold, October 9, 1946, *FRUS,* 1946, vol. 8, doc. 550; and Memorandum to Commanding General XXIV Corps, January 11, 1947, Bertsch Papers, box 1, folder G.

66. "Statement by Lieutenant General John Hodge," Oct. 14, 1946, Civil Disturbance: Department of Labor and Commerce: Strikes and Riots, 9/45-4/47, RG 554, box 62, NARA, College Park, MD.

67. Richard D. Robinson, "Betrayal of a Nation," unpublished manuscript, 1950, p. 163, Harvard-Yenching Library, DS917.52 .R63 1950x, Harvard University Library. There was incentive for the Soviets and north Korea not to interfere in the South. The Joint Commission was on pause but not dead and Soviet officials and the north Koreans didn't want to be held responsible for killing it. As political adviser Leonard Bertsch explained, "There is an apparent desire to go along with the Military Government, possibly in order to have a good record should the Joint Commission reopen."

68. Kim Kihyŏp. "Miguk t'ong Ch'oe Nŭngjin, kyŏlguk ch'ongsal tanghan kkadak ŭn?" [Why Was Ch'oe Nŭngjin, a US Expert, Executed by Shooting?], *P'ŭresian,* December 5, 2011.

69. Kim, *10-wŏl hangjaeng* [The October Uprising].

70. "History of the Department of Police," p.34, History of Police Department, RG 554, box 25, NARA, College Park, MD.

7. Taking a Shot at the Middle

1. Embarrassed by the poll results and afraid of the effect on public morale and the morale of personnel under his command, Hodge ordered the Department of Public Information to stop polling the Koreans on this specific question. Richard D. Robinson, "Betrayal of a Nation," unpublished manuscript, 1950, p. 82, Harvard-Yenching Library, DS917.52 .R63 1950x, Harvard University Library; and A. Wigfall Green, *The Epic of Korea* (Washington, DC: Public Affairs Press, 1950), 97.

2. From USAFIK, Korea from Hodge thru CINCAFPAC, Tokyo Japan, August 19, 1946, RG 165, entry 463, box 249, NARA, College Park, MD.

3. Quoted from George M. McCune, "Korea: The First Year of Liberation," *Pacific Affairs* 20, no. 1 (1947): 3–17, at 16.

4. Robinson, "Betrayal of a Nation," 80.

5. Bruce Cumings, *The Origins of the Korean War,* vol. 1, *Liberation and the Emergence of Separate Regimes, 1945–1947* (Princeton, NJ: Princeton University Press, 1981), 250.

6. "Prospects for Survival of the Republic of Korea," Office of Reports and Estimates, 44–48, October 28, 1948, Korean War and Its Origins Collection, Harry S. Truman Presidential Library, Independence, MO, https://www.trumanlibrary.gov/library/research

-files/prospects-survival-republic-korea-office-reports-and-estimates-44-48?documentid
=NA&pagenumber=1.

7. Leonard M. Bertsch to Dr. Cornelius Osgood, November 10, 1947, Bertsch Papers, box 1, folder H-4-5, Harvard-Yenching Library, Harvard University, Cambridge, MA (hereafter Bertsch Papers).

8. Owen Jones, diary entry for July 20, 1947, folder Diary 7/20/1947–4/7/1948, box 4, Owen T. Jones Papers, Harry S. Truman Presidential Library, Independence, MO.

9. "Memorandum for the Commanding General, XXIV Corps," August 2, 1947, Bertsch Papers, box 1, folder F-26.

10. Political Adviser in Korea (Langdon) to Secretary of State, August 2, 1946, *Foreign Relations of the United States,* 1946, vol. 8, *The Far East,* ed. John G. Reid and Herbert A. Fine (Washington, DC: Government Printing Office, 1971), doc. 536 (hereafter *FRUS,* 1946, vol. 8).

11. Bonnie B. C. Oh, "Kim Kyu-sik and the Coalition Effort," in *Korea under the American Military Government,* ed. Bonnie B. C. Oh (Westport, CT: Praeger, 2002), 103–121.

12. Mark Gayn, *Japan Diary* (New York: William Sloan Associates, 1948), 368.

13. Cumings, *Origins of the Korean War,* 1:256; and Kyu-hyu Jo, "The Rise of the South Korean Left, The Death of Unitary Socialism, and the Origins of the Korean War, 1945–1947" (PhD diss., University of Chicago, 2019), 462.

14. Gayn, *Japan Diary,* 352.

15. Quoted in Oh, "Kim Kyu-sik and the Coalition Effort," 108. According to Oh, Yŏ told Pak he was "too committed" to Kim Kyusik to quit the coalition efforts and would "stay with the project until some conclusion was reached."

16. Leonard M. Bertsch to General A. E. Brown, October 20, 1946, Bertsch Papers, box 1, folder W-11.

17. Cumings, *Origins of the Korean War,* 1:258.

18. The Economic Adviser in Korea (Bunce) to the Secretary of State, August 26, 1946, *FRUS,* 1946, vol. 8, doc. 541.

19. Gayn, *Japan Diary,* 405.

20. "Interview with Lieutenant Bertsch," [1947], Roger Nash Baldwin Papers, series 2: Subject Files, box 18, folder 8, Public Policy Papers, Department of Special Collections, Princeton University Library (hereafter Baldwin Papers).

21. McCune, "Korea," 7, 17.

22. Kiusic Kimm [Kim Kyusik], Letter to Bertsch, October 16, 1946, Bertsch Papers, box 1, folder XYZ-18.

23. Leonard Bertsch to General Brown, November 26, 1946, Bertsch Papers, box 1, folder D-84.

24. W. H. Lyuh, memorandum to Gen. John R. Hodge, Bertsch Papers, box 3, folder T-93.

25. The Political Adviser in Korea (Langdon) to the Secretary of State, December 10, 1946, *FRUS,* 1946, vol. 8, doc. 575.

26. Allan Millett, *The War for Korea, 1945–1950: A House Burning* (Lawrence: University of Kansas Press, 2005), 110–112; and Chŏng Pyŏngjun, *Unam Yi Sŭngman yŏn'gu: Han'guk kŭndae kukka ŭi hyŏngsŏng kwa up'a ŭi kil* [Research on Unam Syngman Rhee: The Formation of the Korean Modern State and the Right] (Seoul: Yŏksa Pip'yŏngsa, 2005).

27. "Prospects for Survival of the Republic of Korea," 9.

28. C. L. Sulzberger, "Foreign Affairs: The Terrible-Tempered Mr. Rhee," *New York Times,* July 21, 1965.

29. Lieutenant John R. Hodge to the Secretary of State, December 31, 1946, *FRUS,* 1946, vol. 8, doc. 579.

30. "One time," according to Bruce Cumings, Hodge "sent a jeep screaming across Seoul to grab Rhee and jail him, an order countermanded by military radio." See Bruce Cumings, *The Origins of the Korean War,* vol. 2, *The Roaring of the Cataract, 1947–1950* (Princeton, NJ: Princeton University Press, 1990), 226.

31. Lieutenant John R. Hodge to Mr. Lyuh, Won Hyung, January 7, 1947, Bertsch Papers, box 2, folder B-3.

32. Hodge hinted at the possible coercion when he acknowledged in his letter to Yŏ that his absence from SKILA "may be due to causes beyond your control." Leonard M. Bertsch, memorandum to General Hodge, October 19, 1946, Bertsch Papers, box 2, folder C-5.

33. Yŏ's ally, Wŏn Sehun argued, as rightist partisans leading the police force, Cho and Chang were a detriment to the coalition movement. Both men had made it clear they opposed the Moscow decision. W. H. Lyuh, Chairman, Coalition Committee, to Major General Albert E. Brown, November 19, 1946, Bertsch Papers, box 1, folder M-7.

34. Won, Sei Hoon [Wŏn Sehun] to Major General Albert E. Brown, November 19, 1946, Bertsch Papers, box 1, folder D-62.

35. Mark E. Caprio, "Colonial-Era Korean Collaboration over Two Occupations: Delayed Closure," in *Japan as the Occupier and the Occupied,* ed. Christine de Matos and Mark E. Caprio (New York: Palgrave Macmillan, 2015).

36. Tony Judt, *Postwar: A History of Europe since 1945* (New York: Penguin Books, 2005), 41–62. The numbers in Eastern European countries, where the Soviets exerted control, were much higher.

37. Quoted in Deokhyo Choi, "Defining Colonial 'War Crimes': Korean Debates on Collaboration, War Reparations, and the International Military Tribunal for the Far East," in *Debating Collaboration and Complicity in War Crimes Trials in Asia, 1945–1956,* ed. Kerstin Von Lingen (Cham, Switzerland: Palgrave Macmillan, 2017), 49.

38. Choi, "Defining Colonial 'War Crimes,'" 48.

39. Leonard M. Bertsch to General Brown, February 3, 1946, Bertsch Papers, box 1, folder W-16. Thirty organizations associated with Syngman Rhee and Kim Ku demanded the establishment of a separate government in the South, insisting it was the "only way to save Koreans from the conditions of slavery under military government." The Political Adviser in Korea (Langdon) to the Secretary of State, January 17, 1947, *Foreign*

Relations of the United States, 1947, vol. 6, *The Far East*, ed. John G. Reid (Washington, DC: Government Printing Office, 1972), doc. 463 (hereafter *FRUS*, 1947, vol. 6).

40. Roger Baldwin, "Why We Fail in Korea," December 1947, Baldwin Papers, series 3: Writings and Speeches, box 22, folder 12.

41. Leonard M. Bertsch, "Rightist Activity," September 19, 1947, Bertsch Papers, box 1, folder A-97.

42. Admittedly it is hard to separate the man from the myth. Kim Tuhan became the subject of numerous movies, books, and television shows in the South. He also fueled his own legend in public appearances and writings. See Erik Mobrand, "The Street Leaders of Seoul and the Foundations of the South Korean Political Order," *Modern Asian Studies* 50, no. 2 (March 2016): 636–674. On rightist youth groups during the occupation period, see Cumings, *Origins of the Korean War*, 2:193–203.

43. Mobrand, "The Street Leaders of Seoul," 650.

44. Hye-Jung Park, "Musical Entanglements: Ely Haimowitz and Orchestral Music under the US Army Military Government in Korea, 1945–1948," *Journal of the Society for American Music* 15, no. 1 (2021): 1–29.

45. Mózes Csoma, Ambassador of Hungary to Korea, "The Fate of a Promising Composer," *Korea JoongAng Daily*, November 10, 2020, https://koreajoongangdaily.joins.com /2020/11/10/national/diplomacy/Kim-Soonam-Korean-composer-Hungary/2020111 0175900423.html (accessed December 19, 2022).

46. Leonard M. Bertsch, memorandum, Bertsch Papers, box 3, folder S-38.

47. Memorandum to General Brown, Subject: Police and Lyuh, Woon Hyung, July 21, 1947, Bertsch Papers, box 1, folder F-37.

48. Captain Richard Robinson, memorandum, October 19, 1946, Bertsch Papers, box 2, folder G-19.

49. Cumings, *Origins of the Korean War*, 2:147.

50. Report to General Lerch, Subject: Kim Hong Sup [Kim Hongsŏp], September 20, 1946, Bertsch Papers, box 1, folder H-26.

51. "Police Drive to Raise 30,000,000 Yen in Seoul Area," translation, March 28, 1947, Bertsch Papers, box 2, folder H-75.

52. Memorandum to General Brown, Subject: Police and Lyuh, Woon Hyung, July 21, 1947, Bertsch Papers, box 1, folder F-37.

53. Pak T'aegyun, *Pŏch'I munsŏ wa haebang chŏngguk: Mi kunjŏng chungwi ŭi nun e pich'in 1945–1948-nyŏn ŭi Hanbando* [The Bertsch Documents and the Politics of Liberation: The Korean Peninsula, 1945–1948, through the Eyes of a US Military Government Lieutenant] (Koyang: Yŏksa Pip'yŏngsa, 2021).

54. Memorandum for the Record, Subject: Political Situation as of May 19th, May 19, 1947, Bertsch Papers, box 1, folder N-18.

55. Cumings, *Origins of the Korean War*, 2:206.

56. Memorandum for the Record, Subject: Political Situation as of May 19th, May 19, 1947, Bertsch Papers, box 1, folder N-18.

57. "Police Corruption South Korea," NARA, RG 554, box 64.

58. Robinson blamed American security forces for focusing their efforts on "ferreting out Communists," while spending little time in investigating "charges of abridgement of civil liberties." He railed against the violation of basic civil rights in the South and accused Rhee, Cho, and the rightist youth groups of being the worst offenders. He asked, "What action has been taken against them which is at all comparable to that taken against Leftist leaders." Richard Robinson to Commanding General, United States Army Forces in Korea, April 17, 1947, Bertsch Papers, box 2, folder G-19.

59. Report of Investigation to Commanding General XXIV Corps, January 11, 1947, Bertsch Papers, box 2, folder G-19.

60. "Draft Statement," April 21, 1947, Bertsch Papers, box 3, folder A-5.

61. After the announcement, Rhee wrote Truman to ask him to "instruct the American military authorities in Korea to follow your policy and abandon their efforts to bring about coalition and cooperation between nationalists and communists." Dr. Syngman Rhee to President Truman, March 13, 1947, *FRUS, 1947*, vol. 6, doc. 474.

62. Pang Kijung, "Nongji kaehyŏk ŭi sasang chŏnťong kwa nongjŏng i'nyŏm" [Ideological Tradition and Agricultural Ideology of Farmland Reform], in *Nongji kaehyŏk yŏngu* [Land Reform Research], ed. Hong Sŏngch'an (Seoul: Yŏnse Taehakkyo Ch'ulp'anbu, 2001).

63. Sung-Chan Hong, "Land Reform and Large Landlords in South Korea's Modernization Project," *Seoul Journal of Korean Studies* 26, no. 1 (June 2013): 23–45, 33. Some Korean landowning families, including brothers Kim Yŏnsu and Kim Sŏngsu, started to make the transition from land to industry during the colonial period. See Carter Eckert, *Offspring of Empire: The Colonial Origins of Korean Capitalism 1876–1945* (Seattle: University of Washington Press, 1991).

64. Memorandum for General Brown, Subject: Land Reform, June 13, 1947, Bertsch Papers, box 4, folder H-40.

65. Roger N. Baldwin, "Prospects in Korea," June 1947, folder 14, box 22, Baldwin Papers.

66. Quoted in Caprio, "Colonial-Era Korean Collaboration," 121.

67. Caprio, "Colonial-Era Korean Collaboration," 121.

68. Quoted in Mark E. Caprio, "The Politics of Collaboration in Post-Liberation Southern Korea," in *In the Ruins of the Japanese Empire: Imperial Violence, State Destruction, and the Reordering of Modern East Asia,* ed. Barak Kushner and Andrew Levidis (Hong Kong: Hong Kong University Press, 2020), 42.

69. Yŏ's daughter told Bruce Cumings that she believed Seoul's Police Chief, Chang T'aeksang, was behind her father's death. On Yŏ's assassination, see Cumings, *Origins of the Korean War,* 2:205–206.

70. Bruce Cumings, *Korea's Place in the Sun: A Modern History* (New York: W. W. Norton, 2005), 192.

71. See Kim Samung, *Mongyang Yŏ Unhyŏng P'yŏngjŏn: Chinbojok Minju chuŭija* [Yŏ Unhyŏng: A Biography of a Progressive Democratic Thinker] (Seoul: Ch'aeryun, 2015), 559–560.

72. "In Memoriam," *Voice of Korea,* August 15, 1947, Bertsch Papers, box 3, folder S-37.

73. Kiusic Kimm, Chairman Coalition Committee, to Lt. Gen. John R. Hodge, US Army, December 12, 1947, Bertsch Papers, box 4, folder H-4.

74. Baldwin, "Why We Fail in Korea."

8. Searching for a Way Out

1. The Secretary of State to the Acting Secretary of State, April 2, 1947, *Foreign Relations of the United States, 1947,* vol. 6, *The Far East,* ed. John G. Reid (Washington, DC: Government Printing Office, 1972), doc. 477 (hereafter *FRUS, 1947,* vol. 6).

2. Commenting on an earlier draft of the letter, Acheson wrote to Marshall, "General tone seems appropriate except that it might be desirable to go further toward placing blame on Soviets." Acting Secretary of State to the Secretary of State, at Moscow, April 5, 1947, *FRUS, 1947,* vol. 6, doc. 479.

3. The Soviet Minister for Foreign Affairs (Molotov) to the Secretary of State, at Moscow, April 19, 1947, *FRUS, 1947,* vol. 6, doc. 483.

4. The Political Adviser in Korea (Langdon) to the Secretary of State, May 17, 1947, *FRUS, 1947,* vol. 6, doc. 492.

5. "In desperation," Langdon wrote, "Rhee, Kim Koo crowd have been trying to stage anti-trusteeship demonstrations, which we have blocked by blanket municipal order forbidding mass political meetings at this time." The Political Adviser in Korea (Langdon) to the Secretary of State, May 17, 1947.

6. The Political Adviser in Korea (Langdon) to the Secretary of State, May 21, 1947, *FRUS, 1947,* vol. 6, doc. 494.

7. Bertsch's Memorandum for Mr. Sargent, March 5, 1948, Bertsch Papers, box 4, folder G-135 Harvard-Yenching Library, Harvard University, Cambridge, MA (hereafter Bertsch Papers).

8. Bruce Cumings, *Korea's Place in the Sun: A Modern History* (New York: W.W. Norton, 2005), 215–216.

9. Leonard Bertsch, Report to General John R. Hodge, Commanding General, December 12, 1947, Bertsch Papers, box 4, folder C-15.

10. Mark Caprio, "The Contradictory Achievement of the 1946–47 US-USSR Joint Commission: Strengthening North-South Korean Divisions," *Proceedings of the XXX International Congress on Historiography and Source Studies of Asia and Africa,* vol. 1 (conference held June 2019), Faculty of Asian and African Studies, University of St. Petersburg, 2021, 334, https://orienthist.spbu.ru/arhiv/2019/Proceedings-HSSAA-2019-2020.pdf.

11. The Political Adviser in Korea (Langdon) to the Secretary of State, May 21, 1947, *FRUS,* 1947, vol. 6, doc. 494.

12. The Soviet Minister of Foreign Affairs (Molotov) to the Secretary of State, May 7, 1947, *FRUS,* 1947, vol. 6, doc. 448.

13. Lieutenant General John R. Hodge to General of the Army Douglas MacArthur, June 2, 1947, *FRUS,* 1947, vol. 6, doc. 506.

14. Lieutenant General John R. Hodge to the Secretary of State, July 7, 1947, *FRUS,* 1947, vol. 6, doc. 535.

15. General of the Army Douglas MacArthur to the Secretary of State, July [9], 1947, *FRUS,* 1947, vol. 6, doc. 538.

16. Lieutenant General John R. Hodge to the Secretary of State, July 17, 1947, *FRUS,* 1947, vol. 6, doc. 547.

17. Leonard Bertsch, Report to General John R. Hodge, Commanding General, December 12, 1947, Bertsch Papers, box 4, folder C-5.

18. Lieutenant General John R. Hodge to the Secretary of State, July 16, 1947, *FRUS,* 1947, vol. 6, doc. 543.

19. Lieutenant General John R. Hodge to the Secretary of State, July 17, 1947, *FRUS,* 1947, vol. 6, doc. 547.

20. The Political Adviser in Korea (Jacobs) to the Secretary of State, July 7, 1947, *FRUS,* 1947, vol. 6, doc. 534. In 1947, there seemed to be a decisive shift in the balance of power to Kim Il Sung and his communist party in the North. See Charles K. Armstrong, *The North Korean Revolution, 1945–1950* (Ithaca, NY: Cornell University Press, 2003),118–120.

21. Lieutenant General John R. Hodge to the Secretary of State, July 3, 1947, *FRUS,* 1947, vol. 6, doc. 530.

22. Owen Jones, diary entry for July 22, 1947, folder Diary 7/20/1947–4/7/1948, box 4, Owen T. Jones Papers, Harry S. Truman Presidential Library, Independence, MO (hereafter Jones Papers).

23. Quoted from Roger N. Baldwin, "Why Democracy Fails in Korea," *The New Leader,* January 24, 1948, Roger Nash Baldwin Papers, series 3: Writings and Papers, box 22, folder 14, Public Policy Papers, Department of Special Collections, Princeton University Library.

24. "The Economic Objectives of the Occupation," 1947, p.10, Report on Occupation South Korea, Part 2: Economics, NARA, RG 554, box 41, NARA, College Park, MD.

25. The Secretary of War (Patterson) to the Secretary of State, April 4, 1947, *FRUS,* 1947, vol. 6, doc. 478.

26. Bruce Cumings, *The Origins of the Korean War,* vol. 2: *The Roaring of the Cataract, 1947–1950* (Princeton, NJ: Princeton University Press, 1990), 58–61.

27. Restoring Japan to a major power was crucial to the strategy, and officials believed that to do so they had to reintegrate Korea and Japan. This involved, as one historian has explained, "making southern Korea a hinterland for Japanese industry and a frontyard

of Japanese defense." The plans required a friendly, anti-communist regime in southern Korea. See Michael Schaller, *The American Occupation of Japan: The Origins of the Cold War in Asia* (New York: Oxford University Press, 1985); and Cumings, *Origins of the Korean War*, 2:50, 59.

28. Quoted in Cumings, *Origins of the Korean War*, 2:46. Other officials argued the US could not "scuttle and run" from Korea without considerable loss to its prestige and credibility with allies not only in East Asia but around the world. Memorandum by the Assistant Chief of the Division of Eastern European Affairs (Stevens), September 9, 1947, *FRUS*, 1947, vol. 6, doc. 601.

29. Letter from General Hodge to Secretary of State, Washington, DC, November 21, 1947, RG 59, Entry CDF 1945–1949, box 7125, 895.01, NARA, College Park, MD.

30. Owen Jones, diary entry for July 28, 1947, folder Diary 7/20/1947–4/7/1948, box 4, Jones Papers.

31. Owen Jones, diary entry for July 28, 1947.

32. The Acting Secretary of State to the Embassy in the Soviet Union, September 16, 1947, *FRUS*, 1947, vol. 6, doc. 608.

33. The Political Adviser (Jacobs) to the Secretary of State, September 26, 1947, *FRUS*, 1947, vol. 6, doc. 623.

34. The Political Adviser in Korea (Jacobs) to the Secretary of State, October 8, 1947, *FRUS*, 1947, vol. 6, doc. 632.

35. The Political Adviser in Korea (Jacobs) to the Secretary of State, September 30, 1947, *FRUS*, 1947, vol. 6, doc. 625.

36. The United States Representative at the United Nations (Austin) to the Secretary General of the United Nations (Lie), October 17, 1947, *FRUS*, 1947, vol. 6, doc. 638.

37. Leonard Bertsch, Report to General John R. Hodge, Commanding General, December 12, 1947, Bertsch Papers, box 4, folder C-15.

38. Even back during his nationalist days, there was complaints Chang was more out for himself than the cause. Chong-Sik Lee and Robert A. Scalapino, *Communism in Korea*, vol. 1, *The Movement* (Berkeley: University of California Press, 1973), 54–55. For the Leonard Bertsch quote, see Bruce Cumings, *The Origins of the Korean War*, vol. 1: *Liberation and the Emergence of Separate Regimes, 1945–1947* (Princeton, NJ: Princeton University Press, 1981), 94. On Chang's wartime collaboration, see Sŏ Chungsŏk, "Chang Tŏksu: Kŭndaehwa chisang chuŭi e maemol toen chaesa" [Chang Tŏksu: A Man Obsessed with the Supremacy of Modernization], in *Ch'inilp'a 99-in* [99 Pro-Japanese Collaborators], vol. 2, ed. Panminjok Munchae Yŏnkuso [The Research Council for Un-Korean Activities] (Seoul: Tol Pegae, 1993); and Yi Kyŏngnam, *Sŏlsan Chang Tŏk-su* (Seoul: Tonga Ilbosa, 1981); Cumings, *Origins of the Korean War*, 2:208.

39. Leonard Bertsch, Report to General John R. Hodge, Commanding General, December 12, 1947, Bertsch Papers, box 4, folder C-15; The Acting Political Adviser in Korea (Langdon) to the Secretary of State, December 13, 1947, *FRUS*, 1947, vol. 6, doc. 679; Cumings, *Origins of the Korean War*, 2:208.

40. United Nations General Assembly, Resolution 112 (II), "The Problem of the Independence of Korea," November 14, 1947, https://digitallibrary.un.org/record/667165.

41. "The Korean Commission," *New York Times,* January 10, 1948.

42. Memorandum of Conversation, by the Acting Secretary of State, January 3, 1948, *Foreign Relations of the United States,* 1948, vol. 6, *The Far East and Australasia,* ed. John G. Reid and David H. Stauffer (Washington, DC: Government Printing Office, 1974), doc. 706 (hereafter *FRUS,* 1948, vol. 6).

43. Quoted in John Price, "The 'Cat's Paw': Canada and the United Nations Temporary Commission on Korea," *Canadian Historical Review* 85, no. 2 (June 2004): 297–324, at 308.

44. The Political Adviser in Korea (Jacobs) to the Secretary of State, November 19, 1947, *FRUS,* vol. 6, doc. 665.

45. Bertsch's Memorandum for Mr. Sargent, January 5, 1948, Bertsch Papers, box 1, folder D-78.

9. Fighting over Separate Elections

1. Richard J. H. Johnston, "U.N. Group Greeted by Korean Throngs: 50 in Commission Party Arrive in Seoul," *New York Times,* January 8, 1948.

2. Richard J. H. Johnston, "Koreans Greet U.N. Commission: Hear Indian Make Plea for Unity," *New York Times,* January 14, 1948.

3. United Nations General Assembly, "First Part of the Report on the United Nations Temporary Commission on Korea," vol. 1, August 1948, 34, https://digitallibrary.un.org/record/703001.

4. UN General Assembly, "First Part of the Report on the United Nations Temporary Commission on Korea," vol. 1, p. 18.

5. *Voice of Korea,* March 20, 1948; Richard J. H. Johnston, "U.N. Korean Group Upset by Politics: Disturbed by Rightist Fete," *New York Times,* January 16, 1948. Johnston reported that "the Commission's delegates were belatedly disturbed by the political complexion of the welcome celebration staged in the Seoul Stadium."

6. United Nations General Assembly, "First Part of the Report on the United Nations Temporary Commission on Korea," vol. 3, Annexes 9–12, August 1948, 26, https://digitallibrary.un.org/record/703004.

7. UN General Assembly, "First Part of the Report on the United Nations Temporary Commission on Korea," vol. 3, pp. 24 and 32.

8. John R. Hodge to Chief, Civil Affairs Division, War Department Special Staff, Jan. 9, 1948, RG 165, entry 463, box 410, NARA, College Park, MD.

9. Owen Jones, diary entry for February 2, 1948, folder Diary 7/20/1947–4/7/1948, box 4, Owen T. Jones Papers, Harry S. Truman Presidential Library, Independence, MO.

10. The Political Adviser in Korea (Jacobs) to the Secretary of State, February 12, 1948, *Foreign Relations of the United States,* 1948, vol. 6, *The Far East and Australasia,* ed.

John G. Reid and David H. Stauffer (Washington, DC: Government Printing Office, 1974), doc. 733 (hereafter *FRUS,* 1948, vol. 6).

11. On the divisions within UNTCOK, see report, "Observation of Election in South Korea of Korean Representatives Which Shall Constitute a National Assembly and Establish a Government of Korea under Resolutions Adopted by UN General Assembly on 14 November 1947 and Participation of United States Army Forces in Korea Therein, 14 November to 26 August 1948," *Taehan Min'guksca Charyojip,* vol. 1, https://db.history.go .kr/contemp/level.do?levelId=ps_004_0810.

12. The Political Adviser (Jacobs) to the Secretary of State, February 12, 1948, *FRUS,* 1948, vol. 6, doc. 733.

13. Lieutenant General John R. Hodge to the Secretary of State, February 26, 1948, *FRUS,* 1948, vol. 6, doc. 754.

14. Lieutenant General John R. Hodge to the Secretary of State, March 17, 1948, *FRUS,* 1948, vol. 6, doc. 770

15. "Report to the President on China-Korea," September 1947, submitted by Lieutenant General A. C. Wedemeyer, September 1947, *Foreign Relations of the United States,* 1947, vol. 6, *The Far East,* ed. John G. Reid (Washington, DC: Government Printing Office, 1972), doc. 612; and Bruce Cumings, *The Origins of the Korean War,* vol. 2, *The Roaring of the Cataract* (Princeton, NJ: Princeton University Press, 1990), 188.

16. Lieutenant General John R. Hodge to the Secretary of State, February 26, 1948, *FRUS,* 1948, vol. 6, doc. 754.

17. David Bercuson, *Canada and the Birth of Israel: A Study in Canadian Foreign Policy* (Toronto: University of Toronto Press, 2014), 137–139.

18. John Price, "The 'Cat's Paw': Canada and the United Nations Temporary Commission on Korea," *Canadian Historical Review* 85, no. 2 (June 2004): 297–324, at 311–313.

19. UN General Assembly, "First Part of the Report on the United Nations Temporary Commission on Korea," vol. 1, p. 27.

20. The Political Adviser in Korea (Jacobs) to the Secretary of State, January 29, 1948, *FRUS,* 1948, vol. 6, doc. 713.

21. The Political Adviser in Korea (Jacobs) to the Secretary of State, February 10, 1948, *FRUS,* 1948, vol. 6, doc. 726.

22. Bertsch's Memorandum for Mr. Sargent, March 4, 1948, Bertsch Papers, box 4, folder G-135 Harvard-Yenching Library, Harvard University, Cambridge, MA (hereafter Bertsch Papers).

23. Bertsch's Memorandum for Mr. Sargent, January 5, 1948, Bertsch Papers, box 1, folder D-78.

24. Leonard Bertsch, Report to General John R. Hodge, Commanding General, December 12, 1947, Bertsch Papers, box 4, folder C-15.

25. Price, "'Cat's Paw,'" 312–313.

26. Lieutenant General John R. Hodge to the Secretary of State, February 26, 1948, *FRUS,* 1948, vol. 6, doc. 754.

27. Memorandum of Conversation, by the Chief of the Division of Northeast Asian Affairs (Allison), March 22, 1948, *FRUS,* 1948, vol. 6, doc. 771; and the Acting Political Adviser in Korea (Langdon) to the Secretary of State, March 12, 1948, *FRUS,* 1948, vol. 6, doc. 767.

28. Sung-Chan Hong, "Land Reform and Large Landlords in South Korea's Modernization Project," *Seoul Journal of Korean Studies* 26, no. 1 (June 2013): 23–45, at 32–33.

29. Bertsch Draft, December 15, 1947, Bertsch Papers, box 1, folder M-23.

30. Memorandum for General Brown, Subject: Land Reform, June 13, 1947, Bertsch Papers, box 4, folder H-40; and Leonard Bertsch, Report to General John R. Hodge, Commanding General, December 12, 1947, Bertsch Papers, box 4, folder C-15.

31. Letter from CG USAFIK (Hodge Sends for Jacobs) to War (Pass to State), Sept. 18, 1947, 091-Korean Summaries, SCAP, RG 331, box 785-5, NARA, College Park, MD.

32. Letter from CG USAFIK (Hodge Sends for Jacobs) to War (Pass to State), Sept. 13, 1947, 091-Korea #5, SCAP, RG 331, box 785-5, NARA, College Park, MD.

33. Quoted from Kim Seong Bo, "South Korea's Land Reform and Democracy," *Seoul Journal of Korean Studies* 26, no. 1 (June 2013): 47–74, at 52–53. The military government's land program gave preference to current tenants, which resulted in the exclusion of the rural proletariat—farmhands and servants—from the program.

34. Chang Sanghwan, "Haebang kwa chŏnjaeng, kŭrigo chŏnjaeng ihu ŭi nongmin undong" [Emancipation and War, Peasant Movement after Korean War], *Nongch'onsahoe* 20, no. 1 (2010): 7–16.

35. Ham Hanhŭi, "Mi kunjŏng ŭi nongji kaehyŏk kwa Han'guk nongmin ŭi taeŭng" [The US-Led Land Reform and the Korean Peasants' Response: Cultural Conflicts and Confrontations], *Han'guk munhwa illyuhak* 31, no. 2 (1998), 430. In 1949, the Kungsam-myŏn peasants, still led by Na Chaegi, petitioned the National Assembly, demanding their land back. After months of investigating, officials concluded that the lands in question were not "enemy," that is, Japanese property. In February 1950, citing the peasants' findings, two assemblymen representing the Naju district put forward a resolution calling for the immediate return of their constituents' lands. It passed overwhelmingly in the National Assembly, but then the Korean War broke out. As the conflict dragged on, the documentation that had been carefully collected over decades was destroyed or lost. The peasants' claim became one of the many casualties of the Korean War. Half the Kungsam-myŏn peasants decided to give up and paid for the land as part of the provisions of the South Korean land reform bill. But the other half, about 2,100 peasants—still led by Na Chaegi—continued their campaign to retrieve their land without payment. They submitted petition after petition to the local and national government throughout the late 1950s and early 1960s, but to no avail. One by one, the remaining Kungsam-myŏn peasants began to make payments for the return of their land. See Pak Yijun, "Naju Kungsam-myŏn t'oji t'alhwan undong yŏn'gu" [Land Ownership Recovery Movement by Naju Kungsam-myŏn Peasants: A History] (PhD diss., Chŏnnam Taehakkyo, 2003), 146–162.

36. In what might come as a surprise, the Taehan Noch'ong demanded land reform on behalf of the peasants. See Hwasook Nam, *Building Ships, Building a Nation: Korea's Democratic Unionism under Park Chung Hee* (Seattle: University of Washington Press, 2011), 41.

37. The Federation of Korean Farmers was established in August 1947, led by former socialist, Ch'ae Gyuhang, and became the dominant farmers' organization in the South after the NFPU was effectively suppressed. See Kim Sŏngbo, "Ippŏp kwa shirhaeng kwajŏng ŭl t'onghae pon Namhan nongji kaehyŏk ŭi sŏnggyŏk" [Characteristics of the South Korean Farmland Reform through the Legislation and Execution Process], in *Nongji kaehyŏk yon'gu* [Farmland Reform Research], ed. Hong Sŏngch'an (Seoul: Yŏnse Taehakkyo Ch'ulp'anbu, 2001), 148–149. Rhee's ability to curry peasant support has been cited as a key element of his political strength (and authoritarianism), though recent scholarship has disputed this claim. For this debate, see Kim Ilyŏng, "Nongi kaehyŏk ŭl tullŏssan sinhwa ŭi haech'e," in *Haebang chŏnhusa ŭi chaeinsik*, vol. 2, ed. Pak Chihyang, Kim Ilyŏng, and Yi Yŏnghun (Seoul: Ch'aek Sesang, 2006), 295–334; Lee Yong-ki, "Taking Another Look at Land Reform in South Korea: A Focus on Kinship Networks," *Seoul Journal of Korean Studies* 26, no. 1 (June 2013): 103–128; Kim, "South Korea's Land Reform and Democracy."

38. Hong, "Land Reform and Large Landlords," 24.

39. Hong, "Land Reform and Large Landlords." See also Pang Kijung, "Nongji kaehyŏk ŭi sasang chŏnt'ong kwa nongjŏng i'nyŏm" [Ideological Tradition and Agricultural Ideology of Farmland Reform], in *Nongji kaehyŏk yon'gu* [Land Reform Research], ed. Hong Sŏngch'an (Seoul: Yŏnse Taehakkyo Ch'ulp'anbu, 2001), 122–125.

40. On the role of *chaebols* in the South Korean economy, see Jung-en Woo, *Race to the Swift: State and Finance in Korean Industrialization* (New York: Columbia University Press, 1992), 148–175.

41. On reforms and the number of prisoners pardoned, see "Report on United States Military Government's Activities in Connection with the Korean Election of May 10, 1948," sent from Joseph Jacobs to the Secretary of State, Washington, DC, July 22, 1948, RG 59, Entry CDF 1945-1949, box 7390, 895.00/7-2248, NARA, College Park, MD. According to Seoul newspapers, 70 percent of all prisoners were being held for violations of strike laws. See Roger Baldwin, "Chaos in Korea," Roger Nash Baldwin Papers, series 3: Writings and Papers, box 22, folder 14, Public Policy Papers, Department of Special Collections, Princeton University Library.

42. The Political Adviser in Korea (Jacobs) to the Secretary of State, April 14, 1948, *FRUS*, 1948, vol. 6, doc. 784.

43. Letter from John R. Hodge to Brig. General William F. Dean, March 24, 1948, RG 59, entry CDF 1945–1949, box 7391, NARA, College Park, MD.

44. United Nations General Assembly, "First Part of the Report on the United Nations Temporary Commission on Korea," vol. 2, Annexes 1–8, August 1948, 70, https://digitallibrary.un.org/record/703002.

45. "Report on United States Military Government's Activities in Connection with the Korean Election of May 10, 1948," Sent from Joseph E. Jacobs to the Secretary of State, Washington, DC, July 22, 1948, RG 59, entry CDF 1945–1949, box 7390, 895.00/7-2248, NARA, College Park, MD.

46. Letter from Brigadier General John Weckerling to Mr. Petrus J. Schmidt, Principal Secretary of the United Nations Temporary Commission on Korea, March 24, 1948. RG 59, CDF 1945–1949, box 7391, NARA, College Park, MD.

47. "Report on United States Military Government's Activities in Connection with the Korean Election of May 10, 1948."

48. George M. McCune, "The Korean Situation," *Far Eastern Survey* 17, no. 17 (1948): 197–202.

49. This would involve a number of steps, as Helen Begley Nixon explained: "The first task was to bring the people to register. After registration, they were taught how to use the ballot, as we in the United States do in the League of Women Voters." Helen Begley Nixon, "Eye-Witness View of Korean Independence," *Alumnae Quarterly*, August 1949, 195–197, Helen Begley Nixon Papers, series 1, Korea, box 1, folder 2, Sophia Smith Collection of Women's History, SSC-MS-00113, Smith College Special Collections, Northampton, MA, https://findingaids.smith.edu/repositories/2/archival_objects/142054; "go to file," pdf pages 40, 41, 42 (hereafter Helen Begley Nixon Papers).

50. Leonard M. Bertsch to Mr. Sargent, April 16, 1948, Bertsch Papers, box 2, folder G-113.

51. Dorothy Todd Foster, "The Koh Sisters of Korea," *International Altrusan*, February 1948, 16–18, Helen Begley Nixon Papers, series 1, Korea, box 1, folder 2, https://findingaids.smith.edu/repositories/2/archival_objects/142054; "go to file," pdf pages 25, 27, 28.

52. Reflecting its low priority, the Women's Bureau offices were in what Nixon described as a "dingy" building on the outskirts of Seoul. On women's rights and their subordination to other political goals during this period, see Yi Imha, *Haebang konggan, ilsang ŭl pakkun yŏsŏngdŭl ŭi yŏksa: Chedo wa kyujŏng, ŏgap e kyunyŏl ŭl naen yŏsŏngdŭl ŭi pallan* [The History of Women Who Changed Everyday Life and Liberation Space: The Mutiny of Women Who Clove through Institutions, Rules, and Oppression] (Seoul: Chŏlsu wa Yŏnghŭi, 2015).

53. Helen Begley Nixon to Bruce and Beatrice Gould, November 11, 1947; and Helen Begley Nixon to Anna Lord Strauss, November 11, 1947, Helen Begley Nixon Papers, series 1, Korea, box 1, folder 2.

54. Dorothy Todd Foster, "Women of Korea Finding Equality in Primitive 'Land of Morning Calm,'" clipping, n.s., n.d., Helen Begley Nixon Papers, series 1, Korea, box 1, folder 2, https://findingaids.smith.edu/repositories/2/archival_objects/142054; "go to file," pdf p. 97.

55. On conservative women's policy agenda, see Yi, *Haebang konggan*; Mun, "Mi kunjŏnggi Han'guk yŏsŏng undong e kwanhan yŏn'gu" [Study on Korean Woman's Libera-

tion Movement under US Military Government (1945–1948)]; and Jeong-Mi Park, "Liberation or Purification? Prostitution, Women's Movement and Nation Building in South Korea under US Military Occupation, 1945–1948," *Sexualities* 22, nos. 7–8 (2019): 1053–1070.

56. Quoted in Mun Chihyŏn, "Haebang hu chwaikkye yŏsŏng undong ŭi panghyang kwa hangye: Chapchi *Yŏsŏng kongnon* ŭl chungsim ŭro" [Post-Liberation Leftist Women's Movement and Their Limitations with a Focus on *Yŏsŏng kongnon*], *Ihwa sahak yŏn'gu* 54 (June 2017): 243–278, at 264.

57. On how the North Korean regime used the trope of the family—and motherhood, more specifically—to maintain conservative gender norms, see Charles K. Armstrong, *The North Korean Revolution, 1945–1950* (Ithaca, NY: Cornell University Press, 2003), 92–98; and Suzy Kim, *Everyday Life in the North Korean Revolution, 1945–1950* (Ithaca, NY: Cornell University Press, 2013), 174–203. On how North Korean women continued to fight for women's emancipation both at home and abroad after the division and war, see Suzy Kim, *Among Women across Worlds: North Korea in the Global Cold War* (Ithaca, NY: Cornell University Press, 2023).

58. Whang Kyung (Evelyn) Koh [Ko Hwanggyŏng], "Women's Status in Korea," typescript, 6 pp., n.d., Helen Begley Nixon Papers, series 1, Korea, box 1, folder 2, https://findingaids.smith.edu/repositories/2/archival_objects/142054; "go to file," pdf pp. 2–7.

59. Kim Ponghyŏn and Kim Minju, *Jeju-do imnindŭl ŭi 4.3 mujang t'ujaengsa charoyojip* [The History of the April 3 Armed Struggle of the Jeju People] (Osaka: Bunyusha, 1963). Quoted in National Committee for the Investigation of the Truth about the Jeju April 3 Incident, Jeju 4·3 Peace Foundation, *The Jeju 4·3 Incident Investigation Report* (Jeju: Jeju 4·3 Foundation, 2014).

60. "Across the nation, disturbances happened and many of your fellow countrymen were victimized by the disturbances. But I think it was very fortunate that there were no similar unhappy disturbances in Jeju because you have the right awareness of the situation," is what Captain Kerry said in his New Year's address to the Jeju people in 1947. Quoted in *The Jeju 4·3 Incident Investigation Report*, 90.

61. Quoted in Cumings, *Origins of the Korean War,* 2:232.

62. Quoted in *Jeju 4·3 Incident Investigation Report,* 171.

63. Quoted in *Jeju 4·3 Incident Investigation Report,* 171.

64. Quoted in *Jeju 4·3 Incident Investigation Report,* 158.

65. The Acting Secretary of State to the Political Adviser in Korea (Jacobs), April 5, 1948, *FRUS,* 1948, vol. 6, doc. 778.

66. The Political Adviser in Korea (Jacobs) to Secretary of State, April 6, 1948, *FRUS,* 1948, vol. 6, doc. 779.

67. *Chosŏn ilbo,* February 10, 1948.

68. The Political Adviser in Korea (Jacobs) to Secretary of State, April 22, 1948, *FRUS,* 1948, vol. 6, doc. 786.

69. "Yŏsŏng haebang chindu chihwi, 6/10 manse undong chudo . . . p'aran manjang haettŏn 'ch'oego miin'" [Vanguard of Women's Liberation, Leader of the June 10th Movement. . . . Trials and Tribulations of 'the Belle'], *Sŏul sinmun*, May 28, 2019; and Im Kyŏngsŏk, "Tongji ŭi son e kkŏkkin 'isanghyang ŭl hyang han kkum'" ["The Dream for a Utopia," Destroyed at the Hands of a Comrade], *P'ŭresian*, August 8, 2005.

70. Andrei Lankov, *The Real North Korea: Life and Politics in the Failed Stalinist Utopia* (Oxford: Oxford University Press, 2013), 15.

71. Richard J. H. Johnston, "North Korea Talks Emphasize Unity: Kim Koo [Kim Ku] Says Separate Polls Must Be Defeated at All Costs," *New York Times*, April 24, 1948; Kim Sin, *Choguk ŭi hanŭl ŭl nalda: Paekpŏm ŭi adŭl Kim Sin hoegorok* [Flying in the Sky of My Homeland: The Memoirs of Kim Sin, the Son of Kim Ku] (P'aju: Tol Pegae, 2013).

72. Armstrong, *North Korean Revolution*, 119.

73. Political Adviser in Korea (Jacobs) to Secretary of State, May 3, 1948, *FRUS*, 1948, vol. 6, doc. 795.

74. Andrei Lankov, *From Stalin to Kim Il Sung: The Formation of North Korea, 1945–1960* (New Brunswick, NJ: Rutgers University Press, 2002), 45.

75. Political Adviser in Korea (Jacobs) to Secretary of State, May 3, 1948, *FRUS*, 1948, vol. 6, doc. 795.

76. Bridget Martin, "American Imperial Sovereignty and Militarised Land Dispossession during the Korean War," *Geopolitics* 28, no. 5 (2023): 2111–2141.

77. Press Conference of General Hodge (off-the record), May 7, 1948, Joseph E. Jacobs Papers, box 1, Hoover Institution Library and Archives, Stanford University, Stanford, CA.

78. The Secretary of the Army (Royall) to the Secretary of State, June 23, 1948, *FRUS*, 1948, vol. 6, doc. 821.

79. Memorandum by the Director of the Office of Far Eastern Affairs (Butterworth) to the Secretary of State and the Under Secretary of State (Lovett), May 11, 1948, *FRUS*, 1948, vol. 6, doc. 797.

10. Strongman Rising

1. Richard J. H. Johnston, "South Korea Is Ready," *New York Times*, May 1, 1948, 1.

2. "United Nations Temporary Commission on Korea: Report of the Sub-Committee on Methods of Observation of Elections," March 19, 1948, NARA, RG 59, entry CDF 1945–49, box 7390, NARA, College Park, MD. For reports on irregularities and fraud during the elections, see "Observation of Election in South Korea of Korean Representatives Which Shall Constitute a National Assembly and Establish a Government of Korea under Resolutions Adopted by UN General Assembly on 14 November 1947 and Participation of United States Army Forces in Korea Therein, 14 November to 26 August 1948," https://db.history.go.kr/contemp/level.do?levelId=ps_004_0810.

3. Memorandum by the Director of the Office of Far Eastern Affairs (Butterworth) to the Secretary of State and the Under Secretary of State (Lovett), May 11, 1948, *Foreign*

Relations of the United States, 1948, vol. 6, *The Far East and Australasia,* ed. John G. Reid and David H. Stauffer (Washington, DC: Government Printing Office, 1974), doc. 797 (hereafter *FRUS,* 1948, vol. 6).

4. Richard J. H. Johnston, "South Korea Turns Out 85% despite Terrorism That Kills 38," *New York Times,* May 11, 1948, 1.

5. Leon Gordenker, "The United Nations, the United States Occupation and the 1948 Election in Korea," *Political Science Quarterly* 73, no. 3 (1958): 426–450, at 446.

6. National Committee for the Investigation of the Truth about the Jeju April 3 Incident, Jeju 4·3 Peace Foundation, *The Jeju 4·3 Incident Investigation Report* (Jeju: Jeju 4·3 Foundation, 2014), 267.

7. "Letter from Ward to Brown," May 19, 1948, box 3, Rothwell H. Brown Papers, US Army Military History Institute, Carlisle, PA, cited in *Jeju 4·3 Incident Investigation Report,* 272.

8. *Jeju 4·3 Incident Investigation Report,* 255.

9. *Jeju 4·3 Incident Investigation Report,* 252–253; and Hun Joon Kim, *The Massacres at Mt. Halla: Sixty Years of Truth Seeking in South Korea* (Ithaca, NY: Cornell University Press, 2014), 30–31.

10. Bruce Cumings, *The Origins of the Korean War,* vol. 2, *The Roaring of the Cataract* (Princeton, NJ: Princeton University Press, 1990), 254. On Mun Hyŏngsun, see Daehoon Kang, "'Life-saving fearsome Toch'aebi': Life of a Police Chief Moon Hyung-Soon [Mun Hyŏngsun] and Conception of Divinity in Jeju Folklore, South Korea," paper presented at the 10th International Conference of NextGen Korean Studies Scholars, Ann Arbor, MI, May 13, 2023.

11. "Korea Vote 'Noted' by U.N. Commission," *New York Times,* June 27, 1948, 12.

12. George M. McCune, "The Korean Situation," *Far Eastern Survey* 17, no. 17 (1948): 197–202, 199.

13. The Political Adviser in Korea (Jacobs) to the Secretary of State, May 13, 1948, *FRUS,* 1948, vol. 6, doc. 799.

14. "Political Summary for June, 1948," RG 59, entry CDF 1945–49, box 7390, 895.00 /7-1248, NARA, College Park, MD.

15. Letter from Arthur C. Bunce to Secretary of State, Washington, DC, August 3, 1948, RG 59, entry CDF 1945–1949, box 7395, 895.011/8-348, NARA, College Park, MD.

16. Joungwon Kim, *Divided Korea: The Politics of Development, 1945–1972* (Cambridge, MA: Harvard University East Asian Research Center, 1975), 118.

17. Joseph Jacobs to the Secretary of State, Washington DC, September 3, 1947, RG 59, entry CDF 1945–1949, box 7395, 895.011/9-347, NARA, College Park, MD.

18. COMEGENUSAFIK Korea to State Department, June 11, 1947, RG 165, entry 463, box 250, College Park, MD.

19. Ernst Fraenkel to Marta Fraenkel, January 24, 1946, Marta Fraenkel Collection, AR 4348, box 1, folder 10, Leo Baeck Institute, Center for Jewish History, New York, https://archive.org/details/martafraenkelcol02frae/mode/1up?view-theater.

20. Jooyoung Lee, "Making Korean Democracy: American Ideals and South Korean State-Building, 1919–1960" (PhD diss., Brown University, 2012), 123; Joseph E. Jacobs to the Secretary of State, Washington, DC, August 16, 1948, NARA, RG 59, entry CDF 1946–49, box 7390, 895.00/8-1648.

21. Quoted in Hwasook Nam, *Building Ships, Building a Nation: Korea's Democratic Unionism under Park Chung Hee* (Seattle: University of Washington Press, 2011), 40.

22. Arthur C. Bunce to Secretary of State, August 3, 1948, RG 59, entry CDF 1945–1949, box 7395, 895.011/8-348, NARA, College Park, MD.

23. On the fight over the drafting of the constitution, see Sŏ Hŭigyŏng, *Taehan Min'guk hŏnpŏp ŭi t'ansaeng: Han'guk hŏnjŏngsa, manmin kongdonghoe esŏ chehŏn kkaji* [The Birth of the Constitution of the Republic of Korea: The Constitutional History of Korea, from the Commonwealth of Peoples to the Constitution] (P'aju: Ch'angbi, 2012), 294–295.

24. Joseph E. Jacobs to the Secretary of State, August 16, 1948, RG 59, entry CDF 1945–1949, box 7390, 895.00/8-1648, NARA, College Park, MD.

25. Yu Chino, *Na ŭi insaenggwan: Chŏlmŭm i kitch'il ttae* [My View on Life: The Days When Youth Vigorously Flaps Its Wings] (Seoul: Sungmun Ch'ulpansa,1984), 219.

26. John J. Muccio to the Secretary of State, September 14, 1948, RG 59, entry CDF 1945–1949, box 7390, 895.00/9-1488, NARA, College Park, MD.

27. Sŏ, *Taehan Min'guk hŏnpŏp ŭi t'ansaeng*, 297–298.

28. According to Ch'oe Kyŏngok, Fraenkel's opinions about the draft constitution were only circulated internally, thus never made known to Korean drafters. Choi laments it as a missed opportunity for a more democratic Korean constitution. Fraenkel's assessment, however, was intentionally limited, focusing on those provisions of the constitution relating to international law. See Ch'oe Kyŏngok, "Mi kunjŏng ha ŭi sabŏppu wa chehŏn hŏnbŏp ŭi sŏngnip kwajŏng: Ernest Fraenkel ŭi nonp'yŏng kwa kwallyŏn hayŏ" [The Department of Justice and the Process of Establishing the First Constitution under United States Military Government in Korea: With Reference to Ernst Fraenkel], *Kongbŏp yŏn'gu* 34, no. 2 (2005): 114–141.

29. Sŏ, *Taehan Min'guk hŏnpŏp ŭi t'ansaeng*, 348.

30. Charles Pergler to the Military Governor, July 16, 1948, RG 59, entry CDF 1945–1949, box 7395, 895.011/7-2648, NARA, College Park, MD.

31. Dorothy Todd Foster, "Women of Korea Finding Equality in Primitive 'Land of Morning Calm,'" clipping, n.s., n.d., Helen Begley Nixon Papers, series 1, Korea, box 1, folder 2, Sophia Smith Collection of Women's History, SSC-MS-00113, Smith College Special Collections, Northampton, MA, https://findingaids.smith.edu/repositories/2/archival_objects/142054; "go to file," pdf p. 97.

32. Kyung Ae Park, "Women and Social Change in South and North Korea: Marxist and Liberal Perspectives," Women in International Development, Working Paper no. 231, Michigan State University, East Lansing, MI, June 1992, https://gencen.isp.msu.edu/files/4814/5202/7066/WP231.pdf.

33. Jackson to Department of External Affairs, June 26, 1948, 1948–49, Australia and the Postwar World, beyond the Region, vol. 16, Australian Government, Historical Documents, doc. 151, https://www.dfat.gov.au/about-us/publications/historical-documents/Pages/volume-16/151-jackson-to-department-of-external-affairs.

34. Memorandum by the Director of the Office of Far Eastern Affairs (Butterworth) to the Under Secretary of State (Lovett), July 20, 1948. *FRUS*, 1948, vol. 6, doc. 843.

35. "Shies at a Presidency: U.S. Citizen, 80, Says That He Will Not Run in Korea," *New York Times*, July 6, 1948, 12.

36. "Korean Trip Barred for Aged Physician," *New York Times*, April 29, 1947, 16.

37. John Dower, *Embracing Defeat: Japan in the Wake of World War II* (New York: Norton, 1999), 353–355.

38. In a related matter, Pergler also found the lack of autonomy for local self-government troubling. "The present system of appointment of the more important local officers is a perfect setup for building up a strong political machine by the Chief Executive and makes possible even the establishment of something in the nature of a dictatorship." Charles Pergler to the Military Governor, July 16, 1948, RG 59, entry CDF 1945–1949, box 7395, 895.011/7-2648, NARA, College Park, MD.

39. Cumings, *Origins of the Korean War*, 2:232.

40. For the history of South Korea's constitution-making, see Sung-Ho Kim and Chaihark Hahm, "To Make 'We the People': Constitutional Founding in Postwar Japan and South Korea," *International Journal of Constitutional Law* 8, no. 4 (2010): 800–848.

41. Letter from Joseph E. Jacobs to the Secretary of State, Washington, DC, August 16, 1948. RG 59, entry CDF 1945–49, box 7390, 895.00/8-1648, NARA, College Park, MD.

42. Letter from Joseph E. Jacobs to the Secretary of State, Washington, DC, August 16, 1948, RG 59, entry CDF 1945–49, box 7390, 895.00/8-1648, NARA, College Park, MD.

43. Arthur C. Bunce to Secretary of State, Washington, DC, August 3, 1948, RG 59, entry CDF 1945–1949, box 7395, 895.011/8-348, NARA, College Park, MD.

44. Letter from Joseph E. Jacobs to the Secretary of State, Washington, DC, August 16, 1948, RG 59, entry CDF 1945–49, box 7390, 895.00/8-1648, NARA, College Park, MD.

45. Paul S. Dull, "South Korean Constitution," *Far Eastern Survey*, September 8, 1948.

46. "Prospects for Survival of the Republic of Korea," Office of Reports and Estimates, 44–48, October 28, 1948, p. 9, Korean War and Its Origins Collection, Harry S. Truman Presidential Library, Independence, MO, https://www.trumanlibrary.gov/library/research-files/prospects-survival-republic-korea-office-reports-and-estimates-44-48?documentid=NA&pagenumber=1; and Cumings, *Origins of the Korean War*, 2:228.

47. Andrei Lankov, *From Stalin to Kim Il Sung: The Formation of North Korea, 1945–1960* (New Brunswick, NJ: Rutgers University Press, 2002), 45.

48. Richard J. H. Johnston, "Korea Set Up as Republic, MacArthur Predicts 'Unity': Third Anniversary of Liberation from Japan Marked by Proclamation Fete in South," *New York Times*, August 15, 1948.

49. Cumings, *Origins of the Korean War*, 2:226.

50. Memorandum by the Director of the Office of Far Eastern Affairs (Butterworth) to the Secretary of State and the Under Secretary of State (Lovett), May 11, 1948, *FRUS, 1948*, vol. 6, 1193, doc 797.

51. The Secretary of State to the Political Adviser in Korea (Jacobs), July 27, 1948, *FRUS, 1948*, vol. 6, doc. 855.

52. Hanson W. Baldwin, "110,000 U.S. Troops 'War' in Sand Hills: 'Strong Man' at War Games in North Carolina," *New York Times*, August 22, 1951, 3.

53. "Rhee in Seclusion on Hawaiian Isle," *New York Times*, June 18, 1960.

54. "Syngman Rhee Dies an Exile from Land He Fought to Free: Body of Ousted President, 90, Will Be Returned to Seoul for Burial," *New York Times*, July 20, 1965; and Cumings, *Origins of the Korean War*, 2:228.

Conclusion

1. "Evacuation from Seoul," June 30, 1950, p. 5, Marta Fraenkel Collection, AR 4348, box 1, folder 11, Leo Baeck Institute, Center for Jewish History, New York, https://archive .org/details/martafraenkelcol02frae/mode/1up?view-theater.

2. Mark E. Caprio, "Colonial-Era Korean Collaboration over Two Occupations: Delayed Closure," in *Japan as the Occupier and the Occupied*, ed. Christine de Matos and Mark E. Caprio (New York: Palgrave Macmillan, 2015), 123–124; and Koen De Ceuster, "The Nation Exorcised: The Historiography of Collaboration in South Korea," *Korean Studies* 25, no. 2 (2001): 207–242, at 214.

3. The nongovernmental Institute for Research in Collaborationist Activities named 4,389 collaborators. See Sang-Hun Choe, "Colonial-Era Dispute Agitates South Koreans," *New York Times*, April 5, 2010, A8.

4. "Evacuation from Seoul," June 30, 1950, p. 6. On Rhee's repressive policies, see Dong-Choon Kim, *The Unending Korean War: A Social History*, trans. Sung-ok Kim (Larkspur, CA: Tamal Vista, 2000); and Su-kyoung Hwang, *Korea's Grievous War* (Philadelphia: University of Pennsylvania Press, 2016).

5. On the Korean War, see Bruce Cumings, *The Korean War: A History* (New York: Random House, 2010); Sheila Miyoshi Jager, *Brothers at War: The Unending Conflict in Korea* (New York: W. W. Norton, 2014); Masuda Hajimu, *Cold War Crucible: The Korean Conflict and the Postwar World* (Cambridge, MA: Harvard University Press, 2015).

6. Kie-chung Pang, "Yi Hun-gu's Agricultural Reform Theory and Nationalist Economic Thought," *Seoul Journal of Koreans Studies* 19, no. 1 (December 2006): 61–89. After a short stint in the National Assembly, Yi returned to the academy. In 1955, he became dean of Tan'guk University, the first private university in South Korea, and a year later, he became the president of Sŏnggyun'gwan University, one of the oldest institutions of higher learning in all of Korea. Disillusioned with Rhee's authoritarianism, Yi joined the progressive opposition party in the late 1950s.

7. On South Korea's democratization movement, see Namhee Lee, *The Making of Minjung: Democracy and the Politics of Representation* (Ithaca, NY: Cornell University Press, 2009); Paul Chang, *Protest Dialectics: State Repression and South Korea's Democracy Movement, 1970–1979* (Palo Alto, CA: Stanford University Press, 2015); Charles Kim, *Youth for Nation: Culture and Protest in Cold War South Korea* (Honolulu: University of Hawai'i Press, 2018).

8. Robert Carlin and Don Oberdorfer, *The Two Koreas: A Contemporary History*, 3rd ed. (New York: Basic Books, 2013).

9. Richard D. Robinson, "Betrayal of a Nation," unpublished manuscript, 1950, p. 53, Harvard-Yenching Library, DS917.52 .R63 1950x, Harvard University Library.

10. John Dower, *Embracing Defeat: Japan in the Wake of World War II* (New York: Norton, 1999), 26.

11. Roger Baldwin to Friends, May 23, 1947, Roger Nash Baldwin Papers, series 3: Writings and Papers, box 18, folder 8c, Public Policy Papers, Department of Special Collections, Princeton University Library.

12. "Draft Statement," April 21, 1947, Bertsch Papers, box 3, folder A-5, Harvard-Yenching Library, Harvard University, Cambridge, MA (hereafter Bertsch Papers).

13. Richard Robinson to Commanding General, United States Army Forces in Korea, April 17, 1947, Bertsch Papers, box 2, folder G-19.

14. "Suggested Revision of Coalition Committee Plan," February 2, 1947, Bertsch Papers, box 4, folder D-19.

15. Roger Baldwin, "Test of American Democracy," June 1948, Roger Nash Baldwin Papers, series 3: Writings and Papers, box 22, folder 12, Public Policy Papers, Department of Special Collections, Princeton University Library.

16. Bruce Cumings, *The Origins of the Korean War*, vol. 2, *The Roaring of the Cataract, 1947–1950* (Princeton, NJ: Princeton University Press, 1990), 226; and Lieutenant General John R. Hodge to the Secretary of State, July 17, 1947, *Foreign Relations of the United States, 1947*, vol. 6, *The Far East*, ed. John G. Reid (Washington, DC: Government Printing Office, 1972), doc. 547.

17. Lieutenant General John R. Hodge to the Secretary of State, December 31, 1946, *Foreign Relations of the United States, 1946*, vol. 8, *The Far East*, ed. John G. Reid and Herbert A. Fine (Washington, DC: Government Printing Office, 1971), doc. 579.

18. Norman M. Naimark, *Stalin and the Fate of Europe: The Struggle for Sovereignty* (Cambridge, MA: Harvard University Press, 2019), 12.

19. "Evacuation from Seoul," June 30, 1950, p. 9.

Acknowledgments

This book is over ten years in the making. I would like to express my deep gratitude to the people and institutions who helped me along the way. I owe an enormous debt to the global Korean studies community, especially in South Korea and North America, whose painstaking research, scholarship, and archiving provided me access to Korean perspectives during a crucial time in their history. As the citations indicate, this book would not have been possible without their works. I'm also grateful to the postliberation-era Korean writers and artists who brilliantly captured the color and complexity of liberation. I have liberally tapped their novels, short stories, images, and songs to provide a visceral sense of how Koreans experienced this brief but intense moment of possibility. Korea had a tradition of creative works long before the current Korean Wave (*hallyu*).

I was fortunate to receive fellowships from the Charles Warren Center at Harvard University, the Academy of Arts and Sciences, the American Council of Learned Societies, and the University of Connecticut's Humanities Institute (UCHI) to support the research and writing of this book. During my time at UCHI, Michael Lynch and Alexis Boylan gave me the idea to write the book for a wider audience. Their encouragement injected new life into the project. I also want to thank the Korea Institute at Harvard University and the Weatherhead East Asian Institute at Columbia University for sponsoring me as a visiting scholar, which gave me access to their rich Korean history holdings.

For reading individual chapters, providing feedback, and sharing research and reading materials, I want to thank Daniel Asen, Daniel Bender, Alexis Boylan, Karen Caplan, Chris Capozzola, Mark Caprio, Paul Chang,

Nancy Cott, Susan Carruthers, the late Mary Dunn, Andrew Jewett, Ruth Feldstein, Susan Ferber, Takashi Fujitani, Andrew Gordon, Jillian Hess, Heather Houser, Chie Ikeya, Chong Myong Im, Jill Lepore, Charles Kim, Ju Yon Kim, Nuri Kim, Sun Joo Kim, Suzy Kim, Erez Manela, Micki McElya, Mae Ngai, Mitch Pak, Albert Park, Sandra Park, Beryl Satter, Andre Schmid, Michael Shin, John Shon, Patricia Spacks, Timothy Stewart-Winter, Whit Strub, Jessica Wang, Barbara Weinstein, the late Marilyn Young, and Jun Yoo. Throughout the project, a remarkable group of research assistants— including Joan Cho, Mi Hyun Yoon, and Juwon Kim—provided superb re- search and translation assistance.

I am lucky to be part of an extraordinary department at Rutgers University– Newark, surrounded by smart and supportive colleagues, many of whom I named above. I want to especially thank Jim Goodman, for his advice on writing, publishing, and beyond. I also want to thank my current and former deans, Jacqueline Mattis and the late Jan Ellen Lewis, for their support. I wish Jan was alive to read the book. A huge thanks to Christina Strasburger, department administrator extraordinaire, who has supported my work in more ways than I can count.

I owe a special mention to Carter Eckert, who contributed to this book in important ways. Carter pointed me to the Leonard Bertsch Papers at the Harvard-Yenching Library, which provided crucial insights into the US military government at the highest levels and how it engaged Korean poli- tics in the South. Further, Carter read the entire manuscript and provided thoughtful feedback, saving me from a number of errors. I also want to thank the press's anonymous reader for their comments.

Daniel Immerwahr also took on the unenviable task of reading the full manuscript in draft form. In addition to his suggestions for argument and organization of the book, his advice on writing and how to tell a better sto- ry was invaluable. He got me thinking about pace and texture and how I might squeeze more out of a story for my readers.

Bruce Cumings's writings on Korea have been an inspiration for as long as I can remember. Even when I thought I was running a fool's errand, Bruce convinced me that I had something important to say about a history he has brilliantly written about for four decades. I am grateful for his sup- port and for patiently answering my countless questions.

My agent, Elise Capron of the Sandra Dijkstra Agency, believed in this project. Her enthusiasm buoyed my spirits when I was having my doubts. I was incredibly fortunate to have Kathleen McDermott as my editor at Harvard University Press. Kathleen's keen editorial eye and sharp pen made this a better book. I want to thank Joseph Pomp, who stepped in as my editor after Kathleen's retirement to get the book across the finish line. I also thank Aaron Wistar and Stephanie Vyce at the press for expertly shepherding the manuscript through the production process. I am grateful to Susan Karani Virtanen, whose attention to detail and insightful suggestions have improved this book. My thanks to Thomas Yu for designing the maps in the book.

My extended family—grandparents, uncles, aunts, cousins, parents, and siblings—inspired me to write this book. I am grateful to them for sharing their stories, thoughts, and delicious food with me. I'm not sure if it will settle the family debate, but I hope that they know that our conversations and arguments made me think long and hard about how to present this history. I thank my friends Kevin Pak, Mitch Pak, and John Shon for needling me about why the book was not finished at every chance they got.

Finally, I want to thank my wife, Laura, and my children, Kate and Carter, who are no doubt relieved that this book is finally finished. They won't have to suffer through hearing me read aloud a passage for the twelfth time and asking them if it was better. My children will also be happy not to see their father hunched over a laptop at the kitchen table when they come back from school, at least for a little while. Laura lived with this book longer than anyone else, listening to my thoughts, commenting on the writing, and providing moral support. For her love and partnership, I dedicate this book to her.

Index

Note: numbers in **bold** indicate a figure. Numbers followed by "n" indicate an endnote.

agreed on by, 136; SKILA members selected by, 136, 138; statement on Yŏ by, 140
Cold War, 2, 7–8, 58, 163, 214, 220n11
Cold War warrior, 7
collaboration: Presidential Committee for the Inspection of Collaboration for Japanese Imperialism, 213
collaborators: Coalition Committee's definition of, 137, 141; confiscation of property from descendants of, 213; defining, 26, 55; drafting legislation to prosecute, 141; election of, 140; expelling, 68; government stacked with, 77; hatred for, 26; identifying and punishing, 29; KDP as party of, 71; notorious, 68, 150; peasant farmers' confiscation of lands of, 36; people's courts established to try, 29; police force members as, 77; pro-Japanese, 26, 68, 72, 77, 82, 177; punishing, 136, 141, 150; purging, 136; removal from public life of, 8, 55, 68; seeking revenge against, 26
collaborators, Japanese, 138, 146; punishments for, 150
colonial rule, Japanese: Koreans defined as "national traitors" under, 131; police force of, 143, 147–148; traditional Korean music banned under, 144; US occupation less preferable to, 130
comfort women, 3
Committee for the Preparation of Korean Independence (CPKI), 19–21, 52–54, 70
Committee of National Mobilization for Anti-Trusteeship, 90, 94
commoner-landowner, 43
communism: anti-communism of Hodge, 6, 8, 79, 82, 95, 130, 148, 216; anti-communist client state of South Korea to be established, 10; Bunce's views on, 97; capitalism versus, 7; in China, 162; cooperatives as middle solution between capitalism and, 112; Kim and Yŏ's disillusionment with, 133; Kim Tuhan's "patriotic" fight against, 144; Korean elections as repudiation of, 197; land reform negatively tied to, 86, 102–103; looming threat of, 76; Meacham's lack of understanding of, 124; Pak Hŏnyŏng's rigid commitment to, 77; Rhee's railing against, 94; Truman Doctrine's anti-communist position, 149; use of colonial police methods in struggle against, 106
communist paradise, Korea as, 77
Communist Party, Korea. *See* Korean Communist Party
concubines, 90, 101

counterfeiting ring, 116; trial related to, 132
Counter Intelligence Corps (CIC), 186
CPKI. *See* Committee for the Preparation of Korean Independence
Cumings, Bruce, 9, 151, 207, 219n1; on assassination of Song Chinu, 237n14; on the Autumn Uprising, 245n59; on Hodge and Rhee, 249n30; on origins of the Korean War, 220n10, 220n11, 264n5; on percentages of Korean population sent abroad during Japan wartime mobilization, 221n3; on Taegu Uprising, 125; on Yŏ's assassination, 250n69

Demilitarized Zone (DMZ), 2
Department of Agriculture (US), 82–83, 98
Division of Land Economics, 82
Djabi, Zeki, **170**, 173
DMZ. *See* Demilitarized Zone
Donner, Francesca, 94, **165**
Dower, John, 6, 214, 233n35
drafting and requisition (military), 12, 27, 115; of Koreans for Japan armies, war crime of, 141; men and women recruited for, 27
drafting of Korean constitution. *See* Korean constitution, drafting of
Dutch East Indies, 3

Eckert, Carter, 225n57
Eisenhower, Dwight, 61
El Salvador, 166, 173, 178
Endō Ryūsaku, 19, 52
Ewha College, 183

Farmers' Association, 113
farmer's associations, local, 112
Federation of Korean Farmers, 180, 257n37
Federation of Korean Trade Unions, 171
Federation of Korean Women, 184
fertilizer, 38; chemical, 102; night soil, 83
59th Army (US), 68
Filipino Independence, 59–60. *See also* Philippines
First Continental Congress (US), 168
First Toilers Congress, 133
food: democratic management of, 112; police supplying rightist youth groups with, 143; sexual favors granted in exchange for, 29; women expected to prepare, 125
food protest, 125
food shortages, 112, 125; anger in Taegu over, 125; chronic, in the North, 108